WRITING ANCIEI

LUKE PITCHER is Lecturer in Classics and Ancient History at the University of Durham. He has studied and written extensively on the subject of historiography in antiquity.

'This is a very good book indeed; general readers, students, and specialists alike will read it with profit and delight. Luke Pitcher ranges over ancient historical writers, both Greek and Roman, from Herodotus to Ammianus, with an impressive grasp of his material, and he has a gift for finding the telling example and making subtle and insightful points with lucidity and punch. He also has a wonderful eye for the modern parallel, and one is as likely to find here illumination drawn from a Patrick O'Brian novel or an episode of Doctor Who as from an extract from Xenophon or Velleius. We meet along the way the diplomat's wife who wrote a universal history while perched in a tree in an embassy garden; and the mad Cornish vicar who deceived Thomas Macaulay with a historical ballad and excommunicated his cat for mousing on a Sunday. No-one after reading this book should venture generalisations about "the modern way" or "the ancient way" of writing history: Pitcher brings out how great are the variations within both, and yet how apparently distant habits of writing may turn out to have parallels within modern culture that make them instantly more intelligible. Pitcher is unusually sensitive to the narrative strategies of the ancient historical writers, and also of all the health-warnings that the modern student needs to bear in mind when reading their works: he makes his readers alert to what he calls the "action of the swan", that is all the work that goes into the shaping of a story but remains beneath the surface of the narrative. Few writers about ancient historiography are so learned, and even fewer carry their learning so lightly: this is a book that anyone interested in ancient history just has to read – and they will thoroughly enjoy it.'

Christopher Pelling, Regius Professor of Greek, University of Oxford

'Luke Pitcher has written an engaging, witty, and accessible study of the complicated relationship between theory and practice in the ancient historians, bringing to the task an impressive expertise in texts that range from archaic Greece to late antiquity. He resists simple contrasts between ancient and modern, presenting the reader instead with finely drawn, convincingly argued analyses of the spectrum of practices employed by ancient historiographers in their treatment of sources, self-presentation, and narrative modes of (re)presenting their pasts. Bearing in mind always that the modern student of the Greco-Roman world is also, in some way, "writing ancient history", Pitcher brings us much closer to the methodologies and reception of these texts through which so much of our understanding of the ancient world derives.'

Christina S. Kraus, Professor of Classics, Yale University

WRITING ANCIENT HISTORY

An Introduction to Classical Historiography

Luke Pitcher

I.B. TAURIS
LONDON · NEW YORK

Published in 2009 by I.B.Tauris & Co Ltd
6 Salem Road, London W2 4BU
175 Fifth Avenue, New York NY 10010
www.ibtauris.com

Distributed in the United States and Canada exclusively by Palgrave Macmillan
175 Fifth Avenue, New York NY 10010

Library of Classical Studies, Vol 1

For full series list see: www.ibtauris.com/LCS

ISBN: 978 1 84511 957 7 (HB)
ISBN: 978 1 84511 958 4 (PB)

A full CIP record for this book is available from the British Library
A full CIP record is available from the Library of Congress

Library of Congress Catalog Card Number: available

Designed and Typeset by 4word Ltd, Bristol, UK
Printed and bound in India by Replika Press Pvt. Ltd.

CONTENTS

INTRODUCTION: OWNAGE BY CLIO

Towards the end of Oliver Stone's 2004 film *Alexander*, Alexander's general, Ptolemy, now king of Egypt, dictates his memories of the great man to a scribe. Suddenly he stops short and instructs the secretary to strike out what he has just said as senile blather. The scribe, cowed by the pharaonic majesty of Sir Anthony Hopkins, hastens to oblige.

An amusing moment, but one that has its implications. The real Ptolemy did write a history. Now lost, it was a source for the later historian Arrian, who made it one of the bases for his own writing about the Macedonian conquest of Persia. This work survives. It is one of the most important documents in modern-day attempts to understand the historical Alexander.

What Ptolemy does not write, Arrian will not read. What Arrian does not read in Ptolemy is not doomed outright – he had other sources and a mind of his own – but its survival in Arrian's own work is less likely. What does not reach the modern world in Arrian's history does not shape that world's perceptions of Alexander. In Hellenistic Alexandria, the mindset of an unimagined future hangs upon one old man's change of mind.

The impact of the past upon the present is a trite theme. It is understood by every parent who warns a child not to eat something because 'you don't know where *that's been*'. Stone's Ptolemy dramatizes a truth more easily forgotten. Today's sense of where humanity has been was determined, in no small measure, by countless individual acts of writerly decision (and, no doubt, of scribal intimidation as well).

Ptolemy is the tip of a very big iceberg. As is the way with icebergs, the troublesome element is invisible, or at the very least difficult to detect. It is hard to tell how much of what we think we know about the ancient world depends on the historical writings of the unregarded or unremembered. We are all, to a considerable extent, owned by Clio, the goddess whom the ancient world eventually saddled with responsibility for writers of history.

Ancient historical works, then, are important. But they are not easy. How, then, is it best to approach them? The modern world has seen two main lines of attack.

The first of these has been focussed upon the relationship between ancient historians and other relevant data about the classical world. Other data may take the form of testimony from other historians, evidence from inscriptions or other physical remains, or non-historical writings. This first approach tends to focus upon the issue of reliability. Its characteristic techniques include comparison between what a historian says (or does not say) with what other evidence attests about a subject and the reconstruction of the sources which the historian had available to him.

The second approach has been focussed upon works of history as literary productions. The emphasis here has been upon the structure of works of history themselves, and how they generate meaning through style, the manipulation of narrative and the use of such devices as allusion and imagery. Its characteristic techniques are those associated with literary criticism. Through close reading of the text, it aims to determine the impact of a history as a work of art.

These two approaches have not always co-existed happily. The first approach is, under certain circumstances, vulnerable to the criticism that it can rest upon rather naive assumptions about the transmission of data. The second, on occasion, stands accused of strategically ignoring the fact that works of *history*, unlike most works of art, place themselves in a very particular relation to what some of us still like to think of as reality.

Such mutual polemic obscures the ways in which each method, thoughtfully applied, can enrich the other. The more sophisticated one's understanding of how a historian shapes a narrative, the better one is equipped to judge his relationship to his data. Contrariwise, proper analysis of histories as works of literature requires due attention to their relationship with the physical universe – the übertext, which not even kings can copy-edit.

This doubled approach is at the heart of the book to come. In what follows, I shall be examining ancient history-writing in action. Above all, what I will be stressing is the importance of decision. Ancient works of history, as Ptolemy shows, are built upon countless decisions. Every history that is written elbows out one that might have been. But decision, likewise, is a responsibility which the reader cannot shirk. How you assess what is written by the historians of antiquity impinges upon the vision of the ancient world which is spawned in consequence. What you see is what you beget.

1

WRITING ABOUT HISTORY
IN THE ANCIENT WORLD

So, if you look at a work of ancient history-writing[1] for the first time, what do you see?

What you see (to continue the theme from the Introduction) is the product of a large number of choices and decisions. The most crucial of these was the historian's decision to compose his work in the first place.[2] This may seem an obvious point, but it is one worth remembering all the same. As we have already observed, the choice *not* to chronicle something can be every bit as significant as the decision to put it on record, and much harder to detect. Examples of such meaningful blanks and absences will appear in Chapter 6.

However, many of the decisions which impact strongly upon the first encounter with a piece of classical historiography were not made by its author. The twenty-first-century reader is most likely to meet with an example of ancient history-writing in the form of a modern printed edition. According to the policy of the editor and/or publisher of this edition, it is likely to contain a reader's introduction, appendices, endnotes and explanatory material. At the very least, the name of the historian and a title for the work itself will appear on the spine, the dust jacket or the title page.

The place where you encounter the work is also the product of decision-making. Bookshop, library, reading list or Internet retailer may well have tagged and classified the work under a rubric such as 'history (ancient)' or 'classical historiography'. Someone, at some point, decided that the work fell into these particular categories, which may be part of the reason you are now looking at it.

These contemporary aids to understanding are, of course, very useful. But they do have an unfortunate drawback. The trappings of a modern edition can easily obscure some fundamental features of ancient history-writing. Again, what is important is what was not there.

The original versions of most prose works in the ancient world lacked, amongst other things, title pages, indexes and page numbers. In fact, the very structure of ancient 'books' was originally very different from the version with a spine and inserted leaves of text which is now so familiar. This book format is known formally as the 'codex'. It only began to make serious headway outside Christian circles in the third century CE, which was some time after the careers of most (but not all) of the historians we shall be examining.

Before the codex took off, the works of the ancient historians, like those of most other classical authors, were preserved on papyrus rolls. The generations which have seen the birth and burgeoning of the Internet need no lessons in how the formats available to transmit data can shape how those data are organized. Papyrus rolls furnish a good example of this.

Titles are a case in point. Twenty-first-century readers find it hard to ignore the title of whatever they are reading. Dust-jacket, title-page and possibly even running heads keep the name of the work constantly before one's eyes. The case with ancient papyrus rolls was rather different. Titles could be written on the papyrus at the beginning and end of the text, on the outside of the roll for easy reference (as on the spine of a modern book), or on a tag, known as a *sillabos*, attached to it. In some of these locations the room for expression was limited, and the titles found on early manuscripts are often terse or cursory.[3]

The result of this is that it is often hard to be as sure of the authentic titles of ancient historical works as the dust jackets of modern editions can suggest. For example, there is a work of the Roman historian Tacitus which is often known as the *Annales* (in Latin) or the *Annals* (in English), or even *The Annals of Imperial Rome* (the title of the popular Penguin translation).[4] In fact, the evidence for the original title involving anything other than the phrase *Ab Excessu Divi Augusti* ('From the Death of the Divine Augustus') is sketchy at best.[5]

It is easy to dismiss this as hair-splitting. None of the titles given above is obviously inappropriate to the work it describes. Tacitus's history does start from the death of the first emperor, Augustus. It is likewise written in the format of 'annals' – a way of structuring histories, particularly associated with Roman historiography, which describes events strictly year by year.

But things are not always so simple. A century-and-a-half before Tacitus, another historian, Sallust, wrote an account of how the disaffected politician Lucius Sergius Catilina, usually known today simply as 'Catiline', launched an insurrection against the Roman Republic. Two titles for this work are in common circulation: *Coniuratio Catilinae* ('Catiline's conspiracy') and *Bellum Catilinae* ('The War of Catiline'). The difference between *these* two titles is by no means insignificant. Almost anyone can put together a conspiracy; a war is a different matter. To call a monograph 'The War of Catiline' is therefore to pass something of a judgment on the character and magnitude of this insurrection, even before the narrative itself begins.

In fact, the titulature of the early manuscripts of Sallust, from which modern printed texts are derived,[6] tends to refer to Catiline's activity as a 'war'. Sallust himself, however, when he initially sets out the subject of his work, writes: 'I am going to describe, in a few words, as accurately as possible, the conspiracy of Catiline.'[7] Moreover, there is an interesting characteristic of Sallust's selection of words in narrating the insurrection. The history is full of people who are described as hoping for war, deciding to go to war, making preparations for war and dreading war. But the narrator himself almost entirely avoids describing what is *actually happening* as warfare. The nearest he gets is when Manlius, who figures in the narrative as one of Catiline's lieutenants, is characterized as the man who 'afterwards was the first to make war'.[8] Even here, war is figured as something which is going to happen later, not at that particular moment in the narrative. Within Sallust's narrative, Catiline's 'war' is perpetually a matter of intention, speculation, hope or fear – even the description of the campaign in which Catiline himself finally dies is hived off into five chapters at the end of the monograph which are collectively shorter than the description of a debate in the Senate that appears just before them.

It will thus be clear that the question of the title of a work of ancient history is not necessarily either trivial or easy to determine with certainty. Some historians, it is true, reveal the name of their opus explicitly in the course of the work itself. Appian of Alexandria, who wrote a history of Rome in Greek during the second century CE, helpfully opens his enterprise with the sentence: 'As I began to write the *Roman History*, I thought it necessary to set out the boundaries.'[9]

Such obligingness should not be taken for granted, however. In some cases, what appears on the dust jacket of the book in the hands of the modern reader represents only a best guess. In others, the weight of tradition has produced a consensus title which is not only unintended by the original author but also rather misleading.

Consider, for example, *The Secret History*, which is the popular name for a work by the sixth-century CE historian Procopius of Caesarea. This is an evocative title. It seems to set the work in explicit contrast to the squeaky-clean, air-brushed world of 'public history' and hints at an authorial interest in the illicit and salacious.

The reader who goes to the work with such expectations will not by any means be disappointed. This is, after all, the book of which Edward Gibbon observed that certain passages should be left in 'the obscurity of a learned language'.[10] But Procopius himself did not advertise any such intent. In fact, the oldest transmitted title for this work is *Anekdota*, which means something like 'unpublished'. This is a name which scholars presume was once accurate, but one unlikely to lend itself to use by writers of intellectual thrillers.[11]

The Secret History is a title that sprays a teasing scent of conspiracy theory onto a text which did not originally smell of it quite that strongly. In a few cases, it seems that the opposite has happened. In these instances, the unambiguous author/title combo on the spine of the modern edition masks deliberate suppression or misdirection on the part of the historian.

The fourth-century BCE Athenian historian Xenophon is an interesting instance of this. Xenophon, amongst other things, wrote an account of an unsuccessful expedition to Asia Minor in 401 BCE to install the pretender Cyrus as the Great King of Persia. There is some evidence that Xenophon originally circulated this account, which is usually known as the *Anabasis* ('March Up-Country') under the pseudonym 'Themistogenes of Syracuse'.[12] What Xenophon hoped to achieve by this imposture is unclear. It certainly, however, has a bearing on how we interpret the work and its purposes. The Greek biographer Plutarch, for example, thought that the pseudonym was intended to give an impression of greater objectivity, since Xenophon himself is an important figure within the account of the expedition.[13]

Some historians even seem to have flirted with the idea of anonymity. Arrian, who wrote a history of Alexander the Great in the second century CE, makes a point of suppressing his own name from the text of his work altogether: 'I have no need to write my name, for it is not at all unknown among men.'[14] Appian, the historian of Rome whom we have already met, makes a self-conscious movement in that direction, but backs down at the last moment: 'As for who I am, the writer of these things, many know and I myself have announced it before, but, to put it more clearly, I am Appian of Alexandria ... '.[15] Since Appian and Arrian were near contemporaries, it is tempting to see some sort of relationship between the anonymity of the one and the last-minute retreat from namelessness of the other, but the exact nature of that relationship is controversial.[16] In any event, it is clear that the straightforward way in which modern editions assert the names and authorship of ancient histories is not always an accurate reflection of their original status.

Modern publishing, then, sometimes resolves ancient ambiguities into certainties where titles are concerned. There is not (usually) anything sinister about this process. We have to call works of ancient history *something*, after all. A name on which tradition has agreed is useful as a point of reference even if it is possibly wrong. Thus, the notes to this book refer to the *Annals* of Tacitus and the *Secret History* of Procopius, because the practice is a simple form of shorthand.

What this question of titles illustrates, however, is that modern readers first start on the works of the ancient historians under a particular set of circumstances. These circumstances render it harder to detect some of the features that make classical history-writing distinctive from its modern counterparts. This is the case even before a work of ancient history is opened. Things become even more complicated once one starts reading it.

The Action of the Swan

We have seen that absences and ambiguities can be caused by the physical texture of ancient books. These are sometimes glossed over or supplemented at a later point by the needs of modern publishing. They are not, however, the biggest problem we face in coming to grips with works of classical history.

A more significant absence is built into the works themselves. One might call this absence the 'action of the swan'. It is perhaps the single most important thing to remember in thinking about ancient history-writing and understanding the arguments of those who interpret it.

Modern works of history usually allow the reader to see their engines in operation. 'Engines', in this context, means how the historian transforms a particular set of data and/or ideas into the finished product that the reader is perusing. Consider, for example, the following passage from A. J. P. Taylor's 1954 work *The Struggle for Mastery in Europe 1848–1918*. Taylor is discussing interpretations of Bismarck's policies at the time of the Treaty of Gastein in 1865:

> There is one strong argument against this more or less pacific interpretation of Bismarck's policy; he was no sooner back in Berlin than he began to drum around for French support. Not content with declaring that he wanted France to expand 'wherever French was spoken in the world', he went off himself to see Napoleon at Biarritz in October. Yet the meeting at Biarritz was far from being a repetition of Cavour's visit to Plombières in 1858. Cavour was resolved on war with Austria; and Napoleon intended to fight it with him ...[17]

In the original text, there is a footnote to the phrase 'wherever French was spoken in the world'. This identifies the source of the phrase: 'Lefebvre de Béhaine to Drouyn de Lhuys, 27 Sept. 1865. Ibid., vii, no. 1590'.[18] 'Ibid.' refers to the *Origines Diplomatiques*, a collection of French diplomatic documents on the origins of the war of 1870.[19] By means of the footnote, Taylor makes it possible for the interested reader to trace back the trail of evidence which enables him to present one argument for the aggression of Bismarck.

Modern writers of history, such as Taylor, usually let the reader see the processes by which their narrative of events progresses. Ancient historians often do not. Like a swan, the narrative of a work of ancient history glides ever forward. But the processes which sustain its momentum remain submerged and invisible. Consider the following passage, which is taken from the account of the Peloponnesian War (431–04 BCE), written by the contemporary historian Thucydides of Athens. It describes the operations of the Spartan general Brasidas in Northern Greece:

> The Spartan Brasidas the son of Tellis happened to be in the vicinity of Sicyon and Corinth at this time, preparing for a campaign in Thrace. When he realized that the walls had been taken, afraid on behalf of the Peloponnesians in Nisaia and fearing that Megara would be captured, he sent orders to the Boeotians to meet the army as quickly as possible at Tripodiskos (a village in the Megarid under Mount Geraneia). He himself went with two thousand, seven hundred Corinthian hoplites, four hundred Phleiasians, six hundred Sicyonians, and those of his expedition who had already gathered together, thinking he would still take the impregnable Nisaia. But when he found out that it was impregnable (for he happened to come out to Tripodiskos at night), selecting three hundred of the army, before he was discovered, he went to the city of the Megarians, undetected by the Athenians near the sea, wanting as a pretext and (if possible) in fact to make an attempt on Nisaia, but especially to enter and secure the city of the Megarians.[20]

Like Taylor, Thucydides depicts the diplomatic operations and restless manoeuvring of a controversial statesman. Like Taylor, he goes to some trouble to set out this figure's motives. Yet the comparison of the two passages illuminates what is missing from Thucydides.

The classical historian repeatedly informs the reader of what is going on in the mind of Brasidas. Thucydides describes the general's fears for the Peloponnesians in Nisaia and the security of Megara. He unfolds how Brasidas discovers the extent of Nisaia's defences. Finally, he asserts complex motives behind Brasidas's approach on the city of the Megarians. The security of Megara is the general's prime consideration, but Brasidas hopes to make an attempt on Nisaia if the opportunity should arise.

What Thucydides does not explain is *how* he arrived at this depiction of the Spartan general's psychology. Thucydides was not Brasidas. He was not even on Brasidas's side in the Peloponnesian War. In fact, Thucydides led Athenian troops (unsuccessfully) against him. Taylor, as we have seen, gives reasons for thinking that Bismarck's intentions in

1865 were not warlike. When he entertains the opposing view, he cites a document which seems to support it. Thucydides, by contrast, purports to tell us in some detail what was going through Brasidas's mind, but he does not lay out what reasons he has to think that this picture of the cogitating Spartan is an accurate one. The narrative glides forward displaying its plumage, but the reader cannot see what is propelling it.

The antithesis I have set up here, like many easy antitheses, does not really do justice to the range of practices throughout ancient and modern historiography. The action of the swan is by no means universal in ancient history-writing and by no means absent from its modern counterparts. As we shall see at greater length in Chapter 2, ancient historians *do* sometimes set out the bases for the version of events that they present. This can take the form of arguing for the plausibility or coherence of their own views against conflicting interpretations, quoting authorities for particular statements that they make, or even bringing in the case of another event to compare or to contrast with the one they are describing. Just as Taylor puts the behaviour of Bismarck after Gastein alongside Cavour's visit to Plombières in 1858 to illustrate how the situation of the one was very different from that of the other, so Tacitus, for example, depicts the people of Rome contrasting the funeral of Augustus in 14 CE with the circumstances surrounding the murder of his adoptive father Julius Caesar in 44 BCE to show how the state of Rome has changed in the interim.[21]

Moreover, the extent to which particular sorts of claims are made without explicit foundation varies a great deal between ancient historians. Herodotus is a striking example of a classical historiographer who shows a considerable readiness to attribute his statements.[22] Levels of fluctuation in the frequency of these claims may also be detected between different passages of the same historian. The depiction of Brasidas is actually an unusual case in Thucydides; the historian supplies motivations for him on a more regular basis than he does for any other individual in the work. The reasons behind this have interesting implications for one's view of Thucydides.[23] For our present purposes, it is sufficient to note that the frequency and confidence with which classical historiographers impute motives to the individuals in their works is subject to considerable variation.[24]

Moreover, it is easy to overstate the extent to which the 'action of the swan' has fallen out of usage in modern history-writing. It is true that a work of historical research which entirely foregoes the use of citations to back up its arguments rarely appears and is likely to raise eyebrows if it does. For example, when Ernst Kantorowicz published his biography of the Holy Roman Emperor Frederick II of Hohenstaufen in 1927, the absence of footnotes to back up his claims generated considerable controversy.[25]

On the other hand, no historical work that has ever been written has spelt out the evidential and logical bases of *every* statement that is made in its pages. And once again, the amount of material that is not explicitly chased back to its sources is likely to vary considerably between authors or between passages by the same author. The narrative histories popular since the Renaissance often avoid much documentation.

This is particularly true of the famous narrative histories written in English before the twentieth century. Consider this passage from Lord Macaulay's *The History of England from the Accession of James the Second,* first published between 1848 and 1859. Macaulay is talking about the declining years of Charles II of Spain:

> His misery was increased by the knowledge that every body was calculating how long he had to live and wondering what would become of his kingdoms when he should be dead. The stately dignitaries of his household, the physicians who ministered to his diseased body, the divines whose business was to soothe his not less diseased mind, the very wife who should have been intent on those gentle offices by which female tenderness can alleviate even the misery of hopeless decay, were all thinking of the new world which was to commence with his death and would have been perfectly willing to see him in the hands of the embalmer if they could have been certain that his successor would be the prince whose interest they espoused.[26]

Macaulay gives no indication of how he knows about the mental state of the dying king, the intentions of his hangers-on or what those hangers-on would have done in the event of being certain of achieving the desired succession.[27] There *are* passages elsewhere in the *History* where he is happy to indicate his sources, it is true. Macaulay's account of the disturbed political atmosphere of London in 1693, for example,[28] is amply footnoted and documented. But the nineteenth-century historian's narrative of Charles II is propelled forward just as invisibly as Thucydides's narrative of Brasidas.

There is, then, no simple contrast between ancient and modern historians when it comes to detailing how they arrive at their accounts of events. Rather, there is a spectrum of practices. This is a pattern which we will see repeated elsewhere. The fact remains, however, that the 'action of the swan' prevails in classical history-writing to an extent that would be unusual in the modern world. What are its consequences?

There are two obvious results of the manner in which ancient histories tend to hide how they work. We might characterize one of these as local and the other as general. On a local level, it is often more difficult for readers to determine the reliability of particular statements which they find in ancient works of history than that of those in the historiography of the modern world. If one wishes to find out whether A. J. P. Taylor was correctly representing Bismarck's rhetoric at the time of the Treaty of Gastein, one can look up the passage in the *Origines Diplomatiques* which he quotes to verify it. If one wants to determine whether Thucydides gives an accurate depiction of Brasidas's thought processes, that avenue of attack is blocked.

This does not exclude other means of assault, of course. As we shall see in Chapter 4, there are a number of different methods by which modern readers can assess the reliability of ancient historiography. However, the action of the swan does tend to complicate such investigations.

The second consequence is a more general issue of methodology. Taylor's references to French documentary records do not just make it possible to check individual facts that bear upon his narrative. They also let the reader see the general principles on which his account is constructed. The footnotes reveal how Taylor operates upon the data of archives and earlier historical accounts to develop his own narrative. They show that he adheres to the canons for assessing and using evidence that (rightly or wrongly) we usually take for granted in modern writers of historiography.

We generally lack any such access to the raw materials of classical history-writing. As a result, the modern reader of ancient historiography has to face a fundamental problem. Are ancient 'histories' really what we think of as history?

At first, this may seem an almost meaningless question. The very word 'history', after all, is derived from the Greek noun '*historiā*'. This is the word which Herodotus of Halicarnassus, whose fifth-century BCE account of the wars between the Greeks and the Persian Empire makes him the earliest fully extant Greek historian, used to describe his work in its opening sentence.[29] Quite apart from terminology, there is also the basic similarity of content and form which, for example, Thucydides on Brasidas shares with Taylor on Bismarck. Despite the differences which we have noted above, the classical Athenian and the twentieth-century Englishman both seem to be presenting their readers with an account of politically significant happenings in the past. How is it possible to doubt, then, that Thucydides and Taylor are engaged in fundamentally identical endeavours?

In fact, the veil that classical histories so often draw over the relationship between the version of events we are reading and the data behind them means that we have to proceed with a little more caution. For modern readers, what makes a history a history is not just a narrative of past events. Nor is it simply that this narrative of past events has to be true. If we discover that certain elements of an account of events in a 'history' are inaccurate, we may think that the history is mistaken, mendacious or simply under-informed. But we will usually still think of it as a work of history.[30] What matters is how we expect the author to handle data to produce the narrative.

This point about expectations is the key. Look at the following paragraph:

> The wind did not hold true. The *Worcester* had barely shipped her new stumps, rattled down the shrouds, completed her water and received the port-admiral's visit before an ominous swell set in, causing her to pitch and roll even in the sheltered Hamoaze and foretelling the great grey swathes of rain driving in on a strong south-wester whose force steadily increased day after day, emptying the Sound, pinning the men-of-war to their moorings in Hamoaze and the merchant ships in Catwater, driving the Brest team off their blockade into Torbay and scattering the shores with driftwood, much of it ancient wreckage, English, French, Spanish, Dutch and neutral. But some was recent, and this was mostly English, for not only were there now far more

English merchantmen than foreigners to be wrecked, but the Royal
Navy, keeping the sea in all weathers, the whole year round, was fast
wearing out, and although new ships were continually being built as
fast as limited treasure and supplies would allow, many others had to
be kept in active service when they were no longer seaworthy –
thirteen had been lost this year, quite apart from those taken by the
Americans or the French.

This narrative of the fortunes of a ship of the line of the Royal Navy gives
no means of verifying its assertions. This, however, does not bother the
reader, because it appears in the second chapter of *The Ionian Mission*, a
1981 historical novel in the Aubrey-Maturin series by Patrick O'Brian.[31]
The reader knows how the rules of what we would call historical fiction
differ from those of 'proper' history-writing. Thus, our expectations
about the relationship between this narrative and extant data about the
Toulon Blockade as it played out in the physical universe are more
accommodating than they would be if *The Ionian Mission* were presenting
itself as 'proper' history.[32] It is not true to say that O'Brian can get away
with anything in his novel. Obviously anachronistic dialogue, technology
or opinions would disquiet in this particular reading context.[33]
Nonetheless, the free intercourse between assertions founded upon historical data and ones for which there is no basis does not bother the
modern reader in a novel, but would certainly do so in a history.

   Novels such as O'Brian's make it easy for the reader to tell what sort
of relationship to historical data they have. O'Brian, in fact, often supplied 'Author's Notes' to make these boundaries explicit, as an example
from another novel demonstrates:

> ... in this case the groundwork of the tale, a little-known campaign in
> the Indian Ocean, is factual; and as far as the geography, the
> manoeuvres, the ships taken, burnt, sunk or destroyed, the battles,
> triumphs and disasters are concerned, the writer has kept to
> contemporary accounts, to the log-books and despatches of the
> officers who fought the actions and to the Admiralty records.[34]

Suppose, however, we encountered the paragraph which I quoted above
from *The Ionian Mission* as a fragment in isolation, without its surrounding

safety-net of context. Above all, suppose we lacked the knowledge that it comes from a novel by an eminent historical novelist. How would we be able to tell what practices in relation to historical data produced it? How would we know what sort of an exercise it actually was?

Interpreting a written narrative becomes a lot harder when one does not know what 'rules' it follows – or, worse, when one's assumptions about those 'rules' turn out to be wrong. In Peter Ackroyd's 1999 novel *The Plato Papers*,[35] for example, the eponymous protagonist, Plato, who inhabits the inscrutable far future of the Earth, makes exactly this sort of category error. Plato discovers a copy of *The Origin of Species* by Charles D————- (the other letters of the surname are effaced in his copy). On the basis of his other fragmentary knowledge about the period, Plato reasonably (but wrongly) assumes that the 'D' stands for 'Dickens'. Ackroyd then shows the consequences when a cultural historian of the far future reads Darwin's masterpiece in the belief that it is a work of creative fiction:

> It opens with a statement by the hero of the narrative – 'When on board HMS *Beagle*, as a naturalist, I was much struck with certain facts ... ' – who then proceeds to tell his remarkable story. By observing bees, and pigeons, and various other creatures around him, he manages to create within his own mind an entire world of such complexity that eventually he believes it to be real. This is reminiscent of another fiction we have recovered, *Don Quixote*, in which the protagonist is similarly deluded. The quixotic hero of *The Origin*, however, is portrayed as being obsessed by 'struggle', 'competition' and 'death by natural selection', in a manner both morbid and ludicrous.[36]

Our situation when we read classical historiography is not altogether dissimilar to Plato's predicament. In fact, Ackroyd highlights possible similarities by including at the beginning of his novel a snippet from a fictional historian of the future written in the style of the opening sentence of Thucydides: 'Myander, a Londoner, wrote the history of a changing world, beginning at the moment of transition, believing that it would mark a great epoch, one more worthy of relation than any that had come before.'[37] Without enough explanatory context, it can, as we have seen, be hard even in the modern world to tell whether a piece of narrative prose purports to be history or simply historical fiction. Because of the general lack of transparency about method that characterizes much of ancient historiography, the difficulties here run much deeper.

Is it safe to assume that the 'rules' of ancient history-writing were identical, or even similar, to those observed by an A. J. P. Taylor? Is it not possible that what we read in the narrative historians of the ancient world is closer to the imaginative recreations of a Patrick O'Brian? And how are we to determine the 'rules' of classical historiography, when the action of the swan makes the relationship between an ancient narrative and the raw historical data at the disposal of its author so hard to tease out?

Writing about History in the Ancient World

There is an obvious place to look in trying to resolve these questions about the essential nature of classical historiography. Examples of history-writing are not all that survives from the ancient world. We also have a number of texts which talk *about* history-writing: what it is; how it works; and what it ought to be. It makes obvious sense to use what these texts say to work out how historiography functioned in the ancient world, and what differences it displayed from its modern counterpart.

This approach has its difficulties, however. In the first place, actual treatises on the writing of history from Greco-Roman antiquity are thin on the ground. References survive to works entitled *Concerning History* or suchlike, by various different authors, including the philosopher Theophrastus. But most of these have been lost.[38]

We still have, it is true, interesting studies from the ancient world of the characteristics shown by particular historians. Into this category fall Plutarch's essay *On the Malice of Herodotus* and the work *On Thucydides* by Dionysius of Halicarnassus.[39] As we shall see in Chapter 6, much in these works is thought-provoking.[40] Neither, however, is as illuminating on wider historiographical issues as one would ideally like.[41]

Perhaps the closest thing that survives to a general, theoretical treatment of historiography from the classical world is a treatise entitled *How History Ought to be Written*, which Lucian of Samosata composed in the second century CE.[42] Apart from Lucian's work, and the author-specific works noted above, reflections upon history-writing mostly have to be unearthed from texts which discuss historiography but do not necessarily take its theory as their main theme. Aristotle, for example, makes some passing (and rather elliptical) remarks on the subject in the course of his *Poetics*.[43] Such remarks can, however, throw up a number of methodological difficulties. These are best illustrated by a practical example.

One of the most extended discussions of historiography that survives from Greco-Roman antiquity is found in *De Oratore (On the Orator)*. This was written by the Roman politician and orator Marcus Tullius Cicero in 55 BCE. *De Oratore* takes the form of a dialogue, an imagined conversation held in 91 BCE between the historical figures L. Licinius Crassus (whom Cicero had known as a boy), M. Antonius, P. Sulpicius Rufus and C. Aurelius Cotta, as well as some others. They discuss the 'power of oratory and the varied accomplishments needed for the orator'[44] over three days in Crassus's Tusculan villa.

The part of this dialogue which has most engaged the attention of readers interested in ancient historiography is in the second book of the work. Antonius, describing what lies within the purview of the ideal orator, lists examples, and the last of these is historiography.[45] There then follows a comparison, again by Antonius, between the early Roman historians and their earlier Greek counterparts,[46] a potted history of Greek historiography[47] and, finally, a description of how an orator should write history.

This description of writing history often forms the centrepiece of discussions of historiographical theory in the ancient world.[48] Many aspects of its interpretation are controversial. The translation given here is that of A. J. Woodman:

> Everyone of course knows that the first law of historiography is not
> daring to say anything false, and the second is not refraining from
> saying anything true: there should be no suggestion of prejudice for,
> or bias against, when you write. These foundations are of course
> recognised by everyone, but the actual superstructure consists of
> content and style. It is in the nature of content, on the one hand, that
> you require a chronological order of events and topographical

descriptions, and also that you need – since in the treatment of
important and memorable achievements the reader expects (i)
intentions, (ii) the events themselves, and (iii) consequences – in
the case of (i) to indicate whether you approve of the intentions,
of (ii) to reveal not only what was said or done but also in what
manner, and of (iii) to explain all the reasons, whether they be of
chance or intelligence or impetuousness, and also to give not only
the achievements of any famous protagonist but also his life and
character.[49]

At first sight, this passage seems to confirm, beyond any reasonable
doubt, that ancient historiography was not very different in conception
from its modern counterpart. The first and second 'laws of historiography' are said to enjoin that histories cleave to the truth and avoid falsehood. Moreover, Antonius notes that the content of history should
include detailed chronological and topographical descriptions. The
emphasis on intentionality and its depiction in history may remind us of
the issues about the handling of motivations in classical historiography
which we have already noted.[50] On the whole, however, there seems to
be little here with which a narrative historian of the twenty-first century
would disagree.

However, this passage is not necessarily as easy to interpret as it looks.
Antonius, as we have seen, is talking about how great a task history is for
an *orator*, and what a challenge it would pose to rhetorical skill.[51] In fact,
Antonius is making a claim for the applicability to history-writing of
some of the features which ancient rhetorical handbooks recommended
for speech-making. Thus, clear chronology is important in a history, as in
a speech, to make the progress of events as lucid as possible. As one treatise on rhetoric put it, 'our statement of the case will be clear if we set
out first whatever happened first, and preserve the order of events and
times'.[52] Likewise the emphasis on topographical descriptions may be
more closely related to the advice of the handbooks that the orator
should demonstrate the fitness of the location for his narrative and
diversify his argument with geographical digressions than to a modern
historian's concern for accurate geography.[53]

The features which Antonius is highlighting fall under the rubric of
inventio, which ancient rhetorical theory defined as one of the various

techniques in which an accomplished rhetorician should be expert. *Inventio* does not mean 'invention'. In fact, the Latin verb from which it derives has the root meaning 'to find', not 'to invent/make up'. *Inventio* is 'the "discovery" of what requires to be said in a given situation, the implied theory being that this is somehow already "there" though latent'.[54] In the context of rhetorical theory, Cicero himself defines this as the 'thinking out of things true or probable, to make a case convincing',[55] and notes that what is convincing is 'that which for the most part happens or which does not strain credibility or which contains within itself an approximation to either of these, whether it be true or false'.[56]

From these considerations, it has been supposed that ancient historiography emerges as a creature very different from its modern successor. As a famous treatment of this passage has put it: 'Since *inventio* makes no distinction between the true and the probable, but accords the same status to the latter as to the former (and sometimes even more), its prescriptions share no common ground at all with modern historiography.'[57] On this reading, the passage from *De Oratore* proves that there is a fundamental difference between ancient history-writing, which, because of its affinities to rhetoric, is mostly concerned with putting an eloquent case for a version of the past and so tends to privilege the plausible, and modern history-writing, which is concerned with methodical investigation of sources and concerns itself only with the true.

This theory of ancient history-writing has a definite appeal. Above all, it provides a panacea for certain aspects of classical historiography which will otherwise tend to strike a modern reader as deeply troubling. These will mostly be the subject of later chapters, but one notes in particular the general prevalence of speeches from the mouths of people in the narrative that may in fact have been composed by the historian himself,[58] and the 'expansion of history' which may have taken place in the historiography of early Rome.[59] If the ancient conception of history-writing was so very different from the modern, such considerations would cease to be problematic.

However, this line of reasoning has a number of significant difficulties. It is evident that Antonius is applying techniques that fall under the heading of *inventio* in rhetorical text books to the writing of history. It is by no means clear, however, that this means he thinks that the whole theory of *inventio* itself is therefore directly applicable to historiography.

17

In fact, there is good evidence to think that Antonius does not regard truth as an irrelevant criterion where historiography is concerned. As we have already seen, he claims that the first and second laws of historiography are 'not daring to say anything false' and 'not refraining from saying anything true'. This is rather hard to square with the notion that he intends the general concern that *inventio* has with the plausible in rhetorical theory to override the truth-claims one might consider appropriate to history-writing.

Attempts to conquer this difficulty have focussed on what immediately follows Antonius's insistence on the importance of not omitting the truth or saying the false: 'there should be no suggestion of prejudice for, or bias against, when you write'.[60] It has been claimed that these words explain those which immediately precede them. Therefore, when Cicero speaks here of 'truth' and 'falsehood', he actually means only that a historian should be impartial.[61] On this reading, Antonius would implicitly be countenancing the inclusion into works of history of material that is not factually accurate, so long as the impartiality of the historian is preserved. Corroboration of the alleged identity between 'truth' and 'impartiality' in this particular context is said to be given by the fact that impartiality is something to which some ancient historians are eager to lay claim, especially in their prefaces, as an example from Tacitus demonstrates: 'Therefore it is my plan to treat in brief Augustus, especially the very end of his reign, later on the principate of Tiberius and the rest, without malice and partiality, for which I am far from having any motives.'[62]

There is a problem with this notion, however. It relies on a hypothesis about the nature of Antonius's train of thought here. This is that the words 'there should be no suggestion of prejudice for, or bias against, when you write' explain *and are co-extensive with* the preceding sentences about the importance of telling the truth and not telling lies.

It is pretty clear that the clause on prejudice and bias is related to what comes before it. It is much less clear, however, that it is simply a *restatement* of the foregoing – which the hypothesis mentioned above assumes.[63] In the Latin, the clause on prejudice follows on from the ones about truth and falsehood without any overt indication of the exact relationship between them. Antonius does not, for example, put in a parenthetical phrase to make it clear that he thinks freedom from prejudice and truthfulness are the same thing; he does not say ' ... the second is not refraining from saying anything true: *that is*, there should be no suggestion of prejudice for, or bias against, when you write'.

Because the exact logical relationship between the clauses is not made clear by the syntax, it is entirely possible that the warning against partiality *is* meant to be the same thing as the instructions to speak truth and avoid falsehood. It can be argued that such a view is compatible with sentiments which Cicero expressed in a letter to the historian Lucius Lucceius in 55 BCE, although that text presents interpretative difficulties of its own.[64] On the other hand, the idea that Antonius is claiming 'impartiality' to be the same thing as 'speaking truth' is by no means the only valid interpretation that the syntax allows. It might equally be the case that avoiding partiality is just a particularly important instance of how the 'laws' concerning truth and falsehood are to be put into operation. When public information campaigns say 'Be smart! Fit a smoke alarm!', we do not believe that the people behind the campaigns think that fitting a smoke alarm is the sum total of what it means to be intelligent. Rather, we infer that fitting a smoke alarm is the most important instance, in this particular context, of being smart. The possibility that there exist other ways of being smart which have nothing to do with fire prevention is certainly not ruled out.

This reading of the passage, which takes Antonius's instructions towards impartiality as a *subset* of his definition of how history should be written rather than the whole of it, certainly coheres better with the attitude towards factual accuracy which is displayed at some points in the ancient historians themselves, or, indeed, in Lucian's treatise on proper historiography. There is no obvious compunction in these texts about criticizing simple 'howlers' in other historians – errors of fact which are clearly the result of blundering or lack of knowledge in the author being criticized rather than the consequence of prejudice or a desire to flatter. Thus Lucian lays into one historian for egregious geographical blunders:

> One man was so careless in gathering his facts that, though he'd never
> met a single Syrian or even, to quote the saying, heard such tittle-
> tattle in a barber's shop, this was what he said about Europus:
> 'Europus lies in Mesopotamia, two days' journey distant from the

Euphrates, and it was founded by colonists from Edessa.' And even this didn't satisfy him, but this splendid fellow picked up my native city of Samosata and transported it, acropolis, walls and all, into Mesopotamia so that it is flanked by the waters of both the rivers passing close to it on both sides and almost touching the city walls.[65]

Note that Lucian does *not* state that this historian was serving any polemical purpose by putting Europus and Samosata in the wrong places. The error does not seem to have arisen out of partiality or prejudice on the part of the censured author, merely incompetence or negligence. Yet Lucian criticizes him anyway. This is hard to square with the idea that it was universally acknowledged in classical antiquity that factual accuracy did not form part of the concept of 'truth' as it pertained to historiography.

Lucian's freedom in criticizing historiographical untruths which do not arise from partiality or prejudice is shared by the practising historians of antiquity. Velleius Paterculus, who wrote a condensed history in two books covering events from the mythic period to the reign of the Emperor Tiberius in the first century CE, criticizes the elder Cato for an error in chronology concerning the date of the foundation of Capua.[66] Velleius does not accuse Cato of perpetrating this error because of his own inclinations or proclivities, and it is hard to envisage a scenario in which that could have been the case. Examples of such criticisms of incompetent chronology in the ancient historians may be multiplied; compare also the lost Roman historian L. Calpurnius Piso's realization that the chronology of the kings of Rome made little sense if one accepted accounts that Tarquinius Superbus was the son of Lucius Tarquinius.[67] A complaint by the biographer Plutarch suggests that in some areas of writing about the past these criticisms were not unusual.[68]

On a broader canvas, Polybius of Megalopolis, whose 40-book history of the rise of Rome, written in the second century BCE, is particularly notable for its comments on historiographical method, devotes much time and attention to cataloguing factual inaccuracies on the part of other historians. He often makes clear that he considers some of these mistakes to be the result of ignorance or incompetence rather than the product of partiality or prejudice. Indeed, he is careful to distinguish between the two, although both are described as needing correction: 'Those, as I have said, who make false statements owing to error should meet with kind correction and forgiveness, but those who lie deliberately deserve an implacable accuser.'[69] There often seems to be more going on with Polybius's strictures than a simple correction of factual error.[70] Nevertheless, it is difficult to see how they could have been made at all against the background of a universal understanding that 'truth' and 'impartiality' were interchangeable terms where ancient historiography was concerned.

It is likewise hard to sustain the notion that Antonius's formulation points to a general denial in antiquity of the need for historians to investigate questions of fact and interpretation. Antonius *may* be envisaging a historian here who 'would have automatic recourse to the rules of rhetoric in which he had been trained ... but ... would be unlikely to be responding to any unanswered questions: he would see himself in the role of advocate and would know in advance, as it were, the case which he would have to make'.[71] As we have seen, it is by no means certain that Antonius *is* actually advocating the wholesale transposition of rhetorical theory into historiography. But even if this is what he is saying, his precepts do not, in fact, square with attitudes to investigation and the assessment of evidence which we encounter at times as we read the historians of the ancient world.[72] Diodorus Siculus, who in the first century BCE wrote a universal history in 40 books covering events from the mythic period to 59 BCE,[73] claims in his preface to have laboured arduously for three decades in preparation for his great work:

> And so we, appreciating that an undertaking of this nature, while most useful, would yet require much labour and time, have been engaged upon it for thirty years, and with much hardship and many dangers we have visited a large portion of both Asia and Europe that we might see with our own eyes all the most important regions and as many others as possible; for many errors have been committed through ignorance of the sites, not only by the common run of historians, but even by some of the highest reputation.[74]

As it happens, there is a good case for scepticism about the complete authenticity of Diodorus's claims here.[75] He certainly fell prey to

Lucian's favourite historiographical blunder: muddling the geography of Mesopotamia (he claims that Nineveh was sited on the Euphrates).[76] What is important for our purposes, however, is that he clearly feels that he has something to gain by making them. Laborious investigation of sources carried prestige, even if a particular claim to such investigations was in fact false or exaggerated. One might also compare Cassius Dio, a historian in whose methodological claims scholars have tended to be more willing to acquiesce. Dio asserts that he spent ten years collecting the information for his work.[77]

The utility of such research could be doubted. Again, Polybius is an important figure here, vehemently criticizing his predecessor Timaeus of Tauromenium for exalting the study of written sources as the most important element in writing history.[78] But Polybius derides Timaeus's book-learning to highlight his own, superior research methodology and investigative equipment, including such important matters as the proper interrogation and assessment of eyewitnesses to significant historical events,[79] and spreading across different sources of information:

> In the same fashion, systematic history too consists of three parts, the
> first being the industrious study of memoirs and other documents and
> a comparison of their contents, the second, the survey of cities,
> places, rivers, lakes, and, in general, all the peculiar features of land
> and sea and the distances of one place from another, and the third
> being the review of political events.[80]

Arguments about the differing status of different sorts of evidence, and how particular pieces of such evidence should be assessed, seem to place Polybius and his ilk a long way away from a historian who 'would be unlikely to be responding to any unanswered questions'.

This brings us to the most fundamental problem with the conviction that Antonius's disquisition on what an orator can bring to history can furnish us with a general definition of how history-writing was tackled in the Greco-Roman world. Even if Antonius does mean to suggest that history is fully explicable in terms of the rules of ancient rhetorical theory – a possible, but by no means inevitable, reading of this passage – such a vision does not seem to map well onto the totality of historiography as it was actually practised. Nor should this surprise us. There are perils in the assumption that a particular work of theory on a given topic will inevitably provide us with a miraculous key that faultlessly unlocks its interpretation.[81]

This is particularly so in the case of Antonius's speech. It is worth stressing a number of points about this which should be obvious but are sometimes elided in critical discussion. Firstly, this is *not* Cicero speaking from his own mouth, but a historical figure acting in a philosophical dialogue. True, Antonius is a figure in whose words one would expect Cicero to want the reader to invest considerable importance. It is worth noting, all the same, that it is a representation of Antonius, not Cicero himself, who is speaking, and that there are certain methodological issues in assuming that a character in a work necessarily speaks for the author without qualification.

The dialogic form of *De Oratore* is not the only interpretative issue here, however. There is a temptation when using a work which pertains to the theory of a subject to assume that what the work is saying was a widely accepted orthodoxy. The temptation can be particularly strong, paradoxically, when there are so few such works surviving that this supposition is impossible to verify. This is, in fact, a special case of the phenomenon which we shall be examining in more detail in Chapter 6: the psychological appeal of the single source.[82]

In fact, the idea that Cicero himself is presenting the consensual view of antiquity about how history should be written, with no axe to grind of his own, is hard to sustain in the light of what we have already seen about the context of Antonius's discussion. The speech is not embedded in a work entitled *De Historia*; the subject of the dialogue is the capacities of the orator. The claim, expressed by Antonius, that history-writing is one more field in which the orator can shine is itself part of the work's own larger rhetorical strategy: the insistence that there are few areas of human endeavour to which the orator cannot make a unique contribution. The exposition of how history ought to be written is therefore not exactly disinterested.

Antonius's masterful rhetoric attempts to impose a certain homogeneity on history-writing in antiquity. But as we have seen by looking at the methodology and claims of the historians themselves, the actual practice of classical historiography was more complicated than that. In what follows, we shall be looking at the many different ways in which the historians of the ancient world grappled with the representation of the past. Many puzzles await the interested student, but each requires consideration on its own terms, and no universal cure-all can explain every one. There is no lack of skeletons in the historiographical cupboard. But there is a distinct lack of skeleton keys.

2

THE NATURES OF HISTORY

Chapter 1 made a case that it is not easy to define the nature of history-writing in the ancient world. Classical historiography does not invariably indicate its relationship to the raw data at the disposal of the historian. Indeed, it does not necessarily indicate whether there is any relationship between the narrative it offers and prior data at all.

Because ancient history-writing often conceals its motive forces in this fashion, it is tempting to look for an easy definition of how it works in theoretical writings on the subject. But these too can prove hard to interpret. We have seen that one can easily leap to generalizing conclusions about the nature of historiography in Greece and Rome which are not supported by evidence from the actual practice of some ancient historians.

Moreover, we have noted that such theoretical texts should not, as a point of method, be elevated to a position of authority which they do not deserve. Statements on the nature of history-writing may reflect the contemporary zeitgeist. But they might equally reflect only the views of an individual – and an individual who is not necessarily disinterested in the vision of historiography which he espouses.[1]

These considerations should not make us despondent, however. It can be perilous (as we have seen) to assume that the experience of the modern world maps neatly onto that of the ancient. Nonetheless, the character of history-writing since the Renaissance would make it surprising if the historiographical production of classical antiquity showed much homogeneity or, beyond the most basic bounding conditions, any common line on how it should go about its business.

It is important to keep sight of this. There has sometimes been a fashion, in the study of classical historiography, for seeing 'the ancient historian' and 'the modern historian' as contrasting but indivisible entities. They may have similarities; they may have differences. Each, however, is self-consistent. There is (or so it is assumed) an 'ancient' and a 'modern' approach to history-writing.[2]

The contrast is rhetorically convenient. Indeed, this is pretty much the antithesis which I erected in Chapter 1, when I set a passage from the modern history of A. J. P. Taylor against one from the ancient Thucydides.[3] The problem is that 'the modern historian', at least, has never been that easy to define. If one investigates the historiography of the modern world, one finds that there are few subjects as likely to engage the attention of a historian as the failure of other historians to write history 'properly'.

> Every schoolboy knows – at least every German high school student
> once knew – what scientific history is and who invented it. Scientific
> history rests on primary rather than secondary sources: Leopold von
> Ranke, the Protestant jurist's son from the wonderfully named
> Thuringian town of Wiehe a. d. Unstrut who became one of the
> dominant figures of the nineteenth-century University of Berlin, was
> its first famous practitioner.[4]

Ranke's self-definition as a historian proceeded through pointed contrast with the faulty methodology and erroneous emphases of his predecessors. So, for example, Sismonde de Sismondi, the earlier historian of the Italian republics, failed to address Ranke's crucial point of historiographical methodology in relationship to his sources: 'who, of these many writers, possesses information that is really original with him: who can offer us real instruction?'[5] Ranke was not the first historian to assert his particular vision of what historiography should be against the ones of his predecessors in history-writing. Debates on the themes, methodologies, narrative structures and relationship to evidence which writers of history should adopt have certainly shown no sign of abating in the almost two centuries since.[6]

The problem of definition is also one which we should not sidestep. Debates on the nature of historiography have often left out modes of historical production which do not sit easily within a particular definition of the subject. It is not hard to think of texts from the modern era which clearly establish and rely upon some sort of relationship with history and the historical past, but do not exactly fit under the conventional rubrics which debates about the nature of historiography try to define. We have already mentioned the case of historical fiction.[7] Other examples are not hard to find: popular histories; collections of the weird and wonderful; even history as comedy. The century which produced Beryl Smalley's *The Study of the Bible in the Middle Ages*,[8] Lewis Namier's *The Structure of Politics at the Accession of George III*,[9] and Fernand Braudel's *The Mediterranean and the Mediterranean World in the Age of Philip II*,[10] also gave birth to *1066 and All That* and *The Book of Heroic Failures*.[11] All of these texts can be found under the classification of 'history' in bookstores or on-line encyclopedias. None, however, exemplifies a conception of unified historiography which is consistent with any of the others.

These observations do not suggest that all modes of historical production are equally valid. What they warn against is the assumption that history-writing, at least in the modern world, is either an entirely uniform enterprise or one the sub-divisions of which can be easily classified. Certainly, to pick out a single textbook or manual on historiography such as the one produced by the French historians Langlois and Seignobos at the end of the nineteenth century, and to take its precepts as supplying the key to historiographical production in the modern era, swiftly emerges as a fruitless exercise.[12] Plato, the historian of the post-apocalyptic future whom we met in the previous chapter,[13] would have reached some surprising conclusions from a reading of Langlois and Seignobos: that historians of the twentieth century believed that history, as a topic for scholarly enquiry, had now ended ('the quantity of documents in existence, if not of known documents, is given; time, in spite of all the precautions which are taken nowadays, is continually diminishing it; *it will never increase*');[14] that geography had no particular relevance to the student of history;[15] and that the history of some portions of classical antiquity would be solved and wrapped up for good in a generation or so.[16]

The obvious solution to this difficulty is examination of ancient history-writing in action. We saw at the end of the previous chapter that the methodological comments of Polybius, Velleius Paterculus and other practising historians refute the idea of a universal commitment to a particular notion of 'truth as impartiality' in the historiography of the ancient world.[17] Can we not extend this strategy? Can not a more accurate notion of how history-writing worked in the ancient world be derived from these insights into, as one scholar has put it with regard to Herodotus, the 'workshops' of the authors themselves?[18]

There is much to be said for this strategy. Indeed, it is one which I intend to pursue for most of this volume. Nonetheless, it is important to keep sight of its limitations.

The biggest problem is what we have already encountered as 'the action of the swan'.[19] Ancient historical texts simply do not, on the whole, announce their methodologies as clearly and consistently as the historians of the modern world. In terms of the classical historiography which has survived to the present day, Polybius is, in fact, unusual in the extent to which he is prepared to discuss at length the ways in which his history-writing functions, especially in what survives of Book 12 of his work, an extended critique of earlier historians. Other historiographers of antiquity are generally less forthcoming, although there are exceptions: both Thucydides and Arrian made important statements of method to which we shall return.[20]

Polybius's loquacity on this subject is very helpful to us, of course. But we should resist the temptation to see his views as inevitably applicable across the historiography of the ancient world. Again, we have to be careful to avoid the notion that a source is authoritative simply because there is so little extant to contradict it.[21]

Another important consideration is that statements about theme and methodology are not necessarily straightforward. This applies even when they refer to the practice of the author who is making the statement. The problem can take a number of forms.

Lie to Me

An author may simply lie about the nature of his enterprise or the methods he has used to undertake it. Examples of this are not far to seek in the modern world.[22] The question becomes a little more complicated where the authors of antiquity are concerned. We have noted the general scarcity of independent testimonies by which we can test the assertions of ancient historians.[23] It is therefore not always easy to establish conclusively when a classical author is telling *deliberate* untruths in the full awareness of what he is doing. Misinformation by lost sources, excessive credulity or incompetence are usually possible alternatives. (A less common one – mental instability or fantasizing on the part of the author – is better attested in modern history-writing and biography than in ancient.)[24]

However, the historians of antiquity were definitely alive to the possibility of deliberate mendacity on the part of their predecessors. They were not slow to allege it – as when the first-century CE author Josephus criticizes the deliberate tampering with Herod's family tree which he detected in the work of Nicolaus of Damascus.[25] And there are certainly cases where, despite a dearth of ancient censure, such an explanation fits the data at our disposal better than any other.

For example, the late collection of imperial biographies known as the *Historia Augusta* (the 'Augustan History') decorates its narrative with frequent and detailed references to documents that are said to back up its claims.[26] Indeed, it contains an alleged record of an argument between scholars who deploy the evidence of coins, imperial edicts and Greek and Egyptian books in support of their assertions,[27] as well as quoting in full a putative letter by the Emperor Hadrian himself.[28] This would seem to offer good evidence for an approach to the writing of history based on the best archival primary sources, an attitude that Ranke himself might have approved. The problem is that there is a compelling case that all of these documents, coins and inscriptions (as well as more than 30 biographers and historians unattested anywhere else) were made up for the purposes of the *Historia Augusta* itself.[29]

Of course, the mere fact that an author's methodological claims are untrue with regard to his own practice does not mean that these claims are not interesting for someone who is trying to unravel what might have been expected from a writer of history in the ancient world.[30] Mendacious authors are usually mendacious for a purpose. In particular, it is likely that the claims a lying historian makes for his work will be playing up to the expectations of his readership. Thus, remarks on methodology in a historian will always tend to have a value for the student of history-writing as a general activity – even if they have to be disregarded by the student of that particular historian.

The Singer and the Song

There is another potential problem in evaluating the status of method-ological statements amongst the historians of antiquity. This arises from the possible disjunction between theory and practice. In other words, the body of a historian's work does not actually seem to cohere with the methodological principles he has stated. Such a disjunction may seem to be simply a restatement of the 'mendacious historian' difficulty. In fact, a lack of exact fit between what a historian professes and what he actually does can have more complex explanations than simple mendacity.

It is not hard to uncover examples from the modern world of method-ological statements which are readily falsified from the works of the author who makes them, but which are nevertheless clearly believed on some level by the writer in question when he does so. The theoretical writings of Richard Wagner offer a case in point. It is disconcerting to discover the man who had already composed *Tannhaüser* and *Lohengrin* and would later compose *Parsifal* declaring that 'Christian art is no true art, because it could relate only to abstract spirit and the grace of God'.[31] Yet this is a statement which Wagner, at this point, felt himself able to make.

Instances from the historiography of the modern world also help us to see the factors which might make the history which an author writes dif-ferent from that which he seems to set out in his statements on his methodology. There is, for example, the phenomenon of what one might call the 'run-away book'. This is where the writer discovers, as he under-takes a work, that its actual proportions or theme are going to be rather different from what he initially stated.

On the one hand, the author may envisage a grand work, of which what eventually appears was at first meant to be only a portion. A library stocked with the histories eminent writers thought they were going to write would be an impressive one: the great history of Hugo Grotius;[32] Edward Gibbon's work on the chronicles of mediaeval England;[33] the intellectual histories of Liberty as a concept by Lord Acton and Arnaldo

Momigliano;[34] Herbert Butterfield's history of diplomacy;[35] and Hugh Trevor-Roper's trilogy on Oliver Cromwell and the Puritan Revolution.[36] Histories take time to write, and a historian's plans for a work may be overtaken by the embrace of new concerns and methodologies, doubts about the viability of the original project, or personal catastrophe.

Contrariwise, it may turn out that the original project needs a scale and a treatment which the author did not fully anticipate or about which he changed his mind. In the field of classical scholarship, this is a phenomenon which seems to be particularly associated with writers of distinguished commentaries.[37] It has never, however, been unique to classicists.[38] Perhaps the most colossal growth of a history from comparatively constrained beginnings is to be found in the *Annales Ecclesiastici*, a history of the first 12 centuries of the Christian Church by the sixteenth-century Italian historian Cesare Baronio. This swelled from sermons the author had delivered to lectures to 12 folio volumes of historiography.[39]

In the modern world, a historian can usually conceal such changes of plan in the text that does appear. We generally find out about the 'histories that did not happen' from the author's graceful revelations of what might have been. Where he or she is less obliging, we are usually dependent upon biographical information released after the author's death.

The situation in antiquity may well have been different. There are certainly cases where one possible explanation of apparent inconsistencies in a historian's work is that he lacked either the opportunity or the inclination to ensure total coherence between the earlier and later portions of his oeuvre. The possibility of dying before completion was certainly a hazard of which classical historiographers were aware. Diodorus, talking about the historical efforts of his predecessors, remarks that 'some did not fulfil the promise of their attempt because they were taken off by fate in mid-life';[40] while Polybius, after explaining the plan for his history, notes 'such is the plan I propose, but all depends on Fortune's granting me a life long enough to execute it'.[41]

It is less straightforward than one might expect to determine how often such fears were justified. The text of Herodotus is a case in point: scholars still debate whether the seemingly odd note on which it ends (a brief flashback story about Cyrus the Great) is the result of authorial intent or an incomplete text.[42] Even if we are sure that our text is incomplete, it will not necessarily be clear whether the author never finished the work or whether the ending has been lost. Nonetheless, our text of Thucydides probably ends in mid-sentence,[43] though even here a case has been made for the text's completeness.[44] The lost history of the first-century CE Roman writer on rhetoric Lucius Annaeus Seneca, covering the period from the Roman Civil Wars of the previous century to the present, appears to have been cut short by Seneca's death.[45] Tacitus seems never to have attempted the work on the reigns of Nerva and Trajan which he claims to be setting aside for his old age at the beginning of his *Histories* ('I have reserved for my old age, if life is spared to me, the reigns of the deified Nerva and of the Emperor Trajan').[46] It can therefore be tempting to explain contradictions between statements which a historian makes at different points, or developments and changes in his methodology, in terms of an evolving work which the author never had the chance or desire to revise.[47] This is a strategy which has often appealed in the interpretation of Thucydides.[48]

In a number of cases, a growth in the scope of a work can be clearly plotted from the programmatic comments of the author himself. Polybius originally announces that he intends to answer the question 'how and by a state with what sort of constitution almost the whole of the known world was conquered and fell under the single rule of the Romans in a space of not quite 53 years'.[49] This chronological span takes him from 220 BCE to the end of the Macedonian monarchy in 167, covering (apart from excursuses and prefatory material) the first 30 books of his history. Subsequently, however, he extends his coverage to include the exercise of Roman domination:

> ... since judgements regarding either the conquerors or the conquered based purely on performance are by no means final ... I must append to the history of the above period an account of the subsequent policy of the conquerors and their method of universal rule, as well as of the various opinions and appreciations of their rulers entertained by the subjects, and finally I must describe what were the prevailing and dominant tendencies and ambitions of the various peoples in their private and public life.[50]

One may also note the related case of historians who cannot, in the absence of clairvoyance, have been entirely sure when their work would finish at the point they started work. Again, Thucydides is a useful example here. We have already noted his claim to have started work when the Peloponnesian War began.[51] If this was so, then exactly how his account of that 27-year conflict was going to develop would have been unknown to him at the beginning of his endeavours, whatever the exact nature of the work he was doing at that time may have been.[52]

Moreover, even where the general pattern of events is known from the start, any history projected on a sufficient scale is liable to course-correction as it proceeds. There is an obvious practical problem in making sure that the work can be completed in one lifetime. We have already seen how Seneca at least seems to have been surprised by death with his historiographical breeches unfastened.[53]

Beyond this, changes of conception, organization, or emphasis in the unfolding opus obviously have the chance to proliferate as its magnitude increases. In post-classical historiography, one might cite the example of Gibbon, who set on record the ways in which he thought his writing changed as the *Decline and Fall* developed: 'The style of the first volume is, in my opinion, somewhat crude and elaborate; in the second and third it is ripened into ease, correctness and numbers; but in the last three I may have been seduced by the facility of my pen, and the constant habit of speaking one language and writing another may have infused some mixture of Gallic idioms.'[54] E. H. Carr, whose *History of Soviet Russia* was 14 volumes and 30 years in the making, likewise commented on the changes in his enterprise as it unfolded.[55]

In the ancient world, Livy, whose history of Rome, as we have already noted, ultimately extended to at least 142 books, is careful to draw notice to the vastness of his historiographical enterprise and the jitters which might assail the historian in mid-course:

> When I reflect that 63 years – the space between the outbreak of the
> First and the end of the Second Punic War – have filled as many books
> for me as were required for the 487 years from the founding of the
> city to the consulship of Appius Claudius (who began the first war
> with the Carthaginians), already I see in my mind's eye that, like men
> who, attracted by the shallow water near the shore, wade out into the

sea, I am being carried on, whatever progress I make, into depths
more vast, and, as it were, into the abyss, and that the task almost
waxes greater which, as I finished each of the earlier portions, seemed
to be growing smaller.[56]

There is certainly more going on here than a simple diagnosis of 'run-away
history'. Livy has other reasons, as we shall see, for intruding his authorial voice thus into his narrative.[57] Nonetheless, the surface meaning retains
its force. A history on this sort of scale can leave even the most self-
confident author thinking that he is going to need a bigger boat.

It is important, then, to remember that historiography can be a process
as much as a product. Statements which a historian makes about the
nature of his enterprise do not necessarily represent his last word on
the subject or depict his subsequent practice with total accuracy. And
even if it *is* his last word, words only get to be last because a lot of
other words, with which they do not necessarily agree, have come before
them.

Author Theatre

We have now examined two possible reasons why a classical historian's
theoretical pronouncements may not be borne out by his practice as a
writer. These have been simple mendacity, and change of conception as
the work progresses. In their own ways, each of these is readily understandable and explicable.

There is, however, a third category of explanation for a mismatch
between theory and practice in classical historiography. This is a little
harder to explain and manifests itself in a greater variety of forms.
Nonetheless, it may account for more cases of apparent 'mismatch' in the
ancient historians than the other two combined.

It is tempting to consider statements of method in ancient historiography in isolation from the work which they purport to illuminate. The
description of them as 'metahistory',[58] which is not uncommon in more
recent treatments of them, is rooted in an important etymological
metaphor that makes this clear. The Greek prefix *meta-*, used in this as in
many similar formulations, originally denoted something that happened

34

after or beyond the thing to which it was attached. Thus, it is easy to slip into the habit of seeing reflections on method within a historical text as slightly divorced from the text itself, standing, as it were, beyond or behind them.

This habit is excusable. However, it should be tempered by an awareness that these pronouncements are still a part of the work on which they offer self-reflection. Methodological statements do not just convey information. In fact, they contribute to the total effect of the text of which they are a part.

Consider, for example, Ranke's comments on historical method, which have already been mentioned above.[59] Ranke does indeed convey what he sees as acceptable methodology through criticism of earlier historians. However, that criticism serves a further function. The inadequacy of his predecessors throws into relief Ranke's own achievement, his sagacity as the person who spotted that Guicciardini, the previously favoured source for historians of the Italian republics, was unreliable: 'if we accomplish that, we will have reached our goal: the Sismondis will have to stop citing Guicciardini at the bottom of every page, and always the same Guicciardini'.[60] The great Ranke derisively deploys an image of faulty historiographers as Sismondi clones (they all look the same to him) in implicit contrast to his own remarkable uniqueness. A statement of method is also a piece of self-promotion, an assertion of singularity. Ranke was not the first to use the trick of demeaning other historians by pluralizing them: 'they are all Thucydideses, Herodotuses, and Xenophons to us'.[61]

Some methodological pronouncements in the historians of classical antiquity are susceptible to a similar analysis.[62] It is particularly notable in the case of Polybius, although by no means unique to him.[63] The Megalopolitan historian is, as we have already noted, remarkably free with comments on acceptable standards of historical practice. A high proportion of the comments are devoted to criticizing the failure to live up to these standards of other historiographers. Indeed, Polybius is fully capable of criticizing a historian (in this case, as in many others, the Sicilian Timaeus) for not knowing how to criticize other historians properly, as when he censures Timaeus's attack on Aristotle: 'I am even ready to concede that Timaeus's account is more probable. But is this a reason why a historical writer whose statements seem lacking in probability must submit to listen to every term of contumely and almost to be put on trial for his life? Surely not.'[64]

Such reflections suggest the superior virtues of the historian who makes them, as we have just seen in the case of Ranke. However, scholars have also noted that the authors whom Polybius singles out for this treatment are often those against whom he has a good reason for personal animosity: Timaeus, who could have disputed Polybius's claim to be the premier Greek historian of Rome; Phylarchus, who wrote approvingly of Cleomenes, the rival of Polybius's own political hero Aratus of Sicyon;[65] Postumius Albinus, who had presided over the Roman Senate in a meeting where the return of Greek exiles (of whom Polybius was one) was discussed, and he manipulated business so that a motion favourable to them was rejected.[66] It is difficult to resist the notion that a simple disquisition on historical method is not all that Polybius is trying to achieve through such criticisms.[67]

It is worth stressing that it is excessively reductive to see these manoeuvres as the *sole* explanation for methodological statements of this type, whether in Polybius or in other works. Comments elsewhere in Polybius's work show that the question of appropriate praise and blame concerned him even when he was not grinding an axe with which to decapitate Timaeus; his explanation of the purpose of his history in Book Three, parts of which we have already noted,[68] concludes with the justification 'that contemporaries will thus be able to see clearly whether the Roman rule is acceptable or the reverse, and future generations whether their government should be considered to have been worthy of praise and admiration or rather of blame'.[69] Ranke *did* expose the weaknesses of attempts to write the history of the Italian republics which based themselves on an uncritical use of Guicciardini and was careful to do otherwise in his own practice. There is no reason to think that a particular statement cannot serve more than one purpose. Models of historiography which assume otherwise are simplistic.

Nonetheless, it is often profitable to ask why a particular methodological statement appears where it does in a history, or why the historian feels moved to emphasize some aspects of what he is doing or to downplay others at a particular point in his narrative. Such considerations can often help to explain differences of emphasis and treatment at other points which would otherwise be puzzling. These differences often make more sense when one considers the effect which the historian wants to achieve in a given passage of his work.

A celebrated example of this occurs in the works of Tacitus. Tacitus's *Histories* and his later *Annals* both make certain claims about the nature of history-writing in Rome in the early principate. The problem is that the claims the historian makes on this subject in the earlier work do not seem to be altogether consistent with those in the later. In the *Histories*, it is stated that serious Roman historiography was quenched by the Battle of Actium in 31 BCE: 'The story of the Roman Republic has been told with equal eloquence and independence. After the Battle of Actium, when the interests of peace were served by the centralization of all authority in the hands of one man, that literary genius fell idle.'[70] The *Annals*, by contrast, seem to set the decline in history-writing rather later, in the latter years of the reign of Augustus: 'there was no lack of fitting intellects to tell of the times of Augustus, until they were put off by swelling flattery'.[71]

Getting these two statements to tally precisely requires some expenditure of ingenuity.[72] It is, perhaps, more helpful to note the rather different contexts of the two pronouncements. In the former, Tacitus is making a general point about the rise of flattery and its destruction of proper history under monarchic rule. This is duly contrasted with the author's own professed freedom from such sycophancy, but otherwise Tacitus has nothing to gain in narrative terms from complicating the clear opposition he has set up between Republican and early imperial history-writing – which has itself been succeeded by the reign of Trajan where, according to the historian, conditions have once more improved: 'it is the rare fortune of these days that you may think what you like and say what you think'.[73] Thus, it makes sense for him to hinge the change on the memorable moment of the Battle of Actium.

In the *Annals*, by contrast, his agenda are a little more complex. Here, Tacitus does not just want to construct a contrast between good and corrupted history-writing. He also desires to justify his decision to start the narrative proper with the last days of Augustus – a decision which enables him to create at the beginning of his work an impression of senility and decrepitude which would not have been so striking if he had devoted a lot of space before it to the vigorous young Augustus instead. Tacitus profits by fostering the impression that he is simply picking up where the 'fitting intellects', the *decora ingenia*, departed. Therefore, the point at which proper historiography is said to have tailed off is permitted to creep forward past the early years of Augustus. The shift conveniently relieves Tacitus of the responsibility of having to say much about them.

Again, what we have here, if this interpretation holds water, is something rather different from either simple authorial mendacity or a genuine change in the historian's mindset as his career develops. The studied vagueness of Tacitus's language about prior historiography in both passages gives him sufficient wriggle-room to avoid a charge of outright lying: it is notable that he does not give any actual *examples* of the authors he has in mind.[74] This, of course, can also be put down to the general avoidance of precise citation which we have already noted as a characteristic of ancient history-writing. Nonetheless, it is difficult to avoid the suspicion that what we see here is the result less of a change of mind regarding the nature of early imperial historiography and more of Tacitus's desire to make a neat start to his own narrative.

Tacitus's authorial statements at the start of the *Annals* relate to the economy of his whole work. The remarks of historians regarding their methodology can also, however, achieve more localized effects. So, for example, when Cassius Dio, who wrote an 80-book history of Rome from its foundations to the date of his own consulship in 229 CE, remarks that he is being purposefully selective in his treatment of Julius Caesar's legislation, he is not just explaining his own criteria for including and excluding material from his history. He is also making a point about the sheer scale and excess of everything associated with the doomed dictator: 'while Caesar was thus engaged he was also enacting many laws, most of which I shall omit, mentioning only those most worthy of record'.[75] Statements about the size, or magnitude or arduousness of their undertaking in the works of classical historians, as in those of their modern counterparts, do not merely point to actual difficulties in historiographical production. They also inculcate in the reader a due sense of the grandeur of the work and its subject matter. The great twentieth-century Roman historian Sir Ronald Syme, whose narrative style was exceedingly influenced by the classical historians, gives multiple examples of this in the prefaces to his works:

The task has been long and laborious (for all that ostensible drudgery can be sheer delight). It has been hampered by various delays and vexations ...

Evidence there was, but miscellaneous and dispersed, infested with all manner of vexatious problems ... much labour therefore and anxieties of selection for an author unable to emulate the easy people 'who write without fear or research'.[76]

In this respect, pronouncements on methodology in historiography can sometimes be in the tradition of Homer's narrator in the *Iliad*, who announces his personal incapability fully to convey the magnitude of his theme and, in doing so, emphasizes how impressive it is.[77] Certainly, Livy's determination to keep the scale of his undertaking firmly in the forefront of his audience's attention, which we have already noted above, makes sense not just as a straightforward comment upon the burgeoning of his work, but also as a reminder of how impressive that work is. His *Proem* has a similar effect: 'my subject involves infinite labour, seeing that it must be traced back above seven hundred years and that proceeding from slender beginnings it has so increased as now to be burdened by its own magnitude'.[78]

The performative aspect to methodological statements in historiography is therefore something which has to be borne in mind when interpreting them. The advantages to authors of playing up or minimizing particular theoretical concerns at particular places in order to produce an effect can be useful in explaining why a historian sometimes seems to sing different tunes at different times. Above all, context is key. There is an obvious temptation for the modern reader, eager to extract a summary grammar of ancient historiography, to pull such methodological statements as there are out of their original places in the ancient historians. But even the most apparently abstruse and rarefied dicta often make more sense in their original setting.

The Pleasures of Herodian

The significance of context to what ancient historians have to say for themselves about writing history is perhaps best illustrated by an extended example. Herodian, who wrote a history in eight books in the third century CE covering the history of Rome from the reign of Commodus to that of Gordian III,[79] is not one of the better-known of classical historiographers. His comparative obscurity, however, makes him a good case-study for examining the uses to which methodological statements could be put by a self-conscious historian. Herodian introduces his narrative as follows:

> Most writers engaged in compiling history, whose concern has been to present a fresh record of the past, have aimed at winning themselves a permanent reputation for scholarship, since they were afraid that if they did not express themselves they would be indistinguishable from the masses. But in their narratives they have shown a contempt for the truth and a preoccupation with vocabulary and style, because they were confident that, even if they romanced a bit, they would reap the advantages of pleasure they gave to their public, without the accuracy of their research being investigated. Some authors, through the excellent quality of their style, have made trivial events acquire a spurious importance with posterity, greater than was deserved by the truth. They have done this either because they were bitterly opposed to tyranny or because they wanted to give flattering praise to an emperor or a city or a private individual. My policy has been not to accept any second-hand information which has not been checked and corroborated. I have collected the evidence for my work with every attention to accuracy, limiting it to what falls within the recent memory of my readers. But I believe that future generations too will derive some pleasure from the knowledge of events which are important and compressed within a brief span of time.[80]

This passage offers rich pickings for the student of ancient historiography. In terms of obvious content, Herodian makes some interesting assertions about his stance as a historian. He claims an attention to accuracy on his own part and an avoidance of uncorroborated material. He also contrasts his own practice with that of (unnamed) historians, subject to prejudice and concerned with style at the expense of accuracy.

These historians may, however, strike us now as rather familiar. Like Ranke's 'Sismondis' and the defective imperial historiographers of

Tacitus's prefaces, they are here to make a point about what Herodian is doing rather than for their inherent interest. Their malfeasance highlights his virtue. Certainly it would be vain to hunt for actual names behind the anonymity of 'most writers'.

The exact way in which Herodian expresses himself also bears further scrutiny. In the Greek, the objection to writers who believed that they would pass muster even if they 'romanced a bit' (*ei ti kai muthōdes legoien*) gives clear evidence of its own prehistory. In fact, the comparatively rare word translated as 'romanced', *muthōdes*, echoes a much earlier methodological statement by Thucydides, in which the Athenian historian said of his account that 'its lack of romance will perhaps seem more unpleasing to the listening'.[81] Herodian, without overt acknowledegment (the action of the swan again), is bolstering his own manifesto as a historian through allusion to the phraseology of an august predecessor. This is another strategy that is by no means dead in latter-day historiography; here, again, the prefaces of Ronald Syme are a case in point.[82] In fact, reminiscences of Thucydidean phraseology saturate the passage.[83] Thucydides, too, makes much of his own accuracy (*akribeia*) near his acknowledgement of the lack of romance in his narrative.[84] He likewise draws attention to the preponderance of earthquakes in the period he proposes to discuss, as Herodian goes on to do just after the passage I have cited.[85]

Herodian's opening remarks on historiography, then, generate an effect beyond their simple content: they make a claim for a place in a tradition of history-writing. 'Association by allusion' is a good example of the performative aspect of the occasions when ancient historians talk about method. This particular manifestation of it – redeploying the methodological statements of earlier historians – is not uncommon. Thucydides is often its subject. For example, Polybius's objection to the ridiculous accounts of the fall of the tyrant Hieronymus of Syracuse in earlier historians labels these writers *logographoi*: 'Some of the *logographoi* who have described the fall of Hieronymus have done so at great length and introduced much of the marvellous ... .'[86] This is exactly the word Thucydides had used to differentiate his own practice from what other authors were doing.

Some interpreters of ancient historiography have been inclined to dismiss apparent 'repetitions' of this nature. They see this as evidence that the later occurrence must simply be the mouthing of what has become an empty platitude or traditional observance in the more recent text. This is, of course, always a possibility, but it is an error of method to suppose that something which is formulaic or hallowed by repetition is *necessarily* meaningless. Polybius, in fact, explicitly defends his own narrative repetitions on the grounds that they are unavoidable in a work of such bulk: 'I may justly be excused if I am found to be using the same style or the same disposition and treatment, or even actually the same words as on a previous occasion ... for in all such matters the large scale of my work is sufficient excuse.'[87] Polybius is speaking of reusing his own descriptions, of course, rather than those of a predecessor. The wider applicability of the statement remains, however; some expressions become formulaic simply because of their enduring usefulness. When a speaker notes that it is a 'great honour and a pleasure' to address a gathering, the mere fact that this is the sort of thing one is supposed to say at the start of a public speech does not mean that the speaker does *not* think it a great honour and a pleasure to be where he or she is.[88] Certainly, scholarly attempts to test Herodian's account against other data relating to the period he covers have tended to indicate that, despite his tendency to become confused about chronology,[89] his practice does not seem to fall ludicrously short of what he claims here.[90]

Moreover, attention to how Herodian's preface fits into the larger disposition of the first book of his history suggests that what he is serving up here is in any event more complicated than reheated Thucydidean leftovers. The exact emphases that emerge in the portrait of the defective historians at the opening of the history bear scrutiny. Herodian depicts these delinquents as obsessed, above all, with their own reputations: 'winning themselves a permanent reputation for scholarship, since they were afraid that if they did not express themselves they would be indistinguishable from the masses'. They set about this by prioritizing style over substance and the sweetness of their discourse over accuracy: 'they were confident that, even if they romanced a bit, they would reap the advantages of pleasure they gave to their public, without the accuracy of their research being investigated'. Herodian, as he quickly makes clear, has no objection to history providing pleasure *per se*.[91] Indeed, he announces that he believes his own work will ensure that 'future generations too will derive some pleasure from the knowledge of events'. However, Herodian is careful to establish that this pleasure will be derived from a narrative of events that are *important*.[92] He says that he has no time for those who 'have made trivial events acquire a spurious importance with posterity, greater than was deserved by the truth'.

Now, if we go on to read the narrative of Herodian's first book, we discover a text where the politics of pleasure and the issue of style over substance are not just important in writing history. In fact, Herodian makes these issues central to his portrayal of Commodus, whose inglorious career the first book of the history chronicles. The Emperor's fall from grace begins when corrupt members of the imperial household lure the new ruler into a life of empty pleasures: 'they reminded Commodus of the soft life of Rome by telling him of the delightful pleasures to be seen and heard and recounting the great wealth of resources there ... By putting such ideas into the young man's head they whetted his appetite for a taste of these pleasures.'[93]

Commodus then descends into debauchery. Moreover, Herodian stresses the disparity in his subsequent acts and imperial gestures between style and substance. When he depicts the Emperor's staged displays of marksmanship, he points out that Commodus, for all his undeniably impressive aim, has carefully arranged matters so as to keep himself out of any physical danger: 'a special raised closure was put up for Commodus's benefit so that he could spear the animals without endangering himself from close quarters, a demonstration of his skill but not of his courage'.[94] When he takes part in gladiatorial contests, he has 'no difficulty in overcoming his opponents in gladiatorial fights by merely wounding them, since they all looked upon him as the emperor rather than as a gladiator and let him win'.[95]

Thus, the portrait of defective historiography at the beginning of Herodian's history is not merely a statement of method. It introduces a theme which will play out in the narrative of Book One. A failing of historians becomes the failing of an emperor, and the defective methodology of Herodian's targets mirrors the defective morality of Commodus. In case the reader continues to doubt the application of historiography to wider issues of practical ethics, Herodian even has a scene where the (accurate) fears of the dying Marcus Aurelius about his son's vulnerability to temptations ('Young men's passions are easily diverted from learning moral values and slip into a life of pleasure')[96] are expressly mediated through the old emperor's awareness, as a 'man much learned in history'

(*anēr poluistōr*), of historical examples of 'rulers in the past who had succeeded to power as young men'.[97] History, Herodian thereby insinuates,
is not some hermetically-sealed compartment divorced from life and
politics. Success and failure in the practice of historiography can proceed
along lines not dissimilar from the conduct of political life. Moreover,
when properly deployed, the one can profitably enrich the other; Marcus
Aurelius thus becomes an example of someone using historiography
within a historiographical text, a phenomenon interesting, for obvious
reasons, to people concerned with how history was read and used in the
ancient world.[98]

Our understanding of Herodian's methodological pronouncements
at the beginning of his history is deepened, then, by seeing how they
interact with the subsequent narrative. What Herodian has to say about
style and substance, and about how historiography should distinguish the
trivial from the important, is significant even by itself. But it takes on
even more interest when one sees its relationship to the story into which
it feeds.

Conclusion

Comparatively uncommon as they are, explicit statements of methodology
or purpose in the ancient historians themselves offer the best hope of
establishing the nature of historiographical texts from the classical world.
Since the use that we can make of these texts depends on what sort of texts
they are likely to be – whether the relationship to data they show resembles that of an A. J. P. Taylor, a Patrick O'Brian, a Baron Munchausen
or someone else – these methodological pronouncements are therefore
very important. They shed much-needed illumination on the swan-like
processes that drive ancient historiography forwards. As a result, much of
the material in the chapters that follow relies upon such statements.

However, we have seen that two factors make it necessary to proceed
with caution. In the first place, we have noted the pluralism of historiographical production in the modern world. Many different themes, styles
and approaches have huddled beneath Clio's skirts since the Renaissance.
We have seen little to suggest that the ancient world was necessarily different. Ergo, generalizing from the statements of individual historians is

a dicey business. This is especially the case when the surviving distribution of these statements is uneven across historians. The possibility that modern ratiocination might populate the historiography of antiquity with a fictitious clone army of Polybiuses is one that should give us pause.

The other consideration is that such statements are themselves by no means straightforward. We have seen various explanations for why an ancient historian's methodological pronouncements might not be consistent with all of his own practice, let alone anyone else's. Conscious deception or a change of tack may both play a part. Also, it has become clear that the relationship between a historian's text and the theoretical comments he makes on it can be more complicated than one might assume.

Nonetheless, the use of authorial comments remains a viable approach. As we have noted, even remarks which are not necessarily reliable in the particular case where they are uttered are significant. This is because they indicate the presence in a historian's readership of assumptions and beliefs which would lead an author to want to make them. Whether or not the early Roman historian L. Cincius Alimentus did actually learn the precise number of Hannibal's troops from the lips of the great general himself, his claim that he had remains significant.[99]

With this in mind, it is time to start interrogating the relationship between ancient historians and their data, and to examine the means by which we can evaluate it. In other words, we need to see, where possible, how ancient historiography interacts with its sources.

3

USING SOURCES – PART I

> I can see the time approach when we will no longer have to base
> modern history on reports, even those of contemporary historians –
> except to the extent that they had first-hand knowledge – to say
> nothing of derivative reworkings of the sources. Rather, we will
> construct it from the accounts of eyewitnesses and the most genuine
> and direct sources.[1]

Ranke's declaration at the opening of his *History of the Reformation in Germany* is a convenient summary of the standards and procedures we have come to expect from one sort of historiography. As we have already seen,[2] history-writing in the modern world is in fact a broad church. However, the notion of source-based history remains basic to the conception of historiography in the present day.

We have likewise seen that contemporary history does not just base itself upon sources. It also tends to make it reasonably easy for the interested reader to tease out the relationship between a particular history's narrative of events and the sources upon which it is based. Modern historiography usually (though by no means invariably) leaves an audit trail.

As the opening chapter of this study made clear,[3] the habitual absence of this audit trail is the single biggest problem we face as students of ancient history-writing. The problem applies on both a local and a general level. Absence of citation makes it hard, at any given point, to determine the evidential basis for what a classical historian is saying. As a wider syndrome, this absence makes it harder than one would like to determine what sort of an enterprise (or enterprises) ancient 'history'-writing actually was. Our assessment of these texts as literature or evidence is likely to change in accordance with exactly how we think they are using, ignoring or making up their source material.

In the second chapter, we saw that methodological statements in the texts of the ancient historians themselves offer a means to penetrate into the often opaque internal workings of classical historiography. It also became clear that there are sometimes dangers in taking such statements at face value, in generalizing them beyond the work of the historian who makes them and in divesting them of their original context in the narrative. Nonetheless, their utility here is obvious. Methodological pronouncements are exceedingly helpful in illuminating the different ways in which ancient writers of history gathered, evaluated and used sources.

However, the usefulness of these statements tends to be confined to the general level. They tell us how ancient historiography operated, true enough. They are less useful, for the most part, to the reader who is trying to evaluate the reliability of an ancient historian at any particular point in his narrative. It is enlightening to know that Tacitus saw the growth in adulation and public flattery under Augustus as a factor that made contemporary accounts of his later years unreliable.[4] This knowledge is less helpful when trying to work out what his sources for that period were or how they were transmuted to form the narrative of the early chapters of the *Annals*.

On this microcosmic level, the 'action of the swan' still makes the hunt for sources a frustrating one. It will therefore be useful to explore the various strategies that post-classical readers have adopted in trying to work out and evaluate the sources of a historian who does not leave an audit trail. Understanding the nature, and the limitations, of these strategies is fundamental to the use of ancient historical texts in constructing a picture of classical antiquity. Before discussing these refined matters, however, it is worth asking exactly what sort of sources were available to those who proposed to write history in the ancient world.

The Nature of the Sources

We have already noted, in passing,[5] Polybius's commentary on some possible sources of information for an aspirant historian in the ancient world. One of these is the use of eyewitnesses to events:

> For since many events occur at the same time in different places, and one man cannot be in several places at one time, nor is it possible for a single man to have seen with his own eyes every place in the world and all the peculiar features of different places, the only thing left for an historian is to inquire from as many people as possible, to believe those worthy of belief and to be an adequate critic of the reports that reach him.[6]

Others are enumerated in his description of systematic history where he notes the need for 'the industrious study of memoirs and other documents and a comparison of their contents' and 'the survey of cities, places, rivers, lakes and, in general, all the peculiar features of land and sea and the distances of one place from another'.[7]

Further categories of evidence may be added, both from elsewhere in the text of Polybius and from the remarks of other historians. Epigraphy is an obvious example. On the basis of Polybius's criticisms, it would appear that Timaeus was particularly noted for his interest in inscriptions: 'it is Timaeus who discovered the inscriptions at the back of buildings and lists of *proxeni* on the jambs of temples'.[8] Moreover, Polybius's sniffy tone here did not prevent him from boasting elsewhere about his own discovery and exploitation of an inscription left by Hannibal in the Temple of Hera on the Lacinian Promontory.[9]

Beyond epigraphy, physical objects and artefacts are also pressed into service by some historians. Herodotus records, during his account of the Lydian king Croesus, offerings which he sent to Delphi.[10] Velleius Paterculus notes not just an inscription, but also a bronze tablet, as evidence for the Roman Dictator L. Cornelius Sulla's piety towards the goddess Diana,[11] and points to an equestrian statue of Augustus raised by a grateful Senate.[12]

It is worth taking some time to examine each of these potential sources of information. Some of them, to be sure, are fairly straightforward. For example, being in a position to assess the terrain at the site of important happenings, as Polybius recommends, is as obviously useful to an ancient historian as to a modern one. On the other hand, the distribution and availability of these sources were not necessarily the same in the classical world as in the present day.

Documents and Archives

Documentary sources are a case in point. Since Ranke, the diligent exploration of documents and archives has often been seen as the cornerstone of proper historiography – though such pursuits certainly did not originate with him: William Camden, for example, whose history of the reign of Queen Elizabeth I was published in two parts in the early seventeenth century, made much of his own archival exertions.[13]

Ranke himself exploited the flourishing market in family records which developed after the revolutions of the nineteenth century.[14] Access to particular classified materials has spurred historiographical activity ever since; one example would be E. H. Carr's *International Relations since the Peace Treaties*, of 1937, which attempted to explain the preceding decades from the vantage point of Foreign Office records which had yet to be declassified.[15] Hard graft in the archives continues to be fundamental to the historian's trade.[16]

Even in the modern world, of course, where these materials are comparatively abundant, the difficulties of handling documentary sources have not gone unnoticed. A. J. P. Taylor, whose *The Struggle for Mastery in Europe 1848–1918* we have already noted for its relationship with its sources,[17] has some pertinent remarks in that work's bibliography about these issues:

> Little of the raw material of history was devised especially for the use
> of historians; and that little is often the least reliable. The historian of
> the middle ages, who looks down on the 'contemporary' historian
> [historiographical turf wars, we may note, did not begin and end with
> Polybius], is inclined to forget that his prized sources are an accidental
> collection, which have survived the ravages of time and which the
> archivist allows him to see.[18]

Taylor's point about access is an important one. It remains the case that full use of all documents relevant to a topic cannot be assumed. The situation in earlier centuries was generally worse. Ranke himself, for example, used official help 'to gain access to what were in the early years still closely guarded archives'.[19] However, strategies for deflecting unwelcome students have continued to be a stock in trade of archives and libraries down to the present day.[20]

Archival research in the ancient world faced the historian with still more acute problems. The comparative difficulty of producing writing materials on a large scale in antiquity did not necessarily preclude extensive documentation. Where writing materials *were* in ready supply, the level of document production was often impressive. Egypt under Roman rule is a case in point.[21] Nonetheless, practical difficulties would generally have tended to keep these levels lower than in the modern world.[22]

A more significant difficulty, however, was access. Many aspects of public record-keeping in the ancient world remain obscure, even for such comparatively well-attested locales as Athens. Nonetheless, it is clear that we should not assume ready access to city archives by curious historians, particularly ones from other cities (and many ancient historiographers either wrote about cities that were not their own or spent time away from them). Polybius, to be sure, does cite an official despatch which a Rhodian admiral sent after the battle of Lade in the course of one of his polemics,[23] but he does not say that he saw it himself.[24]

Even where a historian was dealing with the affairs of his own city, archival access was by no means guaranteed – or necessarily deployed by the historian when it was available.[25] Here, the case of Rome is instructive. The keeping of some public records is attested, although there remains more confusion about details than one would like, and it is by no means clear how extensive or useful such documentation actually was.[26] Antonius in Cicero's *De Oratore*, whose views on historiography we have already noted,[27] has this to say about the most famous example:

> The chief priest, from the beginnings of Roman history down to the
> time when Publius Mucius Scaevola was chief priest, committed to
> writing all the events of each year, and displayed them on a white

tablet and exhibited the tablet at his house, in order that the people might have the opportunity to learn about them. These are the records that even today are called the *Annales Maximi*.[28]

Antonius is in fact using the story of these documents to construct a narrative of early historiography in Rome. Even what remains of that historiography shows this account to be tendentious. For example, Antonius claims that the type of writing which the *Annales Maximi* embodied was adopted by the likes of the Elder Cato, L. Calpurnius Piso Frugi and Fabius Pictor, even though we know that the Elder Cato actually defined his own practice in opposition to such a type: 'I do not care to write what is in the table kept by the high priest: how often grain was expensive, how often darkness or something else obstructed the light of the moon or sun.'[29] Nonetheless, it furnishes an example of a public record which historians of early Rome might have exploited. In fact, it does not look as though historiographers resorted to these records to the extent one might have expected.[30]

The *Annales Maximi,* according to Cicero's Antonius, were originally on public exhibit, 'in order that the people might have the opportunity to learn about them'. From later in Roman history, we have evidence about other sources of documentary information, and the restrictions placed upon them. The key example in this case makes the impact of these inhibitions upon the writing of history explicit. Cassius Dio, writing in the third century CE, notes the consequences of the changes in government introduced by Augustus:

> The events occurring after this time can not be recorded in the same manner as those of previous times. Formerly, as we know, all matters were reported to the senate and to the people, even if they happened at a distance; hence all learned of them and many recorded them, and consequently the truth regarding them no matter to what extent fear or favour, friendship or enmity, coloured the reports of certain writers, was always to a certain extent to be found in the works of the other writers who wrote of the same events and in the public records. But after this time most things that happened began to be kept secret and concealed, and even though some things are perchance made public, they are distrusted just because they cannot be verified; for it

is suspected that everything is said and done with reference to the wishes of the men in power at the time and of their associates. As a result, much that never occurs is noised abroad, and much that happens beyond a doubt is unknown, and in the case of nearly every event a version gains currency that is different from the way it really happened.[31]

Dio's statement is interesting on a number of accounts. It is not just because of the claim he makes for the increasing difficulty of the historian's task after the foundation of the principate and the retreat to the shadows of much significant political activity.[32] Equally instructive is his stress on the possibility, under the Republic, of comparison between competing accounts of what had happened, thanks to the existence of multiple reports and the accessibility of public records. As we shall see, discrimination between multiple sources, and the criteria by which such discrimination should be achieved, were not matters of which ancient historians were unaware.[33]

For our present purposes, Dio's analysis illuminates particular problems of documentary access which obtained under certain circumstances in the ancient world. Even in one city, the provision of records could fluctuate across time (as Dio claims for Rome). Records might also be restricted to certain classes of individual, into which particular historians might or might not fall.

Where Rome is concerned, for example, a question that has exercised modern scholarship is the use by historians of the *Acta Senatus*, the official records of debates in the Senate. These were first published at the instigation of Julius Caesar in 59 BCE,[34] but were suppressed under Augustus,[35] although publication may have resumed under Tiberius.[36] Tacitus mentions using them once: 'I find in the records of the senate that Anicius Cerealis the consul designate spoke in favour of the motion that a temple should be made to the divine Nero as quickly as possible.'[37] So does the biographer Suetonius.[38] These are among the few explicit references to their use.[39] It is, however, likely that they are used at points where (as usual) the source is not directly cited. The extent of this unavowed usage, particularly in the works of Tacitus, continues to be debated.[40]

In any event, both the possibilities and the boundaries of archival study in the ancient world should now be clear in outline – even if the limitations of our evidence mean that they are hardly ever clear in detail. Archives may, in principle, have been a possible source for classical historiography. However, the extent of their availability, the quality of their information, and the use particular historians made of it, usually remain questions for conjecture.

Epigraphy

The line between documentary and epigraphic sources in the classical world is blurred at best. Because of the Greco-Roman penchant for carving important laws or decrees into stone or bronze for public display, inscriptions played as important a part in record-keeping as material recorded on more fragile media. We have already seen that (according to Cicero's Antonius) the *Annales Maximi* were originally displayed 'on a white tablet'.[41] In fact, where antiquity is concerned, there is much to be said for simply applying the term 'documentary' to any record or source of information, regardless of its medium.[42]

The distinction, such as it is, is further muddied by the fact that there is attestation of texts that were originally inscribed being collected and published in manuscript form. Craterus, a Macedonian working at the beginning of the third century BCE, seems to have made such a gathering. This was a collection of official decrees, now almost entirely lost, which extended to at least eight books.[43]

Despite these important caveats, there is a certain amount of sense from a modern perspective, if not an ancient, in taking a moment to consider inscriptions separately from documents on more perishable materials. We have the advantage in this case of being better informed about ancient epigraphic practices than about the mechanics of record-keeping in other media. This is because stone is much more likely to last than any given piece of papyrus or vellum, or a wooden tablet.

Availability is also an issue that plays out differently with inscriptions. As we have seen, access to manuscript archives in the ancient world appears often to have been subject to restrictions. Epigraphy, by contrast, usually indicates a desire to share material with the largest possible number of people.

Most inscriptions in the ancient world, therefore, were designed for public visibility. One should bear in mind that 'visibility' and 'legibility' are not necessarily synonymous. We have already seen how the presentation of statements in a historiographical text can have a strongly performative aspect: how or where something is said, or the fact that it is said at all, can be every bit as important as the actual content of the statement.[44] Similar factors can equally apply to the erection of classical inscriptions. What is important is sometimes not so much that a particular set of data are on record, but that there is a very big and very public chunk of stone or bronze reminding anyone who passes that the data are there. In some cases a religious motivation towards memorializing matter in inscriptions has also been detected.[45] Of course, the performative and informative functions are no more exclusive in the case of inscriptions than we have seen them to be in historiography.[46] An inscription such as the Athenian Tribute Lists, which records the offerings to the goddess Athena from the tribute paid by members of the Delian League during the fifth century BCE on large blocks of marble, both constitutes a potent statement of Athenian power and prestige as the head of the League and makes it possible to determine which states contributed how much.[47]

Despite this distinction, it would be easy to assume that the general accessibility of inscriptions would make them a potent aid to the historian – always allowing that he could travel to the place where they were displayed.[48] Once again, however, there were possible complications. For one thing, inscriptions did not necessarily stay where they were put. A neat illustration of this is supplied by the *Tabula Bembina*, the fragments of a bronze tablet which once belonged to the Renaissance cardinal Pietro Bembo. This tablet contains two important pieces of Roman Republican legislation: an agrarian law, and a law on extortion. For our present purposes, however, the interesting thing about the *Tabula Bembina* is that the two laws are inscribed on opposite sides of the tablet. Thus, the individual who wished to put on the second inscription simply flipped over the tablet so that the original was invisible and then inscribed the second one.[49] Apart from recycling, there was also the possibility of more pointed interference with the epigraphic record. Cicero seems to have tried to have the inscriptions that recorded his embarrassing period of exile from Rome taken down; his political enemy Clodius appears to have opposed this.[50]

Another potential issue was forgery. This was a possibility of which the ancient historians were aware. We have already seen Herodotus's comment on a faked inscription at Delphi.[51] The comments of other historiographers show a similar sophistication. For example, the fourth-century BCE historian Theopompus of Chios, whose works included a 12-book history of Greece from 411 until the battle of Cnidus in 394 BCE and a *History of Philip* in 58 books centring on Philip II of Macedon, denounces a particular inscription recording a treaty (probably the much-debated 'Peace of Callias')[52] as a later fabrication, on the grounds that it was inscribed not in the local alphabet that was used by the Athenians until the end of the fifth century BCE, but the Ionian alphabet, which they officially adopted in 403–2 BCE.[53] As it happens, Theopompus's argument is not certainly right: it is possible that the text he saw was a fourth-century rescript of an earlier original. However, the methodological subtlety he demonstrates here makes plain the by no means uncritical attitude which ancient historians could display to the data at their disposal.

These complications aside, the potential usefulness of inscriptional evidence to the practising historiographer is plain. Once again, the extent to which inscriptions contributed to the underpinning of classical historiography is by no means clear. On the one hand, a preoccupation with inscriptions could easily be portrayed as excessive or vaguely comical. We have already noted Polybius's derisive (and disingenuous) criticism of Timaeus as one who 'discovered the inscriptions at the back of buildings and lists of *proxeni* on the jambs of temples'. Although Polybius is clearly exaggerating for comic effect here, his claims about the odd places where Timaeus is supposed to have found inscriptions is another indication of the strange contexts in which they could end up. Polemon of Ilium, a Stoic writer on geography active in the early second century BCE, attracted the nickname *stēlokopas* (glutton for *stēlai*, the stones on which inscriptions were often placed).[54] On the other hand, these quips demonstrate that such an enthusiasm did exist. Moreover, the texts of the extant classical historians do give explicit examples of the use of inscriptions in argumentation. As well as Theopompus and his peace treaty, one might note Thucydides's use of two dedications to argue that the younger Peisistratus held the archonship under the tyranny of the Peisistratids.[55]

In summary, then, inscriptions are a variety of source where the obscurities which cloud some other types of evidence, such as archives, do indeed lift somewhat. Some of the most enlightening work on ancient historiography in recent decades has centred on the relationship between historiographical narratives of events and extant inscriptions. The illumination of Tacitus which has resulted from the discovery and interpretation of inscriptions from Spain is a case in point.[56]

However, one should resist the temptation to see epigraphy as altogether unproblematic. Because inscriptions are (in some cases) still available to us, and still (again in some cases) easy to read, it is easy to assume that the classical historians, as participants in the cultures which created them, would have found them entirely straightforward to use. In fact (as the example of Theopompus shows), writers of history in the Greco-Roman world could run into difficulty interpreting epigraphic records outside their own immediate context just as easily as modern scholars.

It is also worth remembering that the permanence of most epigraphic monuments does not guarantee the accuracy of texts which purport to record what they say. Even without the considerations of possible forgery or deliberate falsification, the vagaries of textual transmission can garble a report of a monument just as effectively as the words of the historian who talks about it.[57] Nor is accuracy assured even when the text of an author is known to be in good shape. To take an example from the modern world, there is a poem by Geoffrey Grigson, *Bibliotheca Bodleiana*, which uses the inscription at the base of a statue on the side of the Clarendon Building in Oxford in its lyrics: '*Primus Angliae Cancellarius –* he's joined the race of stone'. In fact, the inscription reads *Summus Angliae Summus Academiae Cancellarius*. Visitors to contemporary Oxford can verify the difference with their own eyes. Plato the historian, reconstructing the monuments of our present from fragments of texts in his transfigured London of the far future,[58] might not be so lucky.

Eye-witnesses

This chapter has already shown the consensus between representatives of ancient and modern historiographical traditions as to the importance of contemporary testimony. Ranke's declaration of the true foundation of modern history – 'we will construct it from the accounts of eyewitnesses' –

strikes a similar note to Polybius's dictum that 'the only thing left for an historian is to inquire from as many people as possible, to believe those worthy of belief, and to be an adequate critic of the reports that reach him'.[59]

If we look at Polybius's requirement in context, however, we discover that the Megalopolitan historian is skating on thin dialectical ice. Polybius is insisting on the importance to the proper historian of actually going out and interrogating eye-witnesses. This, he claims, is something which Timaeus signally failed to do, so demonstrating his insufficiency as a historiographer. What Polybius omits to mention is that Timaeus, unlike Polybius himself, did not write what was primarily a contemporary history.[60] In fact, his 38-book *Sicilian History* started in the time of myth, although it did cover events down to the death of Agathocles in 289/8, an event which took place in Timaeus's own lifetime.[61] Polybius, as we have already seen,[62] began his narrative proper at 220, no more than a couple of decades before his own birth,[63] and ended it (probably) in 146/5. Polybius does not explain how he supposed Timaeus might find eyewitnesses of the Trojan War by any means short of necromancy – and claims to have received important historical information by speaking to dead people are reassuringly rare in ancient historiography.[64]

Timaeus's situation was by no means unusual. Many of the extant histories from classical antiquity do bring their narratives approximately down to the historian's present day. The ancient world did not have a special word for this, though in the modern it has been dubbed *Zeitgeschichte*.[65] Besides Polybius, Thucydides and Xenophon are obvious representatives of this tendency. However, many classical works of history did not deal at all with contemporary events: witness Arrian's *History of Alexander*, written in the second century CE, or Arrian's contemporary Cephalion, whose history, though broader in scope, also ended with the reign of Alexander.[66] Moreover, the case of Timaeus shows that even a history that terminated near the present day could cover vast swathes of history before the historian's own lifetime: Livy, Cassius Dio, and the fourth-century Roman historian Ammianus Marcellinus are amongst the other examples.[67] In all these cases, the interrogation of eye-witnesses for the bulk of the work was obviously not a viable strategy.

Even for near contemporary events, eye-witnesses present certain problems. It is true that human memory can reach further back, and with fewer links, than one might incautiously assume. A nice demonstration of this appears in Maurice Bowra's memoirs, talking about old members of Wadham College in Oxford whom he met in the early 1920s:

> The most astonishing was Frederick Harrison. He was ninety-two,
> and his first question to me was, 'When did you come up to Oxford?'
> I told him, 'In 1919', and he answered, 'I came up in 1848'. So indeed
> he had. What is more, he had toured parts of Europe in that year of
> revolutions and had vivid memories of Paris after the fall of Louis
> Philippe. He remembered the accession of Queen Victoria when he
> was seven years old ... Incidentally he provided a link with a still
> remoter past by a neat chain of circumstances. He had as an
> undergraduate met Routh, President of Magdalen, who died in his
> hundredth year soon afterwards. Routh had in his boyhood met an old
> lady, who had in her girlhood seen Charles II exercising his spaniels in
> Magdalen Grove.[68]

The classical world also had a relish for such synchronicities,[69] and enough individuals of conspicuous longevity to bring them about.[70] Ronald Syme's *The Roman Revolution* neatly opens with a reference to a notable one: 'Outlasting the friends, the enemies, and even the memory of his earlier days, Augustus the Princeps, who was born in the year of Cicero's consulate, lived to see the grandson of his granddaughter.'[71]

Syme, characteristically sly, also points to the other side of the coin. The opening of *The Roman Revolution* elaborately echoes the opening chapters of Tacitus's *Annals*. In fact, the very first words of Syme's narrative explicitly reference and echo the beginning of that work.[72] By noting the fact that Augustus had outlasted 'even the memory of his earlier days', Syme revives an insight from early in that work, where Tacitus notes that by the end of Augustus's life popular memory of the old Republic was all but extinct: 'How few were left who had seen the Republic!'[73] The ancient and the modern historian are alike aware of the irony that one of the few remaining witnesses to the system that Augustus replaced was Augustus.[74] Although the *possibility* of there being someone extant who remembered seeing events of particular vintage might remain open for longer than one would expect, access to such an individual was never a certainty.

Nonetheless, the texts of the ancient historians make it clear that reportage from eye-witnesses could and did form part of the fabric of historiographical production in the ancient world. Appian, the second-century CE Alexandrian whose *Roman History* we have already mentioned,[75] paints a vivid picture in his account of the fall of Carthage in 146 BCE of how such recollections might take shape. The Roman troops fall to discussing recent events:

> ... And they chatted through the whole night of how their arms were stripped away and how suddenly, contrary to expectation, they contrived other ones, and how they were deprived of their ships and built equipment again from old wood, and how the mouth of the harbour was shut off and how they dug another mouth in a few days. Also the height of the walls was on their lips, and the sizes of the stones, and the fire, which they often brought against the war-engines. In short, they represented the war to each other as they had lately seen it happening and suited the actions of the body to the images conjured by their words, and they seemed to see Scipio on ladders, on ships, at the gates, in battle, running everywhere.[76]

Appian endows his nameless soldiers with the sensibilities of budding historiographers, and the passage is interesting for the light it sheds on Appian's own practices as a historian.[77] However, the situation it alleges is by no means implausible. One might compare the *Laches* of Plato, the setting of which is a historical fiction, but one which presents a plausible picture of how popular accounts of an ongoing war might be generated, debated and disseminated. The Athenian Laches is talking about martial prowess after witnessing a weapons display by Stesilaus:

> For example, this very Stesilaus, whom you and I have just witnessed exhibiting in all that crowd and making such great professions of his powers, I have seen at another time making, in sober truth, an involuntary exhibition of himself, which was a far better spectacle. He was a marine on board a ship which struck a transport vessel, and was armed with a weapon, half spear half scythe; the singularity of this weapon was worthy of the singularity of the man. To make a long story short, I will only tell you what happened to this notable invention of

the scythe-spear. He was fighting, and the scythe was caught in the rigging of the other ship, and stuck fast; and he tugged, but was unable to get his weapon free. The two ships were passing one another. He first ran along his own ship holding on to the spear; but as the other ship passed by and drew him after as he was holding on, he let the spear slip through his hand until he retained only the end of the handle. The people in the transport clapped their hands, and laughed at his ridiculous figure; and when some one threw a stone, which fell on the deck at his feet, and he quitted of the scythe-spear, the crew of his own trireme also burst out laughing; they could not refrain when they beheld the weapon waving in the air, suspended from the transport.[78]

The *Laches*, as noted above, is itself a fictional dialogue using historical characters, and the historicity of this actual anecdote can be debated. Again, though, what is interesting is the context which Plato sees as generating it. War stories are not restricted to official despatches or formal memoirs. People swapping them, and remembering (with or without advantages)[79] their own role in such critical happenings as the fall of Carthage, their presence at a wiseacre's comedic comeuppance, or an earlier expedition to a particular place,[80] are an obvious possible source for enquiring historians.

The classical historians, and those engaged in related activities, show that this resource was utilized. While it is unlikely that many shared the good fortune of L. Cincius Alimentus, who, as we have already seen, claimed to have established the numbers of Carthaginian troops in a particular engagement by personally asking Hannibal himself,[81] less elevated sources were certainly available. Polybius questioned people who had been present when the great general crossed the Alps in 218;[82] his other informants included, *inter alios*, the friends of King Perseus, whom he quotes in his account of negotiations during the third Macedonian War.[83] The biographer Plutarch, talking about the sources for his *Life of Antony*, makes it clear that informants were often only too willing to share their information, 'whenever they got the chance'.[84]

Historiographers also demonstrate an awareness of the limitations of eyewitness accounts. These, again, are a consideration which the modern reader also does well to remember. Even where the verbal diarrhoea which we have seen vexing Plutarch can be avoided, eliciting the desired information from one's witnesses is no trivial skill. Polybius, ever conscious of his own professionalism as a historian, makes some acute remarks on the importance of a competent interviewer in the proper interrogation of witnesses: 'the interrogator contributes as much to the interview as the informant, since the latter is at the mercy of free association of ideas without the discipline which the trained interviewer brings to the occasion'.[85] It was not (and is not) sufficient just to settle someone down and let them talk.

Eye-witnesses have further limitations. These are particularly acute in a military context. Being in the thick of the action can make it harder, not easier, to tell exactly what is going on, especially if an engagement is large and complex. The scale of some ancient battles is worth remembering. This could vastly exceed the scale usual in the Middle Ages, and in certain cases rival anything from the modern world. The Battle of Ipsus in 301 BCE involved (if the transmitted figures can be trusted) a combined military strength of more than 150,000 men.[86] This is between nine and ten times that attested for the Battle of Hastings. It is not implausible that the Romans suffered more casualties for a single day's fighting at the Battle of Cannae in 216 BCE than any other western army before or since.[87]

It is not surprising, then, that the progress of some ancient engagements could be confusing to the participant. Homer's gods, rubber-necking the Trojan War from mountains in the *Iliad*,[88] or the imaginary observer which the Roman poet Lucretius imagines watching military evolutions with detachment,[89] were considerably better placed to chart developments than the typical combatant.[90] Barring clairvoyance (and Livy did claim to have met a seer in his youth who said that he had watched the Battle of Pharsalus from Padua via his second sight),[91] a comprehensive view of the battle could sometimes be hard to obtain.[92] Indeed, the result of some ancient battles hinged upon uncertainty even amongst the generals as to what exactly was going on. A notorious case of this was the Battle of Philippi in 42 BCE, where Gaius Cassius Longinus, who was commanding troops against Antony and Octavian, seems to have committed suicide under the erroneous impression that his troops had already been totally defeated.[93] The mere presence of an informant at an encounter in no way guarantees a comprehensive understanding of what transpired, as parallels from the twentieth century can readily illuminate.[94]

Of course, not all history is military history, and a great deal of what happened in the ancient world would not have subjected the observer to martial rigours. Even in antiquity, however, the disposition of eye-witnesses to disagree on some subjects was noted as vexatious.[95] The essential limits of human perception are always worth bearing in mind. In particular, one might note the documented fallibility of untrained attempts to 'guesstimate' very large numbers.[96]

Autopsy

The logical consummation of using eye-witnesses is for the historian to be an eye-witness himself. Claims of autopsy (i.e., of having experienced the matter under discussion for oneself) are by no means uncommon in texts of the classical historians.[97] The extreme cases are, of course, to be found when a history is in fact an account of the historian's own deeds, and of those in some way connected to him. The *Commentarii* of Julius Caesar, written in the middle of the first century BCE to describe his conduct of campaigns in Gaul and Britannia and then of his Civil Wars for control of the Roman state, are the most celebrated examples of this; one might also, amongst extant works, instance Xenophon's *Anabasis* (or *March Upcountry*), a work of the fourth century BCE describing an expedition of mercenaries (the 'Ten Thousand') to install the pretender Cyrus as Great King of Persia, the survivors from which Xenophon himself ended up leading back to comparative safety.[98] Amongst lost historiographers, we have already seen Ptolemy at work on his history of Alexander, under whom he had served as a general.[99]

Most extant historians do not dominate the action of their own narratives to quite this extent. Nonetheless, 'Hitchcock moments' for the author of one sort or another are fairly common in classical historiography. Thucydides's account of the Peloponnesian War includes the story of his own career as a general, facing off against the Spartan Brasidas in the contest for Amphipolis,[100] his exile from Athens as a result of his failure[101] and the fact that he had himself earlier fallen victim to the Great Plague of Athens.[102] Polybius recalls how he saw his friend Scipo Aemilianus shed tears at the fall of Carthage in 146 BCE.[103] Cassius Dio's history of Rome reaches an elegant conclusion with the historian's own retirement.[104] Ammianus's adventures during and after the fall of Amida in 359 CE are the focus of the 19th book of his history.[105]

As far as the autopsy of historians is concerned, much the same considerations apply that are obtained in the case of other eye-witnesses. Except where visits to historically significant locales were concerned,[106] it was, of course, only viable for writers of contemporary history. Moreover, even where no conscious bias is skewing their perceptions, historians are no more infallible as observers than anyone else. This is worth stressing. Where historians make claims on the basis of personal experience and we are in a position to be sure from other data that these claims are false, we are understandably tempted to conclude at once that the author is perpetrating conscious fiction or fraud. When Herodotus, for example, produces an account of Egyptian architecture that turns out to be radically defective, there is of course the urge to ask 'could anyone who had ever seen the Pyramids get it all so wrong?'[107] However, while fraud or fancy is always a possibility, due allowance should also be made for failures of observation at the moment of seeing or of recollection at the moment of writing.

Again, a modern example, where the data can be more precisely controlled, may be helpful. This is the case of the nineteenth-century English historian J. A. Froude, whose shortcomings in personal observation were eventually elevated into a syndrome:

> For example, he had visited the city of Adelaide in Australia: 'We saw,' says he, 'below us, in a basin with a river winding through it, a city of 150,000 inhabitants, none of whom has ever known or will ever know one moment's anxiety as to the recurring regularity of his three meals a day.' Thus Froude, now for the facts: Adelaide is built on an eminence; no river runs through it; when Froude visited it the population did not exceed 75,000, and it was suffering from a famine at the time.[108]

Froude was recognized to be an extreme case, but even much more insightful and meticulous observers can fall prey to surprisingly big honest errors.[109] For historians as much as their informants, inadvertent error is always a possible factor to set beside such others as bias and deliberate falsification.

Other Historians

The final big category of sources available to classical historians was, of course, the works of their predecessors and related texts. It is easy to see a distinction between archival records, which we have already considered,[110] and works produced for the public. However, there is a hinterland between these two sources of data, occupied by personal *memoranda* (whether by the historian himself or by others) and family records. Some plausibility attaches to the idea that such accounts of events, given shape and coherence by an individual but not necessarily intended for publication in that form, may have informed the work of some of the extant classical historians. Where family records are concerned, Rome at least offers evidence the interest that aristocratic families took in preserving the memory of their accomplishments: Cicero notes the survival of early funeral orations on the death of distinguished individuals, traditionally delivered by members of their own family,[111] while Livy comments upon inscriptions that were attached to ancestral portraits.[112] The surviving epitaphs of the Cornelii Scipiones also attest aristocratic interest in making sure that a family's deeds were put on record.[113]

Despite these possibilities, the formal compositions of earlier authors remain the most obviously significant source for writers of history in antiquity. Not all of these would necessarily be what the modern world considers historiography. In particular, the poems of Homer remain a potent presence in Greco-Roman history-writing, not just in terms of allusion or structural imitation, but also a source for the mythic period and geography. Herodotus, when discussing the (non-)existence of the river Oceanus, propounds a hypothesis for why the name appears in Homer: 'I know that there is no river Oceanus, but I think that Homer or one of the earlier poets found the name and incorporated it into poetry.'[114] Likewise, Thucydides glances at the reliability of the poet's account of the size of Agamemnon's expedition to Troy,[115] and Appian brings the Homeric account of the Oxen of the Sun into his narrative of the young Octavian's operations in Sicily: 'here, they say, the "Oxen of the Sun" and the "Sleep" happened to Odysseus'.[116]

Nonetheless, published histories, biographies and memoirs were recognized to be a significant source of information for classical historiographers. In many instances, as we have already seen, there would have been few alternative sources of data. And while Polybius decries Timaeus for his reliance on written sources, even he allows 'the industrious study of memoirs and other documents and a comparison of their contents' a role (albeit a subordinate one) in the production of history.[117]

The relationship between historians and their predecessors, especially those whose works have not survived to the present day, has tended to absorb the lion's share of scholarly attention in thinking about the historiography of the ancient world. As such, it will form a significant portion of the next chapter.[118] For the moment, it is, perhaps, expedient to note some of the practicalities of consulting such works in the ancient world which are easy to overlook.

The most significant of these is the need to recognize that the mechanisms which have eroded our own access to the texts of classical antiquity were already active in the ancient world. These mechanisms, and methods to limit the damage that they have done, will be the subject of Chapter 8.[119] For now, it is sufficient to note that the time and expense of producing copies in the age before printing, and the errors which such a copying process tends to bring with it, meant that classical historians could easily suffer from the same sorts of difficulties as readers which afflict their modern student. Texts of useful predecessors might easily be unavailable or, if present, mangled to a greater or lesser extent by the effects of scribal error.

Once again, Polybius shows both an explicit awareness of this problem and a disposition to club a predecessor over the head with it. The target, as so often, is Timaeus:

> ... he falsely accuses Ephorus of making a blunder because he tells us
> that the elder Dionysius began to reign at the age of twenty-three,
> reigned for forty-two years, and died at the age of sixty-three. For
> surely no one could say that the mistake here is the author's, but it is
> obviously the scribe's. Either Ephorus must have surpassed Coroebus
> and Margites in stupidity if he could not reckon that forty-two added
> to twenty-three made sixty-five, or as nobody would believe this of
> Ephorus, the mistake is evidently due to the scribe.[120]

Ephorus of Cyme, the object of Timaeus's criticisms, was writing in the fourth century BCE. Timaeus himself seems to have been born in the middle of the fourth century. In this instance, if Polybius is correct, the garbling of text via scribal error did not take the hundreds of years which some incautiously assume the introduction of mistakes into manuscripts require; there was a lapse of only a couple of generations, or some decades at most, between the publication of Ephorus's history and the creation of the defective copy which Timaeus was using. The classical world was a place where things could go wrong with texts awfully fast. It is prudent to remember this when considering the relationship of historians to their predecessors.

One further consideration, which applies also to the use of informants, is pertinent here. This is the possibility of language barriers. Room for complication here was of course constrained when Greeks restricted themselves entirely to Greek affairs and Romans to Roman. In practice, of course, this was a distinction which could be hard to sustain, even in historiography from the earliest period. The importance of the Persian Empire made *some* treatment of non-Greek speakers unavoidable for particular areas of political history, although Thucydides did his best; the burgeoning of the Roman Empire likewise brought with it the necessity of coping with peoples without Latin. This is to say nothing of such authors as Polybius, Appian, Herodian and Cassius Dio, who all chronicled the history of Rome in Greek.

Issues of language are not often emphasized in extant classical historiography. Nonetheless, there are exceptions, particularly in narratives connected with large mercenary armies and the conduct of campaigns in distant lands.[121] Herodotus, too, makes some attempt to probe the characteristics of foreign languages, although it would be fair to say that his efforts are not crowned with conspicuous success: for example, he asserts, incorrectly, that all Persian names end in the letter 'sigma'.[122] Some writers on historical themes actually note their own competence (or otherwise) in linguistic matters, although it is often hard to tell how much of this is polite self-deprecation. Postumius Albinus, the lost Roman historian who we have already encountered as a butt of Polybian invective,[123] seems to have excused his own inferior command of Greek in his own work, and was roundly abused by Polybius for his pains.[124] From the other direction, the biographer Plutarch claimed to have only an imperfect knowledge of Latin.[125] The possible errancy of historians manipulating sources outside their own comfort zone is a further possible factor that has to be considered in some fields of ancient historiography.

Conclusion

This chapter has illustrated the various different sources of data which were at the disposal of classical historians. Despite the lack of consistent citation practices in ancient historiography, there are enough references to allow a clear general picture to be built up. Eye-witness reports, written accounts, documentary sources, inscriptions, autopsy ... all of these are attested at various points as possible means by which an ancient historian might assemble his own picture of the past. The particular possibilities, and limitations, of these types of evidence have been summarily enumerated.

On the other hand, we have also seen how this general picture can be sadly lacking in specifics. We know, because they say so, that some ancient historians were prepared to make use of certain sorts of sources. What we usually do not know, because of the 'action of the swan', is what sources were available to a particular historian at a particular point in his history, or how he decided what use he was going to make of them. As we have seen, the veil of obscurity is sufficient to leave us uncertain about the general extent of usage even of sources about which one might have expected a clearer picture to emerge. It is still a matter of debate how extensive the public archives at Rome actually were, or who exactly made use of the *Acta Senatus*.

The next chapter will therefore address the question of using sources. The processes by which a given historian generates a particular passage of narrative from the evidence at his disposal are not usually made explicit, true enough. But there are enough cases where ancient writers of history *do* discuss these matters to give us at least some glimpses into the historiographical workshop.

The investigation does not end there, however. As noted in the Preface, making ancient history is a matter of making choices and decisions. An important part of this is the decisions that the classical historians make in putting together their accounts of the past. Equally important, however, are the decisions which we make as readers in trying to assess what these texts are telling us. Thus, the next chapter will also consider the methods which students of antiquity have evolved to make their own decisions about what to do with the texts they read.

4

USING SOURCES – PART II

The last chapter summarized some possible sources of data for those who set out to write narratives of the past in the ancient world. We are aware of these possible sources because of scattered references to them in ancient texts, and (when we are lucky) because the sources themselves still survive. In spite of the optimism traditional amongst poets about the ability of literature to outlast physical monuments,[1] the Pyramids are now in better shape than the text of Livy.

Mere knowledge of these possible sources, however, does not solve the enigma that is central to our attempts to understand ancient historiography. Ancient historians do not consistently quote their sources for their version of events. Thus, it is usually difficult to tell, in any given case, how a classical historiographer cooked up any particular chunk of narrative. We have a cake; we have a sketchy idea of the sort of ingredients that might have gone into making the cake; but we do not have the *recipe* for the cake, or (usually) a precise idea of the particular ingredients that were used to bake it.

Modern attempts to make a history of the ancient world by using the ancient historians proceed, in a more or less explicit form, on the basis of trying to reconstruct recipes by looking at cakes. In other words, they seek to work out how ancient historiographical texts were put together by analysing the finished products. As a procedure, this of course, makes a great deal of sense. But it is important to remember how speculative these attempts can be. As hinted in Chapter 1,[2] it is easy to go astray by mistaking a *theory* about how ancient historiography functions for a doctrine that actually has a weight of evidence to support it.

'Nissen's Law'

This consideration applies particularly to the most famous of modern theories about how ancient historiography functions. Nissen's Law needs to be addressed not just because it is an especially notable example of both the necessity and the perils of theorizing in the absence of data, but also because it lies behind certain assumptions that have continued to be influential in scholarly work on the ancient world.

In 1865, Heinrich Nissen, operating partially under the influence of Ranke,[3] propounded a theory about the relationship between historians and their sources in classical antiquity. According to Nissen, ancient historians usually worked from one, and only one, principal source at a time. Other sources might occasionally be used to correct or supplement this principal source, especially on subjects where it happened to be scanty. However, ancient historians did not exhibit critical judgment when choosing between two sources for the same events – they picked one prior account and stuck with it through thick and thin.

Nissen proposed this idea in the course of his study of Livy. He was, however, at some pains to claim that this model of source use was the general rule – the 'law', in fact – which applied across the historians of antiquity. Livy simply 'reflects the influence of the same fundamental law, which determined all historical writing until the development of modern scholarship'.[4] The thesis arose in part from Nissen's observation of a factor to which we have already alluded: the nature of writing and reading materials in antiquity. Scrolls on the ancient model are much harder to manipulate than the bound volumes of the present day. Hence, Nissen concluded that ancient historians usually spared themselves the cumbersome labour of checking one earlier account against another systematically and adopted the easier route of following a single source wherever possible.[5]

This model of ancient historiographical production has been very influential. It has given rise to a picture of the classical historians as cutting out discrete chunks from earlier writers and sticking them into their own works, with minimal adjustment, wherever they happened to fit. It is often known as a 'scissors and paste' view of historiography, though the present day might perhaps be tempted, on the basis of word processing, to call it 'cut and paste' instead.[6] Outside of classical studies, this model continues to inform popular perceptions of how ancient writers of history, and often pre-modern historians in general, went about their business.[7]

It should be obvious at once, however, that there are certain difficulties with Nissen's theory. The first is the temptation (to which Nissen himself seems to have succumbed) to forget that it is, indeed, a theory. Nissen does not give the evidence to back up his assertion that this was how all ancient historiographers operated. In fact, as we have already mentioned at numerous points in this study,[8] this is exactly the sort of claim which the desultory citation practices of ancient historical texts make impossible to back up. Because classical historians tend not to name sources, and many of the exact sources which they might have used have disappeared, Nissen's 'law' is in fact unprovable.

Of course, it is possible for something which cannot be proven to attain a very high degree of plausibility. If we had access to a sufficient number of cases where we could gather together the text of a historian and the texts of the sources available to him, and in all these cases the historian followed one source faithfully to the exclusion of all the others, then Nissen's 'Law' would indeed start to look like a plausible generalization. The problem is that in the instances where we can do this, the 'law' does not always obtain. In fact, there are a number of cases where historians explicitly state that their methodology is different. Consider, for example, a passage which we have already mentioned in passing:[9] Arrian's explanation, at the outset of his work, of how he set about writing his history of the deeds of Alexander the Great:

> Wherever Ptolemy son of Lagus and Aristobulus son of Aristobulus have both given the same accounts of Alexander son of Philip, it is my practice to record what they say as completely true, but where they differ, to select the version I regard as more trustworthy and also better worth telling. In fact other writers have given a variety of accounts of Alexander, nor is there any other figure of whom there are more historians who are more contradictory of each other, but in

my view Ptolemy and Aristobulus are more trustworthy in their narrative, since Aristobulus took part in king Alexander's expedition, and Ptolemy not only did the same, but as he himself was a king, mendacity would have been more dishonourable for him than for anyone else; again, both wrote when Alexander was dead and neither was under any constraint or hope of gain to make himself set down anything but what actually happened. However, I have also recorded some statements made in other accounts of others, when I thought them worth mention and not entirely untrustworthy, but only as tales told of Alexander.[10]

The principles which Arrian enunciates here bear scrutiny. In the first place, it is quite clear that he openly flouts 'Nissen's Law'. Arrian is not claiming to have found a single source and then clung to it like a life raft. Rather, he uses two major sources, the earlier histories of Alexander composed by Ptolemy and Aristobulus,[11] and goes to some trouble to indicate why he believes them to be more trustworthy: personal experience of Alexander's expedition; lack of incentive for personal gain; and (in the case of Ptolemy) the veracity that befits a king.

The reader may well be inclined to judge some elements of this reasoning a little ropey. Arrian would not have had to read far in his beloved Xenophon to discover that monarchy and mendacity are by no means mutually exclusive.[12] Moreover, propaganda battles amongst Alexander's Successors, of whom Ptolemy was of course one, meant that the value of propagating a particular view of the king's reign would not necessarily dissolve on the king's own death,[13] and Ptolemy and Aristobulus, despite their presence in the army, cannot have been eyewitnesses of all the events they described.[14] Nonetheless, the general thrust of the argument, basing itself on the personal experience of the two historians and the historical context in which they were composing their works, is not something to which even a Ranke would have been able to raise strenuous objections.

Even more instructive, however, is Arrian's statement of policy with regard to *differences* between the accounts of Ptolemy and Aristobulus. Arrian does not, he asserts, adopt a strategy of picking one narrative and sticking to it through hell and high water. Rather, he says that where there are discrepancies he chooses the version 'I regard as more trustworthy and also better worth telling'. Again, the eyebrows of a modern historian may perhaps be raised at the notion of 'better worth telling' as a criterion on which to arbitrate between competing narratives; this policy, in fact, relates to Arrian's views, expressed elsewhere in his work, on the ethical and instructive purposes of history. Nor does Arrian state on what grounds he would judge an account to be 'more trustworthy'.[15] Nonetheless, it remains interesting that Arrian claims to be asserting judgment and discrimination over conflicts in the sources at his disposal.

Moreover, Arrian's practice in the bulk of his narrative does not suggest that this statement of methodology is entirely misleading. It is certainly possible to doubt how thorough-going this process of collation between Ptolemy and Aristobulus actually was.[16] Doubts have also been expressed about his ability to maintain consistency as to which version of events he was accepting.[17] Nonetheless, his practices of citation in the body of his history continue to give evidence that Arrian did assess divergent accounts in his sources. He notes, on several occasions, disagreements on basic matters of fact in earlier texts,[18] including the final fate of Alexander's own court historian Callisthenes: 'As for Callisthenes, Aristobulus says he was bound with fetters and carried round with the army, but at length died of sickness, Ptolemy son of Lagus that he was racked and put to death by hanging. Thus not even those whose narratives are entirely trustworthy and who actually accompanied Alexander at that time agree in their accounts of events which were public and within their own knowledge.'[19] In this instance, Arrian does not make a decision between the two possibilities; elsewhere, in his account of the Battle of the Hydaspes, he not only gives the conflicting accounts of Aristobulus and Ptolemy, but gives his reasons for preferring the latter: 'Nor was it likely that Porus, on learning from his scouts that the Hydaspes had been crossed either by Alexander in person or at least by a part of his army, would have sent out his own son with no more than sixty chariots.'[20] Throughout his work, such questions continue to crop up, and we can plot several points at which he follows Aristobulus rather than Ptolemy, or vice versa. Whatever the exact nature of Arrian's criteria for his decisions, about which there continues to be much discussion,[21] there is much more going on here than just slavish adherence to a single source.

Other glimpses into the processes of historical thinking in the ancient world reinforce the impression that Nissen's Law was, at the very least, a far from universal observance. The Ciceronian commentator Asconius, whose use of the *Acta Senatus* we have already noted,[22] can be seen both noting variation between sources and meditating a decision in his overview of the tangled sequence of events that led to the murder of P. Clodius Pulcher by T. Annius Milo and his associates on the Appian Way in 52 BCE: 'On 18 January – for I think that the *Acta* and the speech, which agrees with the *Acta*, should be followed, rather than Fenestella, whose account has the 17th, Milo set out for Lanuvium, his native town, where at the time he was dictator, in order to appoint a *flamen* the next day.'[23] It is true that Asconius is not himself writing a continuous history. His work is, according to the author himself, intended to guide his sons through Cicero's speeches, and the commentary mode which this enjoins is some way removed from the narrative historiography that is our main (but not sole) concern in this study.[24] Nonetheless, his work shows that the comparison and assessment of different sources in classical antiquity could go some distance beyond picking one earlier account and sticking to it.

The nature of Asconius's work also points up a weakness in the practical considerations which Nissen adduces in support of his thesis. Comparing books (or, more usually, scrolls) was indeed a much more cumbersome operation in the ancient world than it is now. The younger Pliny, for example, in a letter to Titinius Capito, openly bewails the labour that would be involved in collating earlier works: 'You, however, can be considering now what period of history I am to treat. Is it ancient history, which has had its historians? The material is there, but it will be a great labour to assemble it.'[25]

On the other hand, the mechanical toil involved in this task should not be exaggerated or overestimated. A work like that of Asconius took its raison d'être from its reader being able to compare it systematically with another text: in this case, the speeches of Cicero. Another consideration, which the modern sensibility perhaps too easily effaces, is the ready access to slave labour of many elite readers in antiquity. The student of history in the ancient world could call upon the simultaneous application of more pairs of hands than his modern counterpart.

Likewise, there is no compelling basis to the notion that historiographical precision necessarily varies in inverse proportion to the sophistication of the information technologies that happen to be available in a particular epoch. With the advance of the Internet, it is not hard to envisage future students of history (Plato and his associates peering back at the twenty-first century from a magitech world, perhaps)[26] arguing that extensive collation of sources would have been entirely impossible before the advent of computers because of the physical labour involved in hauling around all those bits of dead tree. Accounts of the work habits of Walter Headlam, for example, a nineteenth-century Greek scholar in Cambridge, would be unlikely to inspire these future observers with confidence:

> One morning … his water for shaving was not hot, so after breakfast he put a small kettle to boil over his spirit lamp, and as he waited for that, he sat down in the armchair where he worked and casually looked at a note he had made the evening before. It was about a change of rhythm in a Greek chorus, or perhaps it was a word in his Herondas, which occurred in no dictionary, but which he knew he had seen before in some scholiast on Aristophanes. But where was the particular book he wanted? His room was lined with bookshelves, books that he was using paved the floor round his chair, and the table was piled high with them. There it was underneath a heap of others on the table, and he pulled it out: those on the top of it tumbled to the ground. He put down his pipe on the edge of the table, and as he turned the leaves, he found not just that which he was looking for, but something else he had wanted yesterday. He made a note of this on a slip of paper and picked up his pipe which had gone out. There were no matches, so he folded up the paper on which he had made his note, thrust it into the flame of the spirit-lamp and lit his pipe again. Then he found the passage he had originally started to hunt up.[27]

Headlam was an exceptional case and the passage above was, of course, put together for comedic effect. Nonetheless, it illustrates that the world of books, the physical manipulation of which we still (just about) take for granted, could easily be seen as imposing a strain that made serious and systematic comparison of sources onerous and therefore something to be avoided. Compare Yeats's depiction of his work in the British Library: 'I spent my days at the British Museum and must, I think, have been delicate, for I remember often putting off hour after hour consulting some necessary book because I shrank from lifting the heavy volumes of the catalogue.'[28] We, of course, know that this is not necessarily the case. Students of historiography in a conjectural future, however, might take some convincing. The difficulties of checking sources in the ancient world were certainly not nugatory. But, then as now, they were not insuperable.

As a general principle, then, Nissen's Law lacks confirmation from empirical evidence. Moreover, we have seen cases where it is demonstrably not operating. These observations do not, of course, prove the converse: that classical historiographers *never* adopted a single source and did not budge from it until it ran out. There are certainly instances from the ancient world of historical texts which copy long stretches of their predecessors almost word for word, which we can see when both the earlier and the later text survive and we are able to put them side by side. Likewise, there are cases of authors whose sources have not survived, but whose vocabulary, thematic coverage and other characteristics shift so abruptly and markedly at particular points in their text that a movement from one favoured predecessor to another is at least a plausible hypothesis. Diodorus is one such possible example.[29]

It should, however, be clear that it is a methodological error to assume, in the absence of corroborative evidence, that a particular historiographical text from the ancient world *must* be slavishly following a single (conveniently lost) predecessor for (conveniently long) swathes of its narrative. It is possible that this is the case, but, on the basis of what we have already seen, it cannot be taken for granted. Likewise, confidence that a particular statement in an extant historian can be chased down to its original source when that source is lost and the extant historian does not name it is often misplaced.

It is a regrettable fact of scholarship on ancient historiography that these dubious premises *have* sometimes been assumed. The penchant in some quarters for uncovering the name of a lost earlier historiographer and then asserting the dependence of an extant author upon him, without troubling to consider the theoretical questions which this procedure evades, is now very much reduced (and was often exaggerated for polemical effect by the detractors of source criticism).[30] However, it has produced some notable excesses,[31] and its thoughtless application to authors where hypotheses can be controlled usually has discouraging results.[32]

Quellenforschung

Nonetheless, there is an obvious interest in trying to determine, where possible, the sources from which an ancient historian is deriving his information. If we are intent on constructing our own picture of the historical past, it is clearly to our benefit if we can identify the likely provenance of claims that a historiographer is making. If we are interested in the historian as a thinker or a literary artist, then being able to make educated guesses about the data on which he is working helps to illuminate the processes by which he turns it into a narrative. How, then, can we puzzle out the hidden workings of passages in historical texts, when the 'action of the swan' occludes our view? The attempt to determine the sources of a historical narrative is often known by its German name: *Quellenforschung*. In what follows, we shall attempt to elucidate some of the principal strategies which this procedure can press into operation. Equally important, we shall look at the limitations of these strategies.

Mentioned authorities

As we have already observed, the 'action of the swan' is by no means absolute in its application. Ancient historians do sometimes quote their sources. Our problem is that they do not do so consistently.

However, such citations are a valuable clue, even beyond the original context in which they appear. They are, after all, evidence that a historian has read (or claims to have read) that particular author. It is therefore by no means impossible that information from that author might be deployed *without* acknowledgement elsewhere in the historian's text.

There is a temptation to argue that reference to a source at a particular point implies that elsewhere, where there is no such reference, that source is *not* being used. For example, as we have seen, Tacitus only once actually says that he is using the *Acta Senatus*.[33] Does the uniqueness of this case suggest that he otherwise did not consult them?

In fact, such an argument from silence is usually dangerous. Since ancient historians do not, as a rule, cite consistently anyway, there may well be factors to explain why a source is explicitly cited at some places and not at others. In particular, it is worth noting that named citations have a tendency to cluster at points where different available authorities disagree – above all, where numbers are concerned. So, for example, Appian, discussing the butcher's bill at the end of the Battle of Pharsalus, notes that 'as far as the rest of the army is concerned, those inclined to exaggeration say that 25,000 corpses of Pompeians were found, but Asinius Pollio, who was a general at that battle under Caesar, that 6,000 were found.'[34] As we shall see shortly, there is corroborative evidence that Appian did in fact make use of Pollio elsewhere. The explicit citation is not therefore an indication of a unique recourse to that writer in Appian's histories.

Moreover, the fact that a historian usually criticizes a predecessor when he mentions him explicitly is no guarantee that he does not use him without acknowledgement elsewhere. These considerations apply to post-classical historiography as well. In fact, one of the most cogent surveys of citation practices remains that of Jacob Thomasius, the seventeenth-century German philosopher and jurist, who in 1692 published a *Philosophical Dissertation on Literary Theft* that notes the various ways in which strategic allusion can trick the unwary reader: some authors 'say nothing, at the most significant point, about one whom they then cite only on a point of no or little importance'; others mention their source 'only when they disagree with or criticize him; while yet others accuse the authors they are plagiarizing of the fault which they themselves are engaged in committing'.[35] Thomasius, of course, is actually talking about intentional literary theft, whereas ancient appropriations of sources are in a somewhat different category. Nevertheless, his criticism is worth bearing in mind against the temptation to read too much into the absence of citations from works which do not reliably cite anyway.

'Mentioned authorities', however, can go beyond simple isolated citations of an author's work. Sometimes the presence of an actual historian in a text can be suggestive. For example, the role played by the Caesarean general Gaius Asinius Pollio in Appian's account of the Roman Civil Wars is a striking one: he appears as an important character and emerges in a notably good light in comparison to his colleagues. When we add this to the consideration that Pollio himself wrote a history of the civil wars, that Appian, as we have just seen,[36] quotes his tally of Pompeian casualties at a key point in his narrative, and that Appian's account shows some significant congruities with other extant texts,[37] the pattern becomes rather suggestive.[38]

On the other hand, the mere fact that a historian appears as an actor in a subsequent historical text does not guarantee that the works of that historian will be used to a significant extent by the later historiographer. One example which we have already encountered is that of Alexander's court historian Callisthenes. Arrian was aware of both the man and the fact of his historical output – not to mention his untimely but debatable death.[39] This did not stop him, however, from using Ptolemy and Aristobulus as his main sources. Callisthenes, if Arrian even accessed his text,[40] would have fallen foul of the later historian's distrust of those who wrote during Alexander's own lifetime, in contrast to Ptolemy and Aristobulus, who 'both wrote when Alexander was dead and neither was under any constraint or hope of gain to make himself set down anything but what actually happened'.[41]

Beyond the text of Arrian, examples can be multiplied of cases where allusion to the personal intervention of a historian in a narrative does not necessarily signify reliance on that historian's account of events. This is particularly the case where that historian is himself a very significant agent in the events that are described. Julius Caesar is an obvious instance of this. Since Caesar's own historical works are mostly extant, we are in a position to see that the *other* surviving accounts of his career are not in fact solely dependent on the Dictator's own version of events. There are clear divergences between Caesar on the one hand and later authors on the other as to what actually happened at various points in the Civil Wars; one celebrated case is the famous episode of the crossing of the Rubicon in 49 BCE, which Appian, Plutarch and Suetonius describe in detail and Caesar does not mention at all.[42] We also know that Pollio, whose contemporary history has already appeared as the source for Appian's casualty totals at Pharsalus, went to some pains to flag up his own divergences from his erstwhile general's take on events: 'Asinius Pollio thinks that they (Caesar's *commentarii*) were put together with too little care and too little complete truth, since Caesar had credited several matters rashly, both of his own and others' doing, whether through a lapse of memory or on purpose. And he thinks that he should have rewritten and corrected them.'[43]

Of course, it may well be argued that Caesar is an unusual case. He was, after all, a historian who so obviously had a stake in what he was writing about that his successors in the field of Civil War historiography showed an understandable reluctance to accept his version of what happened unconditionally. We have already seen that Arrian, at least, recognized the pressures that might apply in such a situation.[44] Most historians who appear themselves as players in the drama of history did not operate on quite so exalted a level.[45]

However, the appearance even of less politically significant historians in a later text is still not necessarily a sign that they are being utilized by their successor. Once again, Appian furnishes a useful test case. Appian does mention the activities of the Roman historian Fabius Pictor in the course of his account of the Second Punic War. He even mentions the fact that Fabius wrote historical works about the period he is describing: 'The Senate sent Quintus Fabius, the historian of these events, to Delphi to ask about what was going on.'[46] The conclusion has therefore been drawn that Pictor was the ultimate source for Appian's narrative of the wars against Hannibal.[47] In fact, detailed attention to Appian's account of the Second Punic War demonstrates striking divergences from what we know to have been the version of events which Pictor presented in his lost history of the conflict.[48] Likewise, Appian paints a vivid picture of Polybius at the fall of Carthage;[49] however, this does not in fact come at the climax of an account of the Punic Wars which actually follows his.[50] Not every appearance of a historian is equivalent to a source citation, even when the later writer takes time to mention the earlier's historiographical endeavours – there are thus some methodological issues, with the assumption that Appian's other references to lost historians may be taken as evidence of dependence on their works.[51] Sometimes historians just like to name-check other historians – or to use their appearance as an opportunity to slip in some meta-historical reflection.[52]

References to other writers, then, are something which the student of ancient historiography needs to handle with discretion. They can be exceedingly useful. Even where they do not necessarily unlock all the secrets of the historian under discussion, they at least provide some clues to earlier writing about a particular topic. In particular, they assist in the reconstruction of works which are themselves no longer extant.[53] But the variation in citation practice which we can plot with confidence across some ancient historians should make us pause before we start to hypothesize too recklessly about the sources of others.

Beyond these theoretical issues, however, there is also a problem of practicality. Even if we take into account the name-checking of authors who turn up in narratives alongside explicit citations, the haul of names from classical historiography remains scanty. The 'action of the swan' is a pervasive phenomenon. How, then, does the quest to assess a historian's data fare in the absence of any obvious citations?

Parallel accounts

Absence of overt citation is not necessarily the end of the road where *Quellenforschung* is concerned. It is infrequently the case that an extant historiographical account will share similarities of treatment, wording or phraseology with another extant account of the same topic to an extent which makes it unlikely that they both came up with it independently. At this point, it seems reasonable to conclude either that one of these extant sources is using the other, or that they are both indebted to a lost original.

For example, Appian and Cassius Dio both have accounts of the confusion that ensued at Rome in the immediate aftermath of Julius Caesar's assassination on the Ides of March in 44 BCE. In each case, the individuals who hastened to associate themselves with the Dictator's assassins after that event meet with a particular jibe from the narrator: their plan had almost exactly the reverse of the desired effect, and where they had hoped to win a good reputation for something which they had not actually done, all they managed to do was participate in the subsequent peril without getting a share of the glory.[54] Either Appian and Dio spontaneously came up with identical witticisms at the same point in their narratives, or, as seems perhaps more probable, both of these jests have the same source. It will be noted that a joke or distinctive authorial quip is particularly useful in this sort of investigation, since it is not the sort of textual phenomenon which is likely to arise in the same form independently in two (or more) different writers.

Certain difficulties present themselves, of course. In the first place, it is not necessarily straightforward to determine whether text A and text B are both indebted to a lost text C or whether one is simply using the other.[55] In the case of contemporaneous authors (or of authors whose chronological interrelationship we cannot precisely determine), there is an additional complication: it need not be immediately obvious whether text A is using text B or the other way around.[56] The techniques which help to resolve similar issues in the discipline of textual criticism, such as the practical rule that a descendant will contain all the errors of its archetype and at least one more,[57] do not work so well once one strays beyond the domain of exact copying and into that of use as a source.

Comparison of parallel accounts can, then, be very useful. In certain cases, it may even allow us to gain a fairly accurate picture of the emphases and quirks of a text which is itself no longer extant. However, the circumstances in which it can be deployed are perforce rather limited. Moreover, as we shall see in more detail in Chapter 8,[58] it is wise not to be too sanguine about how much of a lost source can reasonably be excavated on the basis of its traces in later texts, even when there are several of them to act as controls on one another.

Detail, vividness, autopsy

Even where a historian does not explicitly name predecessors, or demonstrate useful similarities with other extant texts that do, scholars have evolved techniques for assessing the likely extent and sources of their information. These usually focus on attention to the character and detail of a historian's account and, in particular, apparent variations in character and detail between one stretch of narrative in a historical work and the next. Once again, this sort of analysis can be instructive. And once again, it is important to stay apprised of the theoretical issues which can vitiate some of its assumptions.

Perhaps the most straightforward application of this methodology occurs in the case of writers of contemporary history. These writers, as we have already seen,[59] often claim to have been eyewitnesses at some of the events they describe. Of course, no one, as Polybius reminds us,[60] can be everywhere at once. Thus, one might reasonably expect fluctuations in the level of detail which a historian can command, based on his personal absence or presence at the events that he is describing. So, for example, Herodian, whose history of Rome we have already examined,[61] claims that 'I have written a history of the events following the death of Marcus which I saw and heard in my lifetime'.[62] If one plots the level of circumstantial detail in his references to what was going on in the city of Rome itself, one discovers that it tends to be highest in the accounts of the years 188–93 and 238 CE. Since, on the basis of biographical evidence about Herodian's own life, these periods coincided with the likely beginning and the end of his career, the conclusion has been drawn that these were the periods when the historian's own administrative career brought him to Rome. At other times, when he was in the provinces, his account was necessarily less detailed.[63]

Where historians who write about non-contemporary history are concerned, the criterion of notable 'vividness' or 'detail' in a narrative is often used to determine whether a particular stretch of a text is derived from the account of an eyewitness. Where a historian's account seems to be more crammed with incidental detail or comment at certain points or on certain subjects than on others, this (it is argued) stems from the fact that the source for this point of the narrative had seen what was going on with his own eyes. So, for example, Appian's account of the Battle of Mutina, with its wealth of picturesque detail, has been held to go back to an eyewitness of the events.[64]

The limitations to this approach should be fairly obvious. It rests on the assumption that detail and vividness are reliable indications of an eyewitness account. Unfortunately, it is, as we have already seen, very nearly as easy (and much more convincing) to make up a vivid and circumstantial account as it is to fabricate a bare and jejune one. Sir Edmund Backhouse[65] and Pooh-Bah were not the only ones who were aware that detail adds artistic verisimilitude to an otherwise bald and unconvincing narrative. For richness of detail and meticulousness of documentation, the manuscript tradition of, say, Velleius Paterculus does not compare to that of the (entirely fictional) *Necronomicon*.[66]

While invented detail, at least when it appears in profusion, is likely to be the result of deliberate fabrication, it is worth noting that 'vividness', too, is a somewhat problematic criterion by which to determine whether a passage stems from an eyewitness account. The difficulty here is that 'vividness' is expressly noted in antiquity as one of the particular virtues to which any historiographical text should aspire. Thus, for example, Lucian, compiling his list of the traits of the perfect historian in *How History Ought to Be Written*, expressly comments on this: 'the task of the historian is similar: to give a fine arrangement to events and illuminate them as vividly as possible. And when a man who has heard him thinks thereafter that he is actually seeing what is being described and then praises him – then it is that the work of our Phidias of history is perfect and has received its proper praise.'[67] Narrative vividness, then, is no necessary index of an original eyewitness account. Both Appian and Herodian (to name but two authors to which this criterion has been applied) seem on the basis of their work as a whole to have been fully capable of generating such vividness through their own literary finesse.[68] We might also remember that the most celebrated and vivid of all fictional accounts of the American Civil War, Stephen Crane's *The Red Badge of Courage*, was written by an author who had not even been born when that conflict ended.[69]

Vividness and detail, then, have to be treated with caution unless they can be controlled by other evidence. An account whose circumstantial details can be corroborated by an independent source, of course, is in a different category. But the mere fact of a wealth of detail or a lively stretch of narrative may say more about an author's literary procedures than the characteristics of his sources.

This extends likewise to the criterion of apparent narrative emphasis. Where an ancient historian devotes what might seem to a modern reader to be a disproportionate amount of space to a topic or period of time, there is a temptation to attribute this to the fact that the historian had a 'good source' for it. This therefore causes him to dilate upon a particular theme to an unusual extent.

The problem with this reasoning is that it assumes in all the ancient historians modern notions of appropriate scale. Even a desultory reading in classical historiography is sufficient to refute such an assumption. It is true that Polybius, for example, does set reasonably clear and consistent targets for the amount of time he is going to cover with a given amount of text: 'these are the principal events included in the abovementioned Olympiad, that is the space of four years which we term an Olympiad, and I shall attempt to narrate them in two books'.[70] Likewise, Lucian satirizes historians whose disposition of material strikes him as eccentric:

> For instance, I myself heard a man cover the Battle of Europus in less
> than seven complete lines, but he spent twenty or even more
> measures of the water-clock on a frigid description that was of no
> interest to us of how a Moorish horseman, Mausacas by name, was

wandering over the mountains because he was thirsty and found some
Syrian country-folk setting out their lunch; at first they were afraid of
him, but then … they welcomed him and gave him food … Long
stories and digressions followed as to how he had gone hunting in
Mauretania and how he had seen many elephants grazing together.[71]

However, even if (as some have suspected) Lucian's anonymous target
here is fictional,[72] the polemic lacks a point if there was not a tendency
of this sort in some quarters to be satirized. Nor are the proportions of
some extant historiographical works from the ancient world quite what
one would necessarily expect, even where simple reliance on a 'good
source' is quite implausible. Sallust, writing about events in his own lifetime at Rome, devotes approximately one-sixth of his entire work on
Catiline's insurrection to a presentation of two speeches[73] and a whole
chapter to a character sketch of a woman who otherwise plays no part in
the narrative.[74] Livy devotes the first two-thirds of Book Seven of his history to a period of 23 years and the last third to a period of only two.[75]

In fact, it is hard not to suspect that classical historians are in fact
designedly upsetting the reader's sense of what ought to be allotted a
large amount of space in their narrative and what should not. Such a
strategy might be compared with that of other Greco-Roman authors,
such as Callimachus, who in his poem *Hecale* relegates the hero Theseus's
quest to slay a monster to the sidelines in favour of an intensely detailed
description of a meal prepared for him by the eponymous old woman
beforehand.[76] The pattern of compressed fights and distended meals
which Lucian criticizes in his historian of the Battle of Europus may
therefore have had a more coherent aesthetic strategy behind it than
Lucian, who argues for a simpler distribution of narrative proportion,
was prepared to admit.[77] Once again, then, the possibility cannot always
be ruled out that artistic intent, rather than the availability of data, is
what determines the nature of the historian's narrative at such points.[78]

There is a larger methodological issue here, which also demands to be
addressed. I have been at pains throughout this study to stress the limitations on what we know *for certain* about the processes which shape the
production of ancient historiographical texts. We have a collection of
finished products, in the shape of the works that have survived to the
present day. But these products and other evidence allude only obscurely

and erratically to the processes that shaped them. Hence my metaphor of the swan to approximate the forward motion of most ancient historio-graphical texts.

On the basis of what we *can* see about the texts we have, we can form theories and models to explain why they are the way they are. The problem we then encounter is that, in the dearth of evidence, multiple models may well turn out to fit the data at our disposal equally well. In the cases we have just seen, for example, the vividness of a particular stretch of narrative in an ancient historian – Appian on Mutina, for example, or Herodian on Caracalla's massacre at Alexandria – *could* be explained by the fact that the passage is derived from the account of an eyewitness. But it might equally be the result of a historian who is writing in line with the notions, espoused by Lucian and others in the ancient world, of the desirability of vividness in a historical narrative. Either (or both) is a plausible explanation for the data at our disposal – the mere fact that a model fits the available evidence does not guarantee that other models do not. The analogy of a detective novel has been usefully deployed in this context: it is not really sufficient, for the purposes of obtaining a conviction, just to produce a version of events that explains the evidence, since such an explanation does not guarantee that there are not other models which do so as well.[79]

The paucity of data from the classical world means that this problem of competing models is one which we often have to address. A Greek historian, for example, uses a word which is very unusual for the dialect or register of diction which he typically adopts. Is this word a remnant of the diction used by his original source, which the historian has simply copied over (a 'source-critical' model)? Is it a conscious decision by the author to variegate his narrative with unusual diction (a 'literary' model)? After all, we know from Lucian that at least one reader of historiography in antiquity was sensitive to variations in dialect,[80] and there are instances in classical literary criticism where the use of a resonant word is explicitly commended.[81] Or is it the case (for reasons we shall examine in Chapter 8)[82] that the word has at some point been copied down incorrectly by a careless scribe and has entered the text by mistake (a 'textual' model)?[83] Or is there a combination of factors at work?

Of course, one should not overstate the problem here. Although different models may well explain the presence of a particular feature in a historiographical text, it may still be the case that other evidence renders one model, in this case, more convincing than another. So, for example, our awareness of Arrian's explicit statements on his methodology with regard to his sources[84] will naturally impact upon what seems the most likely explanation for the idiosyncrasies of a particular passage in his work. In similar vein, we will be less likely to assume that a historian (or his source) is ignorantly muddling up Chalcedon and Carthage in his text if we are aware of the evidence, derived from the study of manuscripts and the historical context of the scribes who were writing them, that this is likely to be a scribal confusion.[85] In other words, the study of ancient historiographical texts, and indeed of ancient history in general, is often a matter of weighing competitive probabilities in this fashion.

Of course, the weighing of these probabilities becomes all the more difficult in a case where there is very little in the way of data to produce a preponderance in favour of a particular model. All one can really do, in these circumstances, is to proceed with a due awareness of the multiple possible explanations for why a historiographical text is the way it is. *Quellenforschung* has one great vulnerability when it is insensitively applied. This is the assumption, convenient to the analyst, but, as we have now seen, not always well supported by control cases, that an extant historian is in essence a defective photocopier of his sources, reproducing them faithfully and without variation at best, misunderstanding, abbreviating and mangling them at worst. This is not to say that there were not authors in the ancient world who did just that.[86] However, the assumption that this must necessarily be the case, and that one can invariably deploy methodologies that only function when matters are so, is clearly a flawed one.

Once one admits the possibility that the historian one is analysing might himself be discriminating between sources, combining different accounts, putting his own slant upon narrative and interpretation, and possibly inserting plausible material of his own devising, the whole enterprise becomes an order of magnitude more complicated, and the 'results' it produces a lot more provisional. The temptation to keep things neat by excluding this possibility is therefore an obvious one. It is unfortunate, however, that we have now assembled compelling evidence to suggest that, where at least a number of classical historians are concerned, this possibility is very plausible.

There is likewise a temptation to flee to the opposite extreme. Since *Quellenforschung* is a hazardous enterprise, and there are often doubts as to the security of its results, it can seem to be a saving of energy to abandon it altogether and restrict analysis to the characteristics of a piece of historiographical literature as it presents itself to the reader. This approach has particular appeal to those who desire to look upon a given history as simply a work of literature and whose principal interest is primarily in the literary techniques by which the author generates his meaning.

The difficulty with this approach is that, in its own way, it again fails to do justice to the particular nature of at least some instances of historiographical production in the ancient world, as indicated by the passages which we have already analysed. Ancient historiography, despite attempts in some quarters to prove otherwise, does not display a consistent indifference to such notions as verification, the assessment of evidence and the reasonable deployment of sources. We have seen examples of ancient historians criticizing one another for factual inaccuracies,[87] discussing appropriate criteria for the use of sources[88] and examining the methodology of interview technique.[89]

These examples do not, of course, demonstrate that fabrication and historical fiction were categories of activity of which the authors of the ancient world were incapable; as we shall see, this was patently not the case.[90] However, they do show that the issue of the relationship between classical historians and the data at their disposal cannot be dismissed wholesale as a shibboleth born of an anachronistic attitude to what the ancient world considered 'history'. The ancient historical text, like the modern, stands in a different relationship to data from that which is occupied by a straightforward work of fiction. This does not entail that the relationship between text and data will always be in accordance with the prescriptions of a Ranke. But it does mean that adequate analysis of the work cannot simply declare the investigation of this relationship as ipso facto irrelevant. While the enthusiast for *Quellenforschung* may succumb to the urge to make life simpler by ignoring the possibilities of textual gene-splicing and mutation on the part of an extant historian, the formalist literary critic is prey to the temptation to efface the possible difference between the operating procedures of fiction and historiography. On the basis of our observation of ancient texts, however, neither of these simplifications is borne out by what we have seen of ancient historiographical practice.

What has emerged from this chapter, then, is the importance of choice and decision-making at all stages in the production and reception of ancient history-writing. We have uncovered evidence of the levels of discrimination which at least some classical historians demonstrated in putting together their narratives. Arrian's dramatization of his own decision-making processes in the matter of writing Alexander's history is, perhaps, unusual in extent and outspokenness. It does, however, serve to illustrate graphically how what an ancient historian commits to papyrus or vellum elbows out another version that might have been.

At another remove, we have seen again the ways in which *we ourselves* as readers are constantly engaged in evaluation and decision-making when we read the historiography of the ancient world. This picks up a theme from the opening chapter. Our first impressions about it are moulded by the decisions that earlier readers of these texts have made about them: how they should be packaged; how they should be titled; and which ones go together.[91]

The primacy of decision-making, it has now become clear, applies equally to our own experience as students of these texts. The use to which we will judge it appropriate to put a particular passage from a Greco-Roman historian will rest upon our assessment of what is going on in that passage. This assessment will, in turn, be informed by the model (or models) which we consider best to explain the nature, at this point, of the historian's narrative. Since so many aspects of the production of historiographical texts in antiquity remain less than pellucid – because of the 'action of the swan' – this exercise of discrimination and decision-making is constant when we read an ancient historian. It is precisely because classical works of history so often make it hard for us to see below the surface of their texts that we must play the investigator and construct hypotheses to account for their unexpected depth.

It is, perhaps, this intersection of acts of decision-making by author and reader which gives the study of historiography its particular fascination. In the next chapter, we shall explore some of the factors which inform these acts of decision-making, both on the part of the historian and on the part of the modern. We shall also begin to explore the (sometimes unconsidered or unnoticed) ramifications which the original decisions of the one can have for the belated decisions of the other.

5

WRITING ANCIENT
HISTORY

In the previous chapters, we have started to get to grips with some of the mechanisms that power the production and reception of ancient historiography. We have noted the common formal features of these texts – above all, their unwillingness consistently to indicate what relationship (if any) they enjoy with prior historical data. We have therefore observed the need, as readers of ancient works of history, to formulate models and hypotheses which can explain why these texts are the way they are, and to test these models against what we can observe of their characteristics. In doing so, we have started to piece together a picture of the sorts of considerations – the bounding conditions, as it were – which sometimes help to determine the nature of these texts. The nature of the sources available to ancient historical authors, and the processes to which they subjected these sources, have both come under the critical spotlight.

In this chapter, the emphasis switches to what ancient historians and their subsequent readers can *achieve* with classical historiography. The title of this chapter, which is also that of this book, is designedly ambiguous. The main focus of concern in this study is of course how authors in the Greco-Roman world wrote history. However, most people who come to the texts of the classical historiographers in the twenty-first century do so because they, too, are engaged in writing ancient history – using these texts to arrive at an understanding of the classical world.

This is, of course, by no means the only reason why one can find one-self approaching ancient historiographical texts. The works of the ancient historians have also been used for many other purposes. In particular, as prose authors with a (usually) straightforward vocabulary, some ancient historians, especially Caesar and Xenophon, formed for many years the basis of teaching the classical languages.[1] They have also been utilized as valuable evidence for the development of the Greek and Latin tongues (Livy being a notable example)[2] and for their application, practical and ideological, in subsequent ages: here, the reception of Tacitus from the Renaissance onwards has proven a particularly fertile field of study.[3] Finally, one might note their status as the targets of allusion and rework-ing in later literature,[4] and as masterpieces of literary artistry: Macaulay (in the context, as it happens, of depreciation of the Roman historians) declared that 'there is no prose composition in the world ... which I place so high as the 7th book of Thucydides. It is the ne plus ultra of human art.'[5] Nonetheless, it would still be fair to say that the most com-mon reason why people encounter classical historiography is because they, too, are writing ancient history – even if the histories they are putting together in their heads never actually make it onto paper or a computer screen.

Climbing Mount Probable

The modern student of classical historiography, then, is writing ancient history. This applies every bit as much to the contemporary reader as it does to the historians he or she examines. Indeed, there can be occasions when the textual operations of the one can bear a striking resemblance to what is attested for the other.

As we have repeatedly noted,[6] it is perilous to generalize from the practice of one ancient historian to that of another. It is likewise impru-dent to set 'ancient' and 'modern' practices in antithesis as if each was a homogeneous and easily classified entity.[7] Nonetheless, it remains rea-sonable to state that some of the procedures which the classical histori-ographers announce themselves as using to decide the nature of their own narratives are by no means as different from what a modern reader is likely to use, as has sometimes been suggested.

A case in point is the famous 'argument from probability'. The popularity of this tool amongst writers of history in the ancient world has often been noticed.[8] Historians, in trying to determine what happened in a given situation, often fall back upon the notion of what is most likely or probable to have occurred.

Of course, such assessments of likelihood are in turn based on a variety of different inductive procedures. One such species of reasoning is the argument from someone's observed character. Tacitus provides two interesting instances of this in action. The first is to be found in his *Histories*. Tacitus is analysing different explanations in his sources for the behaviour of individuals during the contention between Otho and Vitellius for the principate in the 'Year of the Four Emperors' (69 CE):

> In some of my authorities I find a statement that either fear of war or scorn for the two emperors, whose scandalous misconduct grew daily more notorious, led the armies to wonder whether they should not give up the struggle and either negotiate jointly among themselves or refer the choice of an emperor to the Senate. This, it is suggested, was the motive of Otho's generals in advising delay, and Paulinus in particular had high hopes, since he was the senior ex-consul, and a distinguished general who had earned a brilliant reputation by his operations in Britain. For my own part, while I am ready to admit that a few people may have tacitly wished for peace rather than civil war, or for a good and virtuous emperor instead of two who were the worst of criminals, yet I imagine that Paulinus was much too wise to hope that in a time of universal corruption the mob would show such moderation.[9]

The second occurs near the beginning of the *Annals*. Here, Tacitus is discussing conspiracy theories concerning the murder of Augustus's grandson Agrippa Postumus in the aftermath of the Emperor's death:

> Tiberius made no statement about that matter in the Senate: he fabricated orders from his father[10] in which, allegedly, he had ordered that a tribune should be set over those guarding him and that he should not hesitate to put Agrippa to death as soon as Augustus

himself had expired. Augustus had undoubtedly complained much and fiercely about the character of the young man, and had seen to it that his exile was sanctioned by a decree of the Senate. But he did not show indifference to the death of any of his own, and it was not believable that he had brought death upon his grandson in order to assure the well-being of his stepson.[11]

In both of these cases, Tacitus rejects a version of events with which he has been presented. In the first, this is the statement, found in 'some of his authorities',[12] that the armies of the rival Emperors in general, and Paulinus in particular, contemplated giving up their struggle; in the other, it is Tiberius's claim that Agrippa Postumus had been executed on orders from Augustus. In each case, the rejection of this version is based upon Tacitus's assessment of the personality and capabilities of one of the key individuals concerned in the affair under discussion. The historian considers that Paulinus was too smart to have believed that such a plan could work. Tacitus does not *explicitly* present the grounds on which he considered Paulinus 'much too wise' to have overestimated the current appetite for peace. Note, however, that he has already been careful to allude to Paulinus's distinguished record: 'the senior ex-consul, and a distinguished general who had earned a brilliant reputation by his operations in Britain'. This nicely prepares the reader for an interpretation of his behaviour based on his sagacity in the next sentence.

In the case of Agrippa's murder, Tacitus does not just deny the logic of the alleged action ('it was not believable that he had brought death upon his grandson in order to assure the well-being of his stepson'). He also goes to the trouble of backing up his assessment with evidence from Augustus's previous record: the Emperor did not 'show indifference to the death of any of his own'. Tacitus's reading of Augustus's behaviour, based on the accounts known to the historian of how he had acted previously, does not support the allegations of Tiberius, which are therefore rejected. One may also note, in passing, how these passages help to illuminate notions of the consistency of an individual's character and personality in Greco-Roman antiquity.[13]

It is reasonable to object that Tacitus's reasoning may not be particularly cogent here.[14] Nonetheless, the mode of reasoning he employs is not, in fact, unfamiliar to those who have had anything to do with more recent historiography. Consistency of behaviour remains one of the criteria by which later historians choose between interpretations of events. Consider once more, for instance, A. J. P. Taylor on Bismarck's behaviour at the time of the Treaty of Gastein in 1865: 'There is one strong argument against this more or less pacific interpretation of Bismarck's policy; he was no sooner back in Berlin than he began to drum around for French support.'[15]

Now, this is in fact an interpretation which, as we have already seen,[16] Taylor goes on to reject, claiming that Bismarck's subsequent behaviour was in fact something rather different from simple belligerence: 'Bismarck wanted to prevent a French alliance with Austria, not to get one for himself.'[17] What Taylor does not do, however, is deny the essential validity of this sort of reasoning. In fact, he describes as a 'strong argument' the attempt to arrive at a consistent interpretation of Bismarck's behaviour on the grounds that what he did at one point might reasonably be expected to cohere with what he did at another. Just as a Tacitus might reject an account of the motivation of a Paulinus on the grounds that it would be inconsistent with the capabilities he had demonstrated elsewhere, so a Taylor can envisage an argument for the motivation of a Bismarck which founds itself upon the consistency of his behaviour over a period – even if this is an argument which is then rejected in favour of a more nuanced understanding of that behaviour.

The point that I am trying to make here is that some of the arguments we can see Tacitus making as he settles upon his own narrative of events at Rome in the first century CE are not necessarily as alien to the sort of reasoning which one might encounter in much later modes of historiography, as has sometimes been implied. In particular, the disposition in some ancient historians to argue for what is 'plausible' or 'reasonable' has been made the subject of a largely specious contrast with the canons of 'modern history-writing'. The ancient preoccupation with 'likelihood' and 'plausibility', it has been argued, stands in sharp contrast to the procedures of the modern historian, to whom the concerns of verifiable truth and legitimate deduction are paramount.[18]

We have already discussed, at some length, one important flaw which afflicts this model. It implies a uniformity of practice amongst 'ancient' historians (on the one hand) and 'modern' ones (on the other). As we have already observed,[19] this simplification does not in fact seem to map at all well on to the pluralism of historiographical production in the modern world or to what we can see of that in the ancient.[20]

Another flaw, however, should now have become apparent. Demonstrable truth and incontrovertible evidence are not, in fact, commodities in such abundant supply that any historian, ancient or modern, can maintain a robust trade in them. Outside the realms of mathematics and formal logic, the extent of what we can actually *prove* is distressingly limited. I, like a host of others up to and including President James Garfield of the United States, can prove that, in Euclidean geometry, the square of the hypotenuse of a right-angled triangle is equal to the squares of the other two sides.[21] I can likewise prove that the set of prime numbers has an infinite number of members.[22] It is much harder for me to prove, on grounds which admit of no doubt, that I am an academic who has been writing this book for the last few months and not an android planted in front of my computer with a set of false memories by the Ancient Illuminated Seers of Bavaria 20 minutes ago.[23]

The difficulty of *absolute* proof outside the realm of mathematics does not, of course, entail adopting a stance of radical scepticism towards the possibility of attaining any historical knowledge.[24] In the history of historiography, this stance (sometimes known as 'Pyrrhonism', after the great classical philosopher of scepticism) is often associated with some thinkers of the seventeenth century and in particular, though not quite accurately, with the name of Pierre Bayle, the émigré French Protestant who set out, in the 1690s, to compile a dictionary of all the mistakes in other works of reference.[25] It does, however, serve to remind us that there will always be a limit to what historical investigation can achieve on the basis of logical deduction from sources. Since we lack access to the inmost thoughts, motivations and actions of every historical agent who has ever existed, it is never the case that sources and deduction alone can give the historian everything he or she needs to attain an exact understanding of the past. This applies as much in kind to A. J. P. Taylor, forming hypotheses as to the motivations of nineteenth-century European politicians, as it does to Tacitus, puzzling out the tangled power politics of Rome in the first century CE, or, indeed, to the fictional historiographer Plato, brooding over the fragmentary documents of nineteenth- and twentieth-century history in his enigmatic far future.[26]

There has always been, and still remains, a place in historiographical enquiry for assessment of the past on the basis of judgments of probability and the evaluation of explanatory models. We have already seen that we, as readers of ancient historiography, are constantly engaged in devising hypotheses, few of which are susceptible to incontrovertible proof, to explain the characteristics of the texts under our scrutiny. Does such-and-such a feature appear in a passage because of the historian's source, because of the historian's style of treating this particular subject, because something has gone wrong with the text, or because of some other consideration?[27]

It should therefore be unsurprising that similar manoeuvres are replicated in the attempts of modern historians to reach an understanding of the classical world. The need for induction and plausible speculation is particularly pressing in cases where there is a dearth of evidence. It is illuminating, in this connexion, to quote the opening paragraph of a modern scholar's attempt to analyse the economic history of the ancient world:

> This essay is speculative and tentative, a preliminary attempt at exploring a broad territory of Roman economic history over a long period. For the sake of clarity, I have canvassed several probabilities in the form of propositions, but the evidence is so sparse that it is difficult to *prove* that each proposition is right. It is disappointing to confess at the outset that one's case is unproven and that the generalizations advanced are disproportionately large in relation to the supporting evidence. Even so, the experiments made here with both evidence and methods may stimulate others into refuting or reshaping the propositions. And besides, some of the methods can be usefully applied to other problems in Roman history.[28]

Nor is the phenomenon limited to economic history alone. Modern attempts to unravel the inner workings of the established principate under Augustus, where, as we have already seen, the problem of inadequate sources was one which had already begun to vex Cassius Dio,[29] have been particularly interesting in their recognition of the need to supplement the evidence with informed speculation and argument from what the modern historian considers likely or plausible: 'Disturbed though not totally thwarted by the secession of his stepson, Augustus was now intent on conciliating the aristocracy and widening the ambit of his alliances. The situation is clear, the evidence largely missing or conjectural.'[30] Indeed, such attempts have even on occasion preferred the 'likely' or the 'plausible' to the testimony of what evidence there is.[31]

This is not a consideration unique to students of the ancient world either. Andrew Motion's biographical study of the nineteenth-century artist and multitasking criminal Thomas Griffiths Wainewright, for example, tackles head-on the issues involved in writing history or biography where the evidence is seemingly inadequate to the task and a subject languishes in neglect: ' ... unless biographers are prepared to think differently about their work, he is likely to stay there ... But "think differently" how? Clearly, our responsibility to history includes a duty to report on forgotten lives – yet if the material simply isn't there, what can be done?'[32] The final paragraph of Motion's foreword (p.xix) notes that the techniques used in his study, as compared to his previous studies of Philip Larkin and John Keats, raise interesting questions about the nature of biography in general as well.[33] Arguments based on the assessment of probabilities are therefore by no means a phenomenon unique to classical historiography, and accounts of modern history-writing which polemically downplay the element of educated guesswork and 'playing the percentages' which it necessarily involves are misleading.[34]

It may reasonably be objected that the proportional importance attached to arguments from probability, and the ways in which they are presented, is rather different in the bulk of the classical historians from that which is expected in the historical literature of the modern world. Classical historians (it could be argued) do use arguments from probability more often and on less cogent grounds. Moreover, they present the fruits of these arguments with a lot less circumspection than would a modern historical writer under similar circumstances. Modern presentations of speculation and conjecture are usually signposted as such;[35] their relationship to evidence, whatever it may be, is clearly indicated. Andrew Motion is careful to set out the exact nature of the literary strategies that were used in constructing the rest of the work; each chapter provides endnotes which allow the reader to chase down the evidential basis of what precedes it.[36] Classical historiographers may well be a different matter.

There is some substance to such objections. As we have already seen, however, even historical narratives of more modern periods are not always as straightforward in distinguishing the verifiable from the conjectural in their accounts of the past, as one might incautiously assume. We have already observed one example of this: Macaulay's account of the motives that impelled the household of the moribund Charles II of Spain.[37] However, the narrative histories of the nineteenth century hold no monopoly here. Consider this extract from a standard modern biography of Oscar Wilde, which was completed in the 1980s:

> A half-packed suitcase lay on the bed, emblem of contradictory
> impulses. He was tired of action. Like Hamlet, as he understood that
> hero, he wished to distance himself from his plight, to be the
> spectator of his own tragedy. His stubbornness, his courage, and his
> gallantry also kept him there. He had always met adversity head on, to
> face hostile journalists, moralistic reviewers, and canting, ranting
> fathers. A man so concerned with his image disdained to think of
> himself as a fugitive, skulking in dark corners instead of lording it in
> the limelight. He preferred to be a great figure, doomed by fate and
> the unjust laws of a foreign country. Suffering was more becoming
> than embarrassment. Writers, after all, had been prisoners before
> him. Cunninghame Graham and Blunt came to mind. His mind would
> survive, superior to any indignities his inferiors could heap upon him.
> If he was to be immolated, so must be his age. Reveal him as pederast,
> reveal his society as hypocrite. So he waited, defiant. At ten past six
> came the expected knock at the door.[38]

Richard Ellmann, Wilde's biographer, quotes no written evidence in his endnotes to support the picture of what was going through his protagonist's mind at this point. Indeed, since he is dealing here with the mental state of a man almost nine decades dead at the time of publication and who left no formal autobiography, it is hard to see what written evidence there could have been. What we see in this paragraph, then, is actually Ellmann's speculation as to *what would have been* going through Wilde's mind at this particular point, based on the reading of his personality which Ellmann has constructed from the other data about his life.

What makes this passage particularly notable is that it deals not with some quotidian stretch of Wilde's life, but with a pivotal point: the dramatist's decision not to flee the country after the collapse of his libel case against the Marquis of Queensbury in 1895, despite the likelihood of his own imminent arrest and prosecution. Ellmann presents his own interpretation of the factors explaining Wilde's refusal to make a break for France: a desire to confront the hypocrisy of his age, a self-construction as a scofflaw, a sense of inevitable fate. But he does so not as a formal argument, but as a vivid narrative instead. It is, moreover, a narrative which has gone to some pains to invest itself with a Wildean sense of cadence and prose rhythm: one notes the careful assonance of '*canting, ranting* fathers' and the flamboyant apophthegm 'suffering was more becoming than embarrassment'. Ellmann has also carefully laid the ground for this moment by bringing out these thematic elements in his earlier account of Wilde's life: thus, Wilde's interest in the *Agamemnon* of Aeschylus expresses his preoccupation with fate.[39] This is, to be sure, an exceptional case. Nonetheless, the ease with which most biographers claim to penetrate the thought processes of their subjects must, in the presumed absence on their part of the aptitudes enjoyed by a Charles Xavier or a Matt Parkman, give the enquiring reader pause for thought.[40]

Even in the historical investigations of the present day, then, the juncture between evidence and speculation, the verifiable (insofar as that is ever possible in the phenomenal world) and the plausible, is not always as straightforward and easy to detect as one might incautiously assume.[41] In contemporary texts, the join may sometimes be announced by nothing more than an inflexion of tenses: 'x *would have known* this'; 'Y *will have decided* that'. And it is always worth keeping an eye out for cases where it is not announced at all.

In short, the role of the probable is a lot more prevalent in historical writing of every period than has sometimes been thought. There *is* considerable local variation in how arguments from the probable are used, what controls their distribution and how they are announced. Moreover, these variations are not a matter of simple chronology. What is regarded as acceptable practice in one writer of antiquity will not necessarily be approved by another, any more than modern experiments in historiographical form meet with universal approbation.

Talking the Talk

To see this in operation, it is worth taking a moment to examine a feature of ancient history-writing in which this variety becomes particularly obvious. The feature in question is a characteristic of ancient historiography so obvious and so (apparently) alien to modern sensibilities that it deserves attention in any event. This is the prevalence of speeches.[42]

The vast majority of ancient historical texts contain extended versions of what purport to be long, verbatim speeches made by figures within the narrative of the history. Although such speeches are sometimes seen as *the* defining oddity of ancient historiography,[43] they are not, in fact, omnipresent within it. Some historians do not assign more than a couple of sentences of dialogue to any of the figures they describe. So, for example, Velleius Paterculus does not assign extended speeches. In the case of Velleius, this may have been determined partly by issues of scale; his history, as we have already seen, is comprehensive in temporal scope but limited in length. It may also stem from his fondness for setting up one-liners.[44] What remains of the so-called Oxyrhynchus historian also lacks speeches, although it should be stressed that that text is very imperfectly preserved.

In other historians, the frequency of speeches sometimes fluctuates wildly between different parts of their history: there are, for example, none in the eighth book of Thucydides or in Appian's narrative of Roman doings in the Iberian Peninsula, where the longest fragment of direct speech seems to be two sentences from Avarus, leader of the city folk defeated in the Numantine War.[45] However, big speeches do appear elsewhere in the histories of these two historians. Pericles's Funeral Oration in Book Two of Thucydides,[46] and the paired speeches of Julius Caesar and Pompeius Magnus just before the Battle of Pharsalus in Appian,[47] are only the most obvious of the many examples.

At the opposite extreme, speeches can swell to occupy an exceedingly prominent place within a historical narrative. We have already noted how Sallust devotes approximately one-sixth of his narrative of the Catilinarian conspiracy to a pair of speeches;[48] in his *Bellum Iugurthinum*, between one-eighth and one-ninth of the work is devoted to purported verbatim speeches, with only eight words of it coming from the eponymous prince.[49] In the history of Cassius Dio, about one-fifth of book 38 is devoted to a dialogue between Cicero and a (otherwise unknown) philosopher called Philiscus on the subject of the nature of the good life and the desirability or otherwise of temporal power; again, this proportion does not include the other speeches in the book.[50]

Since such fluctuations are a distinctive phenomenon within our texts, various models have been applied, with varying plausibility, to explain them. Some, for example, have postulated that the absence of speeches from the last book of Thucydides is either further evidence of its incompleteness[51] or signs of experimentation by the author with narrative structure.[52] A similar debate has informed the study of Herodian.[53] In other cases, it has been argued that the distribution, and length, of speeches within a historiographical text might be connected with the author's desire to mark out the importance (or insignificance) of whoever is making it or whatever he is saying.[54]

Even when all due allowance is made for such variation, however, the frequency with which long speeches from the mouths of historical figures appear in the works of the ancient historians has always given readers of more modern times pause for thought. Many of these speeches are delivered under conditions which make it hard to see how any contemporary witness could have committed them first to memory and then to a more permanent medium.[55] It is true that examples of prodigious recollection of heard material are attested in antiquity: the opening chapters of the *Controversiae* of the elder Seneca, for example, afford numerous examples, including that of the great Roman Republican orator Hortensius.[56] But even if these stories are reliable, they were clearly out of the ordinary. Moreover, speeches in the work of the same historian often display a conspicuous stylistic homogeneity, even when they were supposedly delivered by different individuals. The natural suspicion therefore arises that most, if not all, of the 'speeches' that appear in the pages of classical historiography were made up for the occasion by the author concerned. This suspicion is borne out by such works as the essay *On Thucydides*, which the critic and historian Dionysius of Halicarnassus composed during the Augustan period. Dionysius's own historiographical output was a history of Rome in 20 books from the foundation of the city to the outbreak of the First Punic War, something over half of which is still extant.[57] His criticisms of the style of Thucydides clearly rest on the supposition that Thucydides himself was responsible for composing the speeches in his history: 'Thucydides assigns to both sides speeches such as each might naturally have made. They are suited to the characters of the speakers and relevant to the situation and neither inadequate nor overdone. He has furnished them with language which is pure, clear, and concise and possesses all the other virtues.'[58]

The picture becomes more complicated, however, if we examine the rare references to the place of speeches in history-writing which we encounter in the works of the historiographers themselves. The attentive reader will not be greatly surprised to learn that one of the most illuminating extant passages occurs in the course of Polybius's criticisms of Timaeus.[59] On this occasion, the facet of Timaeus's ineptitude which is brought under scrutiny is his treatment of speeches:

> But to convince those also who are disposed to champion him I must speak of the principle on which he composes public speeches, harangues to soldiers, the discourses of ambassadors, and, in a word, all utterances of the kind which, as it were, sum up events and hold the whole history together. Can anyone who reads these help noticing that Timaeus has untruthfully reported them in his work and has done so of set purpose? For he has not set down the words spoken nor the sense of what was really said, but having made up his mind what ought to have been said he recounts all these speeches and all else that follows upon events like a man in a school of rhetoric attempting to speak on a given subject, and shows off his rhetorical power, but gives no report of what was actually spoken.[60]

Polybius later illustrates these alleged failings with an example from Timaeus's own practice:

> In confirmation of my charge against Timaeus on this count also, besides that of his mistakes and his deliberate falsification of the truth, I shall give some short extracts from speeches acknowledged to be his, giving names and dates. Of those who were in power in Sicily after the elder Gelo, we have always accepted as a fact that the most capable rulers were Hermocrates, Timoleon, and Pyrrhus of Epirus, and these are the last to whom one should attribute childish and idle speeches. But Timaeus in his twenty-first book ... represents

Hermocrates as speaking somewhat as follows. This statesman, after praising the people of Gela and Camarina first of all for having themselves made the truce, secondly for being the originators of the negotiations, and thirdly for seeing to it that the terms of peace were not discussed by the multitude but by the leading citizens who knew well the difference between war and peace, after this introduces one or two practical reflexions and then says that they themselves must now give ear to him and learn how much war differs from peace ... Apart from his general mistake in devoting the greater part of the speech to a matter that does not require a single word, he employs such arguments as none could believe to have been used by, I will not say that Hermocrates who took part with the Lacedaemonians in the battle of Aegospotami and captured the whole Athenian army with its generals in Sicily, but by any ordinary schoolboy.[61]

Polybius, then, subjects the speeches of Timaeus to a twofold charge. In the first place, he reports as historical speeches things which were simply never said: 'he has not set down the words spoken nor the sense of what was really said'. In the second place, the made-up speeches which he does perpetrate are entirely unconvincing as the works of their putative authors. The statesman Hermocrates is made to spout arguments which, in Polybius's estimation, would have shamed a schoolboy.[62]

Polybius, then, *does* object to Timaeus's generation of fictitious speeches. This is an objection of principle which he makes at various points in his history.[63] Nor is this objection unparalleled in later historiography from the ancient world.[64] Pompeius Trogus, who wrote a 38-book history in the Augustan period, criticized Sallust and Livy for the fabrication of historical speeches as well.[65]

Once again, then, the spectrum of tolerance for particular practices across classical antiquity emerges as wider than a limited number of theoretical statements would suggest. As another indication of this spectrum, one might profitably bring in the case of Tacitus, who at one point produces his own version of a speech of Claudius, which is partly preserved on a bronze tablet in Lyons.[66] Tacitus's version is sufficiently close to the inscription to show that he was familiar with the speech, but it is likewise possible to map various changes which he made to it. The speech in the *Annals* has a distinct and intriguing relationship to what

Claudius seems to have actually said.[67] But it is by no means a verbatim transcription.

Once again, too, the treatment of speeches in history-writing shows that there is not necessarily an easy concinnity between an author's methodological statements and his own historiography. Not all of the speeches in Polybius's own work can easily be swallowed, on various grounds, as the straightforward records of 'the words spoken' which Timaeus is criticized for failing to produce.[68] Polybian theory and Polybian practice, here as elsewhere, do not necessarily demonstrate an exact fit.

The fact remains, however, that Polybius's open criticism of the way in which prior historiography has managed itself is another compelling indication of something which has emerged as a recurring theme in this study. We have noted at several points that history-writing in the ancient world presents itself as neither a homogeneous nor a straightforward pursuit. Evidence has already accrued that different historiographers could have very different preoccupations, methodologies and tolerances from each other.[69] These writers were not all singing from the same theoretical hymn sheet. Some of them may not even have been singing hymns at all.

The other important consideration, however, is one which pronouncements like those of Polybius above make very clear. Even within the thought-world of a particular historian, historiography was not necessarily a straightforward activity. I do not mean this simply in the sense that writing history was potentially hard work, a theme on which ancient (and modern) historians are often keen to expatiate.[70] Rather, it is important to note that even a single author may exhibit tensions, stresses and contradictions over what history-writing is and how one should go about it. Polybius's somewhat uncomfortable position within a tradition of extensive speechifying in historiography, and the ways in which he tries to cope with it, are a case in point. In fact, this very unease about the methodology of speeches does itself have a historiographical precedent, in the much earlier statement on the subject which Thucydides makes near the beginning of his own history:

> With reference to the speeches in this history, some were delivered
> before the war began, others while it was going on; some I heard

myself, others I got from various quarters; it was in all cases difficult to carry them word for word in one's memory, so my habit has been to make the speakers say what was in my opinion demanded of them by the various occasions, of course adhering as closely as possible to the general sense of what they really said.[71]

The translation and interpretation of this passage remain, it should be stressed, exceedingly controversial and keenly debated topics.[72] It should be clear, however, that there is at the very least a potential tension between Thucydides's decision to write down *ta deonta*, which the translation above renders as 'what was demanded of them', while 'adhering as closely as possible to the general sense of what they really said'. Whether one thinks that Thucydides means by *ta deonta* that he is reporting the particularly *important* and *vital* elements of the speech – the necessary core, as it were – rather than presenting *everything* that was actually said,[73] or whether one supposes instead that he has composed what he thinks the particular occasion demanded of the speaker, there is still an obvious tension here. On one interpretation, there is an issue of selectivity; on the other, one of keeping the composition of speeches in line with 'what they really said'. We may also note (and anticipate the theme of Chapter 8) that the translation which I used above clearly adopts the second interpretation. This sentence is a particularly good example of the interpretative aspect to translation – the fact that a rendering of a potentially ambiguous or debatable passage is liable to reflect the way in which the translator understands it.[74]

On any reading of the passage, though, Thucydides not only notes a tricky issue of methodology in the relating of speeches, but goes to some trouble to advertise it. He displays awareness, at a very early stage of the Greek historiographical tradition, of methodological difficulties in the discipline he is helping to shape. What we are certainly not seeing here is a placid acceptance of particular automatic conventions.

In short, the use of speeches in the historical production of the ancient world reveals itself as a much less unified phenomenon than one might anticipate. This is a pattern which continues, to a greater extent than is always acknowledged, in more modern historiography. The continued popularity of speeches composed by the historian in the mediaeval period is, perhaps, unsurprising.[75] So too is its appearance in the Renaissance, which Ranke subsequently deplored; he noted, for example, that none of Guicciardini's set-piece orations could be proved to have been delivered as the earlier historian claimed.[76] But the history-writing of the post-Ranke age has still found space for invented speeches. One particularly interesting example is that of the great nineteenth-century legal historian F. W. Maitland,[77] whose epochal *History of English Law* conveys the situation regarding pasture rights in the Middle Ages by means of an imaginary harangue from a peasant to his lord and fellow tenants.[78]

Again, arguments of proportion, context and authorial management are important here, of course. Unlike the ancient historians, Maitland does not present the speech of his peasant as something which was said on a particular historical occasion by a particular historical individual. The speech is a device to convey vividly the sorts of arguments that could have been used in the situation generated by the state of the law in a particular period. Nor is it a formal device which Maitland regularly uses.

Nonetheless, it remains worth noting that recourse to what the historian infers people *would have been saying* remains a device that modern historiography is not always averse to employing. History-writing in the contemporary world does (usually) shy away from the attribution of extensive fabricated speeches to historical individuals; in the rare event of such speeches being used, they are clearly marked as such. However, a related technique of ancient historical texts has continued to display a notable vitality. This is the presentation of the alleged responses of groups of people to unfolding events. Amongst ancient historians, this is a technique particularly associated with Tacitus, a celebrated example being his presentation of popular attitudes to the death of Augustus in the first book of his *Annals*:

> One opinion was as follows. Filial duty and a national emergency, in which there was no place for law-abiding conduct had driven him to civil war – and this can be neither initiated nor maintained by decent methods ... The opposite view went like this. Filial duty and national crisis had been merely pretexts. In actual fact, the motive of Octavian, the future Augustus, was lust for power.[79]

The technique is, however, by no means limited to Tacitus in the ancient world.[80] It is a resource of which post-classical historians have not been slow to avail themselves either, when their aim is to invoke their vision of a particular zeitgeist. Once again, the example of Syme's *The Augustan Aristocracy* is instructive here. Syme's conjectural narrative of the Augustan principate bristles with imagined readings of events on the part of contemporary observers.[81] While there is certainly an evidential basis for the circumstances under which Syme envisages these readings taking place,[82] the tone of these discussions is the product of the historian's inferences.

The extent of this phenomenon should not be overestimated. We have now examined numerous examples of cases where history-writing in the modern world avails itself of techniques and strategies – inference, judgment from probability, the presentation of the plausible but unverifiable in narrative form – on which one might incautiously assume ancient historiography to have a monopoly. It would not be unreasonable to claim, however, that there has been a shift in what one might call the horizon of expectations where history-writing is concerned. Plausible reconstruction has its limits in the modern world, and works that aim to be described as history which stray too close to that limit are likely to prove controversial, as evinced by a recent exploration of the religious experience of the ancient world through the tropes of time travel and the epistolary novel.[83]

All the same, the case of speeches brings out more sharply, perhaps, than any of our previous investigations the fact that historical production, across the ages, has accommodated a spectrum of techniques, tolerances and expectations. A simplistic model might have led us to expect, for example, that the ancient world showed a unified tolerance towards passages of plausible fabrication on the part of the historian himself, while the world after Ranke would austerely eschew it. In fact, we have seen that the ancient world included objections from Polybius and (at the very least) unease from Thucydides to such practices, while the modern has furnished evidence for the continuing viability of certain modes of historical expression and the inescapability of the plausible or reasonable as a criterion for the historian. Above all, the notion that historiography, in any age, is characterized by an easy consensus as to what it is and how it should be conducted has been strongly challenged.

Historiography, ancient or modern, whether inscribed on papyrus, vellum or hard drive, or alternatively put together in the head of the attentive reader, is not a matter of automatic programmes. Cultural context and writing traditions have their force. But the idea that prescriptions culled from the writings of a single author will necessarily map onto the historiographical procedures of an entire age is a will-o'-the-wisp.

We have now examined some local examples of the decision-making which informs all attempts to write ancient history, whatever the epoch of the writer who is doing it. In particular, the role of plausible conjecture and hypothesis has been scrutinized. It is now time to turn our attention to larger structures. How do the historiographers of the classical world organize their narratives? And what consequences do the structural decisions which this organization involves have for the modern student of ancient history?

6

THE ENDS OF HISTORY –
PART I

In 1952, the German historian Arno Peters published the first version of his *Synchronoptische Weltgeschichte* ('Synchronoptic World History').[1] This took the form of a chronological chart in which each century from 3000 BCE was allotted equal space on the page. The format led, as one of Peters' obituarists was later to remark, to some interesting characteristics: 'The 29th century BC received as much space as the 20th century AD, and the story of the Incas of Peru covered as many square inches as the history of Europe in the Middle Ages.'[2]

Peters subsequently found more fame through his espousal of the so-called Peters Projection,[3] a map of the Earth which avoids some of the distortions of representation in the 'Mercator Projection', the form of world map with which most people are familiar from school atlases and the like.[4] In the Mercator Projection, for example, the representation of Greenland is larger than that of Africa, although the latter is in fact 14 times the size of the former. The Peters Projection attempts to redress such inequities (at the cost, it is fair to add, of some distortions of its own).

The point to observe here is that Peters' earlier historical work makes a similar ideological point to his later geographical one. Projection of the oblate spheroid Earth onto a flat surface entails certain distortions: some things look bigger than they really are, others smaller. Peters' chronographical chart, in a like vein, seeks to redress the clustering of attention on certain areas and periods in Earth's history. It may well be the case that there is a large war going on somewhere in the world. But that does not mean that anything much is happening in Cyme.

Cyme, it should be explained, was in antiquity the most important of the Aeolian cities on the seaboard of Asia Minor.[5] Its significance in this context stems from the fact that it was the hometown of the lost, fourth-century BCE Greek historian Ephorus. We have already encountered Ephorus in the undignified capacity of a polemical football in Polybius's ongoing historiographical match against Timaeus.[6] His relevance here lies in the fact that, according to later writers, the patriotic historian's accounts of exciting events in the world at large would be punctuated with the words 'During this period the people of Cyme were at peace'.[7]

This trait of Ephorus provoked mirth in antiquity, which is why we still know about it. Hilarity aside, however, it focusses attention on a significant question of historiographical decision-making. How, given the limited extent of the written word and the limited life-span of the historian who is writing it,[8] does a historiographer decide which portions of time and space he is going to give the lion's share of attention in his history? What are the consequences for the times and spaces he neglects? And how, if he is managing a narrative across a wide chronological or spatial range, is he going to organize the material at his disposal?

Polybius, unsurprising to relate, had strong views on such issues. These emerge in the course of a discussion, early in his history, of the part played by Fortune in human affairs:[9]

> We can no more hope to perceive this from histories dealing with particular events than to get at once a notion of the form of the whole world, its disposition and order, by visiting, each in turn, the most famous cities, or indeed by looking at separate plans of each: a result by no means likely. He indeed who believes that by studying isolated histories he can acquire a fairly just view of history as a whole is, as it seems to me, much in the case of one, who, after having looked at the disseuered limbs of an animal once alive and beautiful, fancies he has been as good as an eyewitness of the creature itself in all its action and grace. For could anyone put the creature together on the spot, restoring its form and the comeliness of life, and then show it to the same man, I think he would quickly avow that he was formerly very far away from the truth and more like one in a dream. For we can get

some idea of a whole from a part, but never knowledge or exact
opinion. Special histories therefore contribute very little to the
knowledge of the whole and conviction of its truth. It is only indeed by
study of the interconnexion of all the particulars, their resemblances
and differences, that we are enabled at least to make a general survey,
and thus derive both benefit and pleasure from history.[10]

Polybius, then, criticizes histories that deal only with 'particular events'
as providing an entirely partial perspective, one which does not have sufficient scope to permit any conclusions useful to the contemplative
reader. Many of the historical productions of the ancient world, both
before and after the time of Polybius, would have fallen into this category. Such histories are usually described in modern scholarly literature
as 'monographs', although it is worth pointing out that this term is not
itself of classical vintage; it seems to have arisen in the late eighteenth
century to describe a 'separate treatise on a single species, genus, or
larger group of plants or animals' and to have been generalized thence as
a term for a 'detailed written study of a single specialized topic'.[11]
Polybius's term for the object of his censure here is actually *historiā kata
meros* (literally something like 'history bit-by-bit'). Extant examples
might include Sallust's works on the Catilinarian conspiracy and the war
against Jugurtha – narratives which deal with a sequence of events
strictly delimited in space and time.

A contrasting format in Greco-Roman antiquity was a history which
dealt with events across the known inhabited world (sometimes known
in Greek as the *oikoumenē*) over a wide sweep of time, such as Polybius's
own history, or the *Library* of Diodorus.[12] This sort of work tends nowadays to be called a 'universal history'. Once again, this is a term which
requires some circumspection in its deployment. Although ancient
authors certainly contrast a comprehensiveness of approach in history-
writing with historiography on a more limited scale, they do not use a
consistent term to do so: Diodorus, in a passage praising works of such
sweeping scope, calls them *koinai praxeis* (literally 'common matters'):
'most writers have recorded no more than isolated wars waged by a
single nation or a single state, and but few have undertaken, beginning
with the earliest times and coming down to their own day, to record the
events connected with all people (*koinas praxeis*)'.[13] Polybius describes

this order of composition as *graphein hatholou* ('writing comprehensively').[14] In addition, not all the works which scholars have got into the habit of categorizing as 'universal histories' are, in fact, of exactly similar scope. Polybius's history, as we have already seen, does not deal in a systematic way with events before 220 BCE, despite its geographical sweep. Diodorus, by contrast, covers events from mythological times to 60 BCE and explicitly notes variations in temporal scope:

> ... for while some have closed their accounts with the deeds of Philip, others with those of Alexander, and some with the Diadochi or the Epigoni, yet, despite the number and importance of the events subsequent to these and extending even to our own lifetime which have been left neglected, no historian has essayed to treat of them within the compass of a single narrative.[15]

Some histories were more universal than others.[16]

Nonetheless, writers in antiquity did perceive a possible distinction between historiography on a catholic scale and works devoted to discrete topics. Polybius does not deny outright, in the passage quoted above, that such limited histories might have the capacity to entertain. The point of the last sentence in the passage above is that it is only when a truly synoptic view is taken that *both* pleasure and utility (always by far the more important element of the pair to this historian)[17] will be on the reader's menu at the same time – though the emphasis on the 'comeliness' of the live animal in his metaphor surely hints that universal history will be more pleasurable as well. Ephorus, in fact, is the one prior writer who escapes Polybius's censure on this account. His history was of a sufficient sweep and inclusivity that the later historiographer is prepared to describe him as 'the first and only writer who really undertook a general history'.[18] Even Ephorus, however, is vulnerable to Polybius's implication elsewhere that universal history only begins to make sense during Rome's rise to dominance, which (conveniently enough) would further imply that Polybius himself is the first person to do worthwhile universal history properly.[19]

We have already noted that it is perilous to accept the strictures of Polybius as a reliable guide to historiographical thinking throughout antiquity.[20] In fact, Polybius himself did write a historical monograph, probably after the completion of his larger *History*. This was on the Numantine War, in which his friend Scipio Aemilianus had played a notable part; and may have been a source for Appian's account of that conflict.[21]

All the same, the terms in which Polybius phrases his critiques of 'monograph' historiography, a theme to which he returns at several points in his history, are thought-provoking and deserve attention. Apart from the problem of limited perspective, which we have seen him criticizing above, he raises an interesting point about alleged distortions of scale in histories on discrete matters. This comes out in his discussion of the fall of Hieronymus of Syracuse, in which he contests the view that this dynast displayed prodigious savagery. According to Polybius, previous historians had been responsible for inflating Hieronymus's undoubted viciousness: 'the fact, as it seems to me, is that those who write narratives of particular events, when they have to deal with a subject which is circumscribed and narrow, are compelled for lack of facts to make small things great and to devote much space to matters really not worthy of record'.[22]

In Polybius's view, then, writing a 'narrative of particular events' lends itself particularly to the temptation to get things out of proportion. It is not merely that form of narrative, however, which extorts from him censure for failure to preserve an appropriate sense of scale in historiography. Amongst the many, many grounds on which he criticizes Timaeus,[23] for example, is the older historian's inflated sense of the importance of Sicilian politics in the wider scheme of things: 'Timaeus was sure that if Timoleon, who had sought fame in a mere teacup, as it were, could be shown to be worthy of comparison with the most illustrious heroes, he himself, who treated only of Italy and Sicily, could claim comparison with writers whose works dealt with the whole world and with universal history.'[24]

The element of self-service in this tirade should, by now, be too obvious to need much in the way of comment. The implications of Polybius's criticisms, of Timaeus and others, remain intriguing. In particular, one notes the way in which Polybius claims a historian's sense of self-worth can be bound up in the significance of his subject matter ('he himself ... could claim comparison with writers whose works dealt with the whole world'), and that the scale of *coverage* of particular events within a historical work can mislead readers as to the scale of *importance* of the events that are thus described (hence the popular misunderstanding as to the true level of Hieronymus's savagery).

Polybius was by no means alone in this perception, of course. One might compare Sallust's reflections on the putative importance of Athens near the beginning of his *Bellum Catilinae*: 'I do not doubt that the exploits of the Athenians were splendid and impressive; but I think they are much overrated. It is because she produced historians of genius that the achievement of Athens is so renowned all the world over; for the merit of successful men is rated according to the brilliance of the authors who extol it.'[25] It is a perception which becomes particularly significant, however, for the reader of what remains of the historiography of antiquity at the beginning of the twenty-first century. Even more than Polybius or Sallust, we have to stay vigilant against the seductive fallacy that the importance of an event or a period bears a necessary correlation to the amount of extant historiography which deals with it.

It takes very little investigation to demonstrate that this is fallacious, of course. A good counter-example is the principate of Augustus. Tacitus, as we have already seen,[26] begins his *Annals* in the dying days of Augustus. The books of Livy which dealt with the opening decades of his primacy have been lost, as have the works of most of the early imperial historians who may have covered the period.[27] Moreover, there appear, as noted above, to have been issues concerning access to information which rendered the gathering of data for this epoch troublesome to the historian.[28]

As a result, the student of the period is thrown back upon: the third-century Greek narrative of Cassius Dio (for which the extant text has substantial gaps after it reaches 6 BCE);[29] the extremely condensed account of the reign in Velleius Paterculus's two-book history, written during the reign of Tiberius;[30] the second-century biography of the emperor by Suetonius (another biographical account, by Nicolaus of Damascus, probably did not extend beyond the mid-20s BCE);[31] and Augustus's own version of his achievement, the *Res Gestae Divi Augusti* ('achievements of the divine Augustus'), an inscription erected on bronze pillars at the entrance to Augustus's mausoleum in the Campus Martius at Rome, although the version now extant is actually taken primarily from a copy set up at the temple of Rome and Augustus at Ancyra.[32] There is also a ragbag of remarks in other historiographical works; and, of course, evidence from outside the realm of formal historical production. Hence the level of necessary speculation and conjectural reconstruction which beset modern attempts to write the narrative history of what by most standards would be considered a significant epoch: Rome's transition from republic to empire.[33]

The extent of this problem can be overstated, of course. A relative dearth of extant narrative historiography concerning a period can be compensated by a richness of other surviving evidence. For example, some stretches of the first-century BCE Roman Republic, while somewhat better served by surviving narrative historiography than the Augustan period, because of the addition of Sallust's *Bellum Catilinae*, Julius Caesar's war narratives and Appian's *Civil Wars* to the histories mentioned above,[34] are still not as well off in that regard as one would like. However, the survival of Cicero's speeches and correspondence, not to mention the contribution from archaeological evidence and epigraphy, has ensured that the period remains richly documented. In a similar vein, the history of fourth-century BCE Athens is not dependent on Xenophon's *Hellenica*, Plutarch's biographies of a few key individuals, the relevant stretches of Diodorus[35] and the fragments of the lost historians of that period,[36] thanks to the large corpus of surviving speeches by Athenian orators of the age and (again) inscriptional evidence.

On the other hand, there are certainly historical epochs where the lack of extant historiographical coverage has, perhaps, had its consequences for their subsequent reception and prestige. One oft-cited example of this is the history of the Hellenistic world between the death of Alexander the Great and the rise of Rome. The disappearance of almost all Hellenistic historiography, including such notables as Timaeus and Hieronymus of Cardia, makes it hard to write detailed narrative histories of the period. It has been argued that it is this dearth which led to a general lack of scholarly interest in this age, persisting in some cases well into the twentieth century.[37]

Of course, there are good pragmatic reasons for focussing attention upon periods for which there is an abundance of sources rather than those for which there is little. No amount of belated regret is going to bring back vanished sources. What is important, however, is to bear in mind the distribution of extant evidence in relation to any larger claims we may wish to make. This may be as apparently straightforward as, say, contemplating the very large contribution made by Cicero to the extant sources for the Late Roman Republic, and therefore making due allowance for the possible distortions introduced by the worldview of an orator not always notable for a due sense of proportion.[38] Or it may entail an awareness of the considerable blanks in our coverage of antiquity. It is not always straightforward to keep track of what one does *not* know.

Keeping it in Proportion

The examples in the previous paragraphs have mostly concerned cases where the survival or disappearance of whole histories might skew subsequent perceptions of the ancient world. As Polybius makes clear, however, issues of scale and proportion within a given text can also manipulate a reader's perception of historical significance, through a propensity 'to make small things great and to devote much space to matters really not worthy of record'. This is an element of historiographical design and structure which it is therefore worth taking a moment to comment upon, particularly as it is one which can easily be missed if one is using the reading strategies which are often most convenient to the modern student of the ancient world.[39]

We have already encountered Lucian's sarcasms at the expense of historians whose allotment of space within a work strikes him as ill-considered: as, for example, in the case of the author whom he alleges to have spent less than seven lines describing the Battle of Europus and an immense amount of space on the adventures of a wandering horseman called Mausacas.[40] Historiographical compression *tout court* likewise meets with his scorn: 'one fine historian compressed all that had happened from beginning to end in Armenia, Syria, Mesopotamia, by the Tigris, in Media into less than five hundred lines, incomplete at that, and after this says he has composed a history. Yet the title that he attached to it is almost longer than the book: "A description of recent exploits of Romans in Armenia, Mesopotamia and Media, by Antiochianus the victor sacred to Apollo".'[41] Issues of appropriate scale and inclusivity were potentially a matter for debate and decision amongst the historians of antiquity. How do they pan out, then, in the extant historiographers of Greece and Rome?

Post-Renaissance historiography, of course, is by no means uniform where considerations of scale are concerned. On the one hand, one might instance the *Historia Sui Temporis* of the French historian Jacques-Auguste de Thou, which covered the period from 1544 to 1607 and comprised (in the first complete edition published shortly after his death) 138 books.[42] On the other, one can call upon the numerous examples of abbreviated one-volume histories of the world, an exercise which has exerted, amongst others, such notables as H. G. Wells[43] and the great art historian Ernst Gombrich, who wrote his originally for the young daughter of a pair of his friends, so proving that the instruction of young relatives and friends as a motivation for historiographical production was not a phenomenon unique to antiquity.[44]

In the ancient world, as we have already seen, there was likewise a considerable fluctuation in general scale, although there are no obvious examples of a work that devotes quite so much space to quite so limited a time-span as de Thou. Some examples of historiographical production on a massive scale are well-attested – one might note the 142 books of Livy's history, most of which has now disappeared, or the 144-book history composed by Nicolaus of Damascus, which seems to have covered events down to the death of Herod the Great.[45] These, however, dealt with periods of considerably more than de Thou's 63-year span. Perhaps the most expansive examples in antiquity of comparably limited time-spans were the lost autobiographical writings of L. Cornelius Sulla the Dictator (extending to 22 books) and Ptolemy Euergetes II (in 24 books); the *History of Philip* by Theopompus of Chios, which was largely (but by no means exclusively) concerned with the career of Philip II of Macedon, originally ran to 58 books.[46]

By contrast, we still have a number of very abbreviated histories. Lucian's Antiochianus has gone (if he ever existed at all),[47] but a number of ferociously condensed accounts of long stretches of time remain, such as Velleius Paterculus's account in two books of events down to the consulship of Vinicius in 29 CE, or Florus's 'Abridgment of all the wars over seven hundred years', also in two books.[48]

Velleius is, in fact, a very good example of the ways in which fluctuations of scale *within* a particular text can be used by the historian to make points about his subject-matter. It is true that chunks of the first of his two books are missing. This means that assessments of the proportional space he allotted to particular subjects are in some cases rather conjectural,[49] since the exact size of Book One, and what was covered in its missing portions, cannot be determined with certainty. Most attempts to calculate the length of the missing portion of Velleius's Book One proceed on the assumption that its original bulk was broadly comparable to that of Book Two (which is preserved intact). This assumption, however, is not well-founded, since 'books' of ancient authors (like chapters of modern ones) fluctuated tremendously in length. In the case of Florus (a two-book history where both parts *are* fully extant), the first book is more than one and a half times the length of the second one.

Nonetheless, few who have read what remains of Velleius's work in its entirety have failed to note the interesting proportions in his treatment of different epochs. Book One covered history from the time of mythology down to the Roman sacks of Carthage and Corinth in 146 BCE (with digressions on the foundation of Roman colonies and the nature of cultural efflorescence).[50] Book Two devotes a little under half of its bulk to Roman history between these events and the death of Julius Caesar (a period of a little over a century). The remaining portion of the history is devoted to the rise of Octavian, his ascendancy as Augustus and the subsequent reign of Tiberius.[51]

It is not hard to spot that the early Roman Principate eats up a very large proportion of the space in what purports to be a comprehensive account of history. Velleius is, as it were, the antithesis to Arno Peters. The twentieth-century historian's fanatical insistence on the exact correspondence between temporal duration and space on the page is opposed by a luxuriance in the treatment of material which Velleius considers particularly interesting and significant: the rise of Augustus and the present disposition of the Principate.

Velleius seems, at least as far as extant classical historiography is concerned, to have been a somewhat unusual case. However, interesting variations in the space allotted to different topics or time-periods within a historiographical text were not his preserve alone, by any means. Moreover, variations in proportion can be all the more effective when they are more subtle. 'Present-bulge', the tendency of coverage in a historical work to bulk out as it approaches the historian's own day, is observable in more extensive historians as well. Ammianus Marcellinus, for example, wrote a history of 31 books covering the period from the reign of Nerva to the Battle of Adrianople in 378, as we have already seen.[52] Again, Ammianus's work is imperfectly preserved, since the first 13 books have disappeared, which, as with Velleius, complicates arguments of proportion somewhat. Nonetheless, the apparent variation in the scale of coverage remains striking: the first 13 books (to judge from the point at which Book 14 begins) dealt with matters from the late first century to the year 353, while the remaining (and surviving) 18 books are devoted to a period of only a quarter of a century.

Of course, 'present-bulge' or other differences of proportion do not necessarily represent a conscious effort on the part of the historian to exalt (or condemn) recent times at the expense of what has gone before. Although, as we have noted, differences in the scale of coverage of events within a history are by no means unambiguous markers of the nature of the source-material at the disposal of the historian,[53] it is not hard to see how a comparative abundance of data and a livelier interest in the almost contemporary might swell coverage of the near past. Nonetheless, comparative scale of coverage does potentially represent one of the more subtle means of (de-)emphasis at the command of a historian.

The most extreme manifestation of this technique, of course, is to be found when a historian simply omits material which for one reason or another he considers to be uncongenial, uninteresting or simply irrelevant. As we noted at the beginning of this study,[54] a historian's decisions about what he is going to leave out are every bit as significant as his treatment of what he chooses to include. Every history that is written elbows out one that could have been.[55]

In antiquity, a particularly notable (or, to be more accurate, a particularly notable *and still detectable*) exponent of the art of strategic omission was Xenophon. In his *Hellenica,* for example, he omits any reference to the foundation of the second Athenian Confederacy, despite the implications of that organization for the nature of policy at Athens in a dicey period for inter-state relations.[56] Attempts to plot the passage of time in his *Anabasis* run into a curious discrepancy, whereby a period of at least three months in the course of the march of the Ten Thousand seems to have been skipped in the narrative. This may be attributed to inadvertence, or a failure of memory concerning events that may have happened decades before.[57] But the suspicion that something might have happened during this period which Xenophon (who by this point, as we have seen,[58] was leading the survivors) preferred not to talk about has been hard to resist.[59]

Selectivity of treatment operates at a much more local level as well, of course. Once again, the impact upon the effect of a narrative of what is *left out* is easily underrated.[60] Viewed in a positive light, omission sorts the wheat from the chaff of narrative exposition. Under other circumstances, it can constitute an exceedingly effective means of *suggestio falsi*.

The large omissions of Xenophon's which we have just noted can be rectified by other evidence. In the case of the second Athenian Confederacy, this mostly takes the form of epigraphic evidence. Where the missing months of the *Anabasis* are concerned, it is more a matter of plotting dates, distances, travel times and, in one case, considerations of botany, then noting how they do not match up.

The omissions of a work where there is less in the way of corrective material can be more inscrutable. Hence a difficulty to which we have already alluded earlier in this study: the problematic allure of the 'single source'. How, for example, can we know what Thucydides (who is, after all, the principal source for a great deal of what he has to say) is not telling us?[61] How can we guard against the temptation to swallow uncritically a version of events which may simply happen to lack other evidence by which we can control it?

It has been one of the contentions of this study that what we as modern readers are *not* told by the historiographical texts of antiquity is one of the most important factors that contribute to the complexity of our response to them. At the level of the individual text, this manifests in a way in which the concealment of the workings which generated it (the 'action of the swan') lead to the need for us to evolve and evaluate hypotheses as how it got the way it is. At a larger level, however, a factor which often shapes our responses to classical historiographical texts in a way which is less commonly the case with more modern history-writing is this frequent absence of comparative material. The modern student of the ancient world finds himself or herself having to use a single text as an evidential life-raft more often than one would like.

The solution (unsatisfactory and unspectacular as it is) is to maintain an awareness of the nature of the source provision for what we are examining, and a rigorously evaluative attitude towards these sources. In the case of the *Anabasis*, as we have already seen, *internal* inconsistencies within Xenophon's narrative can point towards the significant void somewhere in the wilds of Book Four. Black holes, by definition, do not allow light to escape. But their existence can still be determined by the distortions they entail for surrounding matter.

On a more general level, examination of an author's thematic preferences and narrative practices can also supply a clue as to the sort of material which is unlikely to have made the cut into the final draft of his history. In the case of Thucydides, the example of this which is often cited is his indifference to religion and religious observances.[62] Other historiographers can also display idiosyncrasies, across a range of topics. Appian, for example, shows a slight tendency to shy away from the treatment of amatory or erotic matters in the extant portions of the *Roman History*, a preference particularly obvious in his account of the career of Julius Caesar, and one which makes it all the more frustrating that the extended account of Antony and Cleopatra promised for his (now lost) books on Egyptian history is no longer extant.[63] In line with what we have seen elsewhere about other historiographical trends, it should come as no surprise that a tendency towards avoidance of the unpalatable is not a phenomenon limited to the ancient world, either. Plotting the silences in modern history-writing can also be an intriguing exercise: H. G. Wells's gargantuan *An Outline of History*, for example, is notable for amongst other things its general suppression of *American* history (the USA disappears almost entirely from his narrative for half a century after the War of Independence) and omits almost any reference to women (with the exception of the female pharaoh Hatshepsut).

There are, however, perils in an excess of readerly paranoia. Selectivity, it is worth stressing, is not always tantamount to suppression. In particular, a disposition to censure the historians of antiquity for not being interested in the same things we are and not talking about material which we would consider interesting is not, on the whole, constructive or particularly useful.

The converse of Lucian's strictures about excessive abbreviation in historical matters, which we have already quoted, was an equal aversion from a historian's excessive indulgence in detail about what Lucian considered trivia: 'He described all cities, mountains, plains and rivers in the most detailed and striking way, as he thought ... For example, he only

just got through his description of the emperor's shield in a whole book
... Because of weakness in matters of importance or ignorance of what to
say, they turn to this sort of description of scenery and caves.'[64] It is true
that we have noted the methodological issues in assuming that such strictures in a treatise would necessarily map easily onto historiographical
practice in antiquity.[65] Indeed, we have already seen how some ancient
writers of history can demonstrate ideas about proportion within their
texts that may perhaps strike us as surprising.[66]

Nonetheless, Lucian's point that, in any extended work of historiography, selectivity of treatment is a necessity rather than an option retains
its force.[67] The failure of Tacitus to display the conscientiousness in the
detailing of military minutiae which would make the work of the modern historian of the Roman army easier,[68] or Herodian's general lack of
interest in topographical matters or the routes taken by the protagonists
in his history,[69] need to be understood in terms of the historian's own
aims and concerns rather than those of the convenience of the contemporary scholar. It is a fallacy to suppose that omission or a seeming dis-
proportion in an ancient historiographical work must stem from blithe
indifference, incompetence or wilful malice on the part of the historian.

It is not hard to multiply examples from the history-writing of antiquity where the author explicitly points out his awareness of issues involving scale, the avoidance of needless repetition, or the problems of what
to include or exclude. Diodorus pointedly limits an oenophile digression
so as not to omit more significant matters.[70] Cassius Dio announces his
selectivity in recording the details of the ascendancy of Julius Caesar.[71]
Herodian notes his reasons for not duplicating material about the
Emperor Severus that is readily available in other historians.[72] Velleius
Paterculus makes authorial comments at the point where the progress of
his narrative becomes complex or bogged down in necessary expansion
or detail;[73] Thucydides can note the regularity of a particular occurrence
to avoid later iterations.[74] Even though such remarks often form a part of
the 'author theatre' by which a historian can generate particular effects,[75]
they nevertheless indicate the level of awareness and thought which classical historiographers could bring to their selectivity – and not always
with a narrowly polemical aim in view.

The Necessary Arrangements

Besides decisions as to what material is to be omitted or included, the composition of a historical narrative poses other challenges. In particular, the problem of what should be described where is seldom absent. This is especially the case when a history covers multiple events transpiring simultaneously in different regions.

Again, this was a problem with which some writers of antiquity make it clear that they were entirely familiar. Dionysius of Halicarnassus, for example, has this to say on Thucydides's way of structuring his narrative, in the course of the essay on that historian which we have already quoted:[76]

> It is surprising how he [sc. Thucydides] failed to see that a narrative
> which is broken up into small sections describing the many actions
> which took place in many different places will not catch the 'pure
> light shining from afar'; as is clearly shown by what happens in
> practice. Thus in the third book (I shall confine myself to this single
> example) he begins his account of the Mytilenean episode, but before
> completing this he turns to the activities of the Lacedaemonians; and
> he does not even round these off before describing the siege of
> Plataea. This in turn he leaves unfinished and recounts the Mytilenean
> War; then from there he transfers his narrative to Corcyra and
> describes the revolution in which one side brought in the
> Lacedaemonians and the other the Athenians. He then leaves this
> account, too half-finished and says a few words about the first
> Athenian expedition to Sicily. He then begins a narrative of an
> Athenian naval raid on the Peloponnese and the Spartan land
> expedition against Doris and proceeds to the exploits of the general
> Demosthenes around Leucas and the war against the Aetolians. Then
> he goes off to Naupactus and, leaving these wars on the mainland also
> unfinished he touches on Sicily again, and after this purifies Delos and
> brings to its conclusion the war that is being waged by the Ambraciots
> against Amphilochian Argos. What need I say further? The whole of
> the book is broken up in this way, and the continuity of the narrative
> is destroyed. Predictably, we wander here and there and have difficulty
> in following the sequence of the events described, because our mind is
> confused by their separation and cannot easily or accurately recall

the half-completed references which it has heard. But history should
be presented as an uninterrupted sequence of events, particularly
when it is concerned with a large number of them which are difficult
to comprehend. It is clear that Thucydides's principle is wrong and ill-
suited to history: for no subsequent historian divided up his narrative
by summers and winters, but all followed the well-worn roads which
lead to clarity.[77]

Dionysius's criticisms, here as elsewhere in his essay, are not always
particularly well-focussed.[78] His account of the action in the third book of
Thucydides is at some points rather sketchy, and it is not in fact
altogether true that 'no subsequent historian divided up his narrative by
summers and winters'.[79] He does, however, present (in a rather one-
sided fashion) one of the inherent difficulties in a narrative which has to
cope with important events transpiring in multiple diverse locales simultaneously. It is this need to cope with plural theatres of activity which
gives Thucydides's narrative the 'jumpiness' that Dionysius is criticizing.[80]

What Dionysius does not really offer, of course, is much in the way of
practical suggestions on how such a complicated narrative is to be handled. It is all very well to declare that 'history should be presented as an
uninterrupted sequence of events', but this dictum is not particularly
helpful when one 'sequence of events' feeds into another elsewhere, or
when two different 'sequences' split off from each other. It is also, perhaps, notable that while Dionysius is eager elsewhere in his essay to supply his own 'improved' versions of how Thucydides should have handled
certain passages, he is conspicuously silent (beyond the vague instruction
already noted) on how the narrative of Book Three might actually have
been rearranged.

Perceptions of such structural problems were sometimes more constructive. For example, Appian's objection to being whisked willy-nilly
from place to place by a narrative as the chain of events demanded
informed the unusual structural principles of his own opus on the deeds
of the Romans:

Many of the Greeks and Romans have written about these things, and
the history is much greater than that of Macedonia, the very greatest
of those that went before. But despite my enthusiasm and my desire to

see their virtue complete against each people, the writing took me often from Carthage to the Iberians and from the Iberians to Sicily or Macedonia or to embassies or alliances happening with other peoples, then again it led me to Carthage or Sicily like a wanderer, and again from these still lacking resolution, until I brought the parts together, whenever they waged war or sent ambassadors or did anything regarding Sicily, until they brought it to its present order, and whenever they waged war against or made treaties with the Carthaginians, or sent embassies to them or received embassies from them, or whatever they did or suffered at their hands, until they levelled Carthage and brought Africa into its present state. And I made this arrangement by each people because I wished to comprehend the deeds of Romans in regard to each, in order to comprehend the weakness of endurance of the peoples and the prowess or fortune of those who had conquered, or any other circumstance that obtained.[81]

Appian, in other words, claims that he wished to contemplate Roman valour as it displayed itself in continuous engagements against discrete peoples. This contemplation would be difficult in a narrative form which (like Thucydides's, but on a wider scale) darted from place to place as it described events. Appian's solution was to pursue the history of Roman involvement with a particular area, from beginning to end,[82] without diversions to cover what was going on in other parts of the world at the same time. Once this regional narrative is completed, he moves to another region, winds back chronology to the point of Roman first engagement with *that* people and begins again. These were not, as we have already seen, the organizational principles of his whole history. His account of the Roman Civil Wars, for example, is a more-or-less discrete chronological narrative devoted to the internal crises of Rome itself in the Late Republic, albeit one with strong thematic ties to what has gone before. Nonetheless, these principles do inform the first half of his work.

This method of structuring a large work of history has some affinities with Dionysius's (somewhat vague) description of what he sees as one of the earlier, more sensible alternatives to Thucydidean narrative management. Thucydides too might have benefited, according to Dionysius, from taking 'the places in which events occurred as his basis for division, as Herodotus, Hellanicus,[83] and some of his other predecessors had done'.[84] Nonetheless, it is an approach which brings with it its own complicated considerations.

Most obvious are the consequences for chronology. With each new area, as we have already seen, Appian rewinds time to the point at which Rome makes contact with it.[85] This can (and does) lead to a tension between 'narrative time' (i.e., the order in which one reads the history) and 'historical time' (the order in which events actually happened). So, for example, the reader who tackles Appian's history in its original order will encounter the detailed account of Scipio Aemilianus's conduct of the Numantine War in 133 BCE in his book on the history of the Iberian peninsula before the vivid account of the same general's destruction of Carthage at the end of the Third Punic War 13 years earlier, which comes at the end of the book on the affairs of Africa later in the *History*.[86] Appian does limit possible confusion by including verbal cues and references to events elsewhere, when they are sufficiently significant or important for the present narrative.[87] Nonetheless, the narrative complexity is clear – though this is a complexity which certainly offers possibilities of its own to a sagacious historian.[88]

Another, more subtle, consideration is the problem of demarcation. Although Dionysius places great store by the recording of an 'uninterrupted sequence of events' in the same place, he offers little clarification of how one determines where such a 'sequence' begins, where it ends and what one does if (a possibility we have already noted) it becomes implicated with events occurring elsewhere. Appian is a particularly interesting test-case in this respect, because his criteria for where he begins and ends the narratives of his 'geographical' books are both reasonably clear and illustrative of the tricky issues which the apportioning of narrative space entails.

As hinted in the passage from his *Proem* which we have already quoted, Appian usually begins the narrative proper of a book in the geographically-structured portion of his history with the point at which the Romans first make contact with the area, and then pursues it to the point at which, according to Appian, it reaches its current disposition: in the *Proem*, he talks about reaching the points at which Africa was brought into its 'present state' (lit. *es ta nun onta*, 'to the matters now being') and Sicily settled to its 'present order' (lit. *es ton kosmon ton paronta*, 'to the present arrangement'). At one end, Appian's choices as to where to put the first contact between Romans and indigenes can sometimes seem a little curious. At the other, his decisions as to what constitutes a definitive conversion to 'the present order' sometimes, to another perspective, seem to gloss over later complications. In the case of the Iberian peninsula, for example, Appian appears to place the crucial moment of settlement at the end of the Second Punic War, which in turn entails his interpretation of the further history of the area as a series of rebellions.[89] The imperatives of narrative form, then, can have their implications for interpretation of events and vice versa.

Appian is the principal example of this means of structuring a history in antiquity that remains substantially extant, although he was certainly not unique in adopting it. (Ephorus, for one, seems to have been another exponent of this location- and people-based means of organizing a narrative, although the extremely fragmentary nature of our evidence for his work makes this a somewhat fiddly question.)[90] This particular response to the problems of handling narratives that entail reporting chains of events occurring in different localities simultaneously appears to have been comparatively unusual.

The problem itself, however, did not go away, in the ancient world or the modern. (Margaret Ann Tyrrell, for example, devoted her life work to 'the composition of a new kind of parallel history, simultaneously tracing events in all parts of the world from 2000 BC to modern times', often ensconced in the upper branches of a tree in the grounds of her husband's embassy.)[91] Polybius, lucid as so often on matters of methodology, notes at one point both his own way of dealing with the problem and the temporal fiddling it entails: 'as I give an account of events that happen contemporaneously throughout the world each year, obviously the result will on occasion have to be recounted before the beginning, whenever in fact the general pattern of my work and the progress of my narrative requires the locality which is the scene of the conclusion of some action to occupy an earlier place than that which witnessed its initial stages'.[92]

Polybius was not alone in alluding to this difficulty. Diodorus, also, expatiated on the problem: 'In life many different actions are accomplished at the same time, but those who record them have to interrupt the narrative and to parcel out different times to simultaneous events.'[93]

It is worth noting, too, that the difficulties which any narrative text experiences in representing events happening in two places simultaneously are not limited to histories which are consistently dealing with multiple theatres of operations. Nor indeed is this an issue for historiography alone; one might, for example, compare the differing ways of handling apparently simultaneous events in Homer (on the one hand) and Apollonius Rhodius (on the other).[94] Whenever two things happen at the same time, someone who is reporting them will have to make a decision as to which is told first.

Tacitus's *Annals*, presents an interesting, small-scale case-study here. The report of the death of Augustus in 14 CE, which is described early in the first book of the *Annals*, helps to inflame two separate mutinies amongst the Roman legions. One of these happens in Pannonia, the other in Germania. Tacitus describes them both, but notes when he begins to detail the latter that in fact they happened at approximately the same time: 'at about the same time and for the same reasons the German legions were disturbed'.[95] It is by no means implausible to suppose that the German mutiny may in fact have begun slightly later than the Pannonian one, if only because the news of Augustus's decease would have taken longer to reach Germania than Pannonia.[96] However, Tacitus's remark would at least seem to indicate that there was a period when they were running in tandem, since he does not introduce the mutiny in Germania with a simple '*then* the German legions were thrown into confusion'.

Thus, Tacitus has had to make a decision about how to handle the presentation of simultaneous events. What he does, as the transitional phrase at 1.31.1 makes clear, is treat the Pannonian mutiny in its entirety, from its first inception under the influence of the rabble-rouser Percennius to its extirpation by Drusus, in one discrete chunk of narrative.[97] Then he turns to the disturbance in Germania and subjects it to a similar treatment.[98]

This decision has its consequences for the impact which Tacitus's narrative has on the reader. Students of narratology (the investigation of how narrative structures are put together and function) usefully distinguish between the 'story' of a text (which is the events of the narrative as they are 'dispositioned and ordered in the text') and the 'fabula' ('all events which are recounted in the story, abstracted from their disposition in the text and reconstructed in their chronological order').[99] Although narratology was initially developed to deal with straightforward fictional texts, its insistence on the effect that ordering and sequence can have on a narrative is useful for historiography as well.[100]

In the case of Tacitus's text, the subordination of the 'fabula' (the order in which things actually happened) to the 'story' (the order in which they appear in the narrative) enables the historian to generate an effect of escalation which would not have been possible if he had run the accounts of the two mutinies in tandem. Tacitus, we note, is at pains to stress how much *worse* the mutiny in Germania was than the Pannonian uprising. Immediately after noting the near-simultaneity of the German uprising with the other revolt, he characterizes it as 'the more violent in proportion to its greater numbers';[101] shortly thereafter, he picks out the respects in which factors that hamper the Pannonian revolt leave this one unconstrained: the trepidation of the other soldiers is absent, and the solitary demagogue Percennius is replaced in Germania with 'many mouths and voices of sedition'.[102]

All of these touches combine to form the impression that, in terms of Tacitus's narrative, things are getting progressively worse for Rome: the bad happenings in Pannonia are succeeded by worse in Germania. In fact, as attention to the actual chronology of what happened makes clear, 'bad' and 'worse' as historical events were running more or less simultaneously. Tacitus's choice as to how to structure his narrative enables him to craft an effect of rising tension within the first book of the *Annals* which would not have been the case if he had handled it otherwise.

As we have already noted, Tacitus's engineering of his narrative chronology in this fashion is a very localized instance of the decisions which a narrative historian has to make about how to organize events within his history, and the consequences which these decisions have for a work's impact. The stories of the two mutinies are soon told. Moreover, it is one which Tacitus himself, through his insertion of an explicit chronological marker, makes it very easy to spot.

Structural decisions on a larger scale are often more difficult to detect. Sometimes this is because they do not announce their presence; sometimes this is a result of the fact that, once one is accustomed to a text being a particular shape and size, it is often hard for the reader to remember that it could potentially have been organized very differently. Moreover, these decisions can have consequences for subsequent interpretation, of both a work of historiography and of the events that it describes, which a shrewd reader does well to keep in mind.

We have already seen how Appian's favoured means of structuring the narratives in the 'geographical' books of his *Roman History* have implications for the way in which he interprets some of the events that take place in them.[103] This phenomenon is by no means unique, though. Again, Thucydides, as read through the spectacles of Dionysius, presents an interesting case. In particular, Thucydides's organization of his war narrative, and how it looks subtly but meaningfully different when hastily précised by someone with a different set of priorities, repays attention.

We have already quoted Dionysius's extended paraphrase of the action of Thucydides's Book Three.[104] Apart from the characteristics which we have already noted, a striking feature of this précis is the later critic's comparative freedom with the notion of individual 'wars' within the events which the historian describes. Dionysius talks happily about 'the Mytilenean War', 'the war against the Aetolians' and the 'wars on the mainland'.[105]

If one looks at Thucydides's own narrative, however, the cumulative effect is rather different. Thucydides is conspicuously less free than Dionysius with the notion of 'the x war' or 'the war against x' in his descriptions of what is going on in Book Three of his work. People 'go to war' a great deal in Book Three and indeed elsewhere in Thucydides's history. The historian, however, is much less inclined than Dionysius to multiply the number of semi-discrete named 'wars' within his narrative. In Book Three, for example, the nearest Thucydides gets to such a local-ized notion of war is when he describes the Athenian response to events in Sicily as aimed at 'putting an end to the war there (*ton ekei polemon*) faster'.[106] Thucydides is content to mention *historical* wars (the conflict with Persia being the obvious example) and he talks, with careful emphases, about 'the x war' or 'the war against x' when he is dealing with the conflicts that arose during the Peace of Nicias when the 'main' war was, in his perception, 'on hold' (though not dead).[107] But during the periods when war between Athens and the Peloponnesians is overt, he seems to steer clear of blithely sub-dividing the conflict after the fashion of Dionysius.

Further investigation into Thucydides's methodology and his decisions as to how to organize his history soon uncovers a possible explanation for this preference. Thucydides's history is very heavily invested in his perception of the *unity* of his subject matter: the Peloponnesian War. We have already seen how the opening words of the work make the focus of attention plain from the outset: 'Thucydides the Athenian composed the history of the war of the Peloponnesians and the Athenians, how they warred upon each other, beginning from the point of its first inception.'[108] The issue of *unity*, the fact that Thucydides considers the conflicts he covers to be a unified phenomenon, comes out more clearly at a significant point later in the narrative, which it is worth quoting at length:

> Though for six years and ten months they [sc. the Spartans and the Athenians] kept off from invading each other's territory, they harmed each other a great deal abroad in a truce that was not secure. Finally, forced to break the treaty made after the ten years, they again became involved in open war.
>
> The same man, Thucydides of Athens, has written in order these events too, as each happened, by summers and winters, until the Spartans and their allies put a stop to the empire of the Athenians, and took the Long Walls and the Piraeus. In all, the war lasted twenty-seven years. If anyone will not think fit to regard the interval of treaty as war, he will not judge rightly. Let him look at it as it is divided up by its events, and he will find that it is not reasonable for it to be considered a peace, as they neither gave nor got back all that they had agreed, and besides this there were violations by both sides with regard to the Mantineian and Epidaurian Wars, and in other respects ... [109]

The context here is very significant. Thucydides's narrative has just reached the Peace of Nicias, which brought a conclusion to the first ten years of the Peloponnesian War and ushered in the period of uneasy truce to which the historian is alluding in the passage above until the second phase of open war erupted again. The point of this authorial interjection here is that this is the moment in Thucydides's work where the unity of his subject matter, the Peloponnesian War (and so of Thucydides's own opus), might look most suspect.[110] What makes a war which has a period of treaty in the middle one war rather than two? After all, if a period of treaty can be discounted *simply* because there is tension during it and some of the people on both sides ended up fighting again, one could argue that the twentieth century witnessed one World War, 1914–45 (which would still be only four years longer than Thucydides's Peloponnesian one).

Thucydides, therefore, feels the need to defend his interpretation of events and the structure of his history, which here are closely implicated: 'Peloponnesian War', not 'Peloponnesian Wars'. This stress on the unity of his endeavour, I would suggest, also lies behind his more conservative approach to the sub-division of the conflict in semi-discrete smaller 'wars', which emerges when one compares it with Dionysius's somewhat 'war-ette'-happy précis. Thucydides has no intention of letting his readers lose sight of the big picture and does a thoughtful and intelligent job of defending the essentially monolithic quality of his subject-matter. Nonetheless, it is at least an interesting exercise to consider how one's interpretation of events would differ if the second half of the Peloponnesian War were regarded as a free-standing conflict, related (of course) to what happened before, but seeking explanation on its own terms.

The structures of classical historiography, in short, have to be understood in terms of a broader issue that faces all writers, readers and interpreters of history. This is the phenomenon of 'periodization'. An 'uninterrupted sequence of events' is not the straightforward proposition which Dionysius presents it as being. Every such sequence entails a decision about where it should begin and where it should end, and, indeed, of how one determines what events are actually *in* the sequence and which are epiphenomenal. The decision as to where one should place the boundaries of one's enquiry and exposition tends to have knock-on effects as to the picture which that exposition will present.

A lot of the most interesting work in thinking about history comes from 'unthinking' assumptions about the patterns into which events 'naturally' fall, or in unravelling structures which may have only the opinions of one individual or even an accident of dating systems to commend them. Thucydides unthinking the assumption that he was dealing with two wars rather than one is not altogether dissimilar from those modern historians unthinking the sausage-slicing epochs of established chronology to use the 'long' eighteenth or nineteenth centuries as units for analysis.[111]

It is true that a great deal of the reflection on these topics which we find in the texts of the ancient historians is not straightforward. Some are perhaps subtle pieces of 'author theatre'; others may well be simple grand-standing. Classical historiographers, like most authors, have a vested interest in establishing the target of their attention as the biggest, the best, the most significant of matters in need of exposition or interpretation. When Polybius and Diodorus bewail the necessary complexities of their narrative manner, they are also drawing attention to the intricacy and grandeur of their own endeavours and how far these endeavours surpass histories conceived on a smaller scale.

All the same, ancient reflections on how history is to be expressed, and meditations on where the appropriate starting and ending points for their works should fall, indicate both the unavoidable decision-making involved in writing narrative history and the need for the reader to bear these decisions in mind when reading it, or works which are in some way indebted to or based upon it. The most insidious patterns are the ones that do not announce themselves. Again, it is worth remarking that one of the hardest things to remember when looking at a historiographical text is to remember that it did not *have* to have the shape, or scope, that it currently possesses. It is hard to spot what someone has chosen not to say.

It should be clear, too, that the question of the ends (and beginnings) of history in turn brings up a further question. How *does* one determine that a 'sequence of events' belongs together? What are the appropriate criteria for making such a decision? And what alternative ways were there in antiquity for using the historical past, beyond the confines of the political historiography which has been the main focus of our concern thus far. These are all considerations which will be tackled in the next chapter.

7

THE ENDS OF HISTORY – PART II

Mapping the reception of a particular event or personage in later ages has never been a straightforward enterprise. There are perils in generalizing excessively about the knowledge, or ignorance, of past times in any given epoch. Nonetheless, it is probably not going too far to assert that General Sir Charles James Napier GCB (1782–1853) is, in the opening years of the twenty-first century, not exactly a name to conjure with.

Sir Charles Napier was a British major general and subsequently Commander-in-Chief in India during the 1840s. Those who do remember anything about him often recall an anecdote about his behaviour after subjugating the province of Sindh in 1843. Napier is said to have despatched on this occasion a telegram to the Governor-General which consisted of the single Latin word *peccavi* – 'I have sinned (Sindh)'.

As it happens, this story was almost certainly made up for a cartoon in the satirical magazine *Punch* the following year.[1] Nonetheless, it continues to make a regular appearance in histories and biographies of the period, not always with acknowledgement that it is most likely apocryphal.[2] Napier's other contemporary monument is his statue, the work of George Cannon Adams, in London's Trafalgar Square. This was erected in 1855 and was the subject of controversy in October 2000 when the then mayor of London suggested that it should be removed because he did not know who Napier was (the nearby statue of Major General Sir Henry Havelock came under similar criticism).[3] Statues and other forms of monumentalization are not as reliable an indication of a lasting reputation as some might think.

Sir Charles Napier is a useful example for the purposes of the present study because he illustrates how one individual or sequence of events can generate many different forms of historical and para-historical production. At the more expected end of the spectrum, there is the reverential 'life' of the subject, *Life and Opinions of Charles Napier*, produced by Napier's brother and encomiastic even by the sometimes accommodating canons of nineteenth-century biography: 'This shall be the story of one who never tarnished his reputation by a shameful deed: of one who subdued distant nations by his valour and governed them so wisely that English rule was reverenced and loved where before it had been feared and execrated.'[4] There are the snapshots in encyclopaedias and reference works which gather the potted achievements of famous personages, such as the *Dictionary of National Biography*.[5] There are the appearances in histories of the period or (as we have already seen) in the biographies of others, often in the context of troubled relations with Robert Peel and the Board of the East India Company.[6]

There are also, however, the other, more diverse, avenues available for making use of the past. Towards this end of the spectrum we might place the statue in Trafalgar Square, or the adoption by his former regiment, the 22nd Cheshire, of the marching song 'Wha wadna Fecht for Charlie' in his honour;[7] the classicist might be tempted to compare the martial songs which attended upon the careers of such successful ancient generals as Julius Caesar, Aemilius Paullus and Sulla.[8] And then there is the *Punch* cartoon, which represents a piece of satirical para-history, an exploitation of the possibilities for an epigram suggested by a particular historical moment, and places itself with self-conscious irony into a hallowed and ultimately classical tradition of terse military messages back to base in doing so. Napier in this cartoon appears as the spiritual heir to the famously laconic generals of ancient Sparta: 'one hears it said by Lacedaemonians that Lysander wrote to the ephors thus: "Athens is taken"; and that the ephors wrote back to Lysander: " 'Taken' were enough". '[9]

There are many ways of putting to use the various building blocks with which historical events present contemporaries and subsequent generations. The case of Napier has the advantage that he is sufficiently well documented, from our twenty-first-century perspective, for us to be able to observe the different treatments his career spawned with some clarity. In particular, we can see the interesting possibilities for *cross-fertilization* that exist between these different modes of response to the past. The apocryphal *Punch* anecdote begins, after a due interval, to work its way into more orthodox treatments of Napier's career, sometimes accepted at face value, sometimes deployed more subtly as indicating the tenor of the times and the contemporary reception of his behaviour.

Demarcation between different methods of processing the past is not always, then, a clear-cut endeavour. To give another nineteenth-century example, one might instance Macaulay's (apparently unwitting) straightforward use of the 'Song of the Western men' to evoke the contemporary atmosphere of popular unrest at the detainment of Sir Jonathan Trelawny in 1688:

> All over the county the peasants chanted a ballad of which the burden
> is still remembered: 'And shall Trelawney die, and shall Trelawney
> die?/Then thirty thousand Cornish boys will know the reason why.'
> … this fact was communicated to me in the most obliging manner by
> the Reverend R. S. Hawker of Morwenstow in Cornwall.

In fact, Hawker (an eccentric clergyman whose other claims to fame included the reputed excommunication of his cat for mousing on Sundays) was the author of the ballad.[10]

We have already noted the variety of possible approaches, subject matters and methodologies that have characterized the history-writing of the modern world. It was emphasized early in this study that modern historiography is a broad church. 'History' is a rubric which accommodates the geophysically and demographically informed *longue durée* analyses of long-term historical structures that characterize the French *Annales* school of historians as readily as the intricate prosopographical studies of the House of Commons under George III that formed part of the work of Lewis Namier.[11]

What we also observed in passing, however, was the proliferation of rather different works of a different mould to these forms of historiographical production. The modern world displays an impressive variety of ways of engaging with its past which are outside the realm of 'academic' historiography. Historical fiction, of course, is an obvious example. Our opening chapter examined Patrick O'Brian's engagement with history amidst the cut and slash of his tales of nineteenth-century naval warfare.[12] Aside from other historical novels, one might instance plays, poems, films and, indeed, comics and graphic novels.[13] There is also, however, an intriguing hinterland between the academic historiographical monograph and obvious historical fiction. Accounts of history-writing sometimes filter out the impact of 'popular' histories, summary histories, collections of weird and wonderful historical facts, and even works which use historical excerpts or a historical narrative to body forth humour or satire.[14]

The impact of such alternative modes of processing the past is easy to overlook. It is, however, unwise to do so. The case of Sir Charles Napier has already illustrated how fluid the lines between different modes can be. Surprisingly unusual instances of historiographical production can end up having an impact on subsequent historical thought.

The history-writing of the ancient world is no exception. The Camden Chair of Ancient History in the University of Oxford, for example, is an institution deeply implicated in the stories of some of the many eminent historiographers that have already flickered through the pages of this study. It was instituted in 1622 by William Camden, whose musings on historiographical method in the course of his work on the reign of Elizabeth I we have already examined on a number of occasions.[15] Its holders have included amongst others Sir Ronald Syme, whose works have likewise enabled us to illuminate the various methodological possibilities in writing narrative history.[16]

This association with some of the leading lights in history-writing across a space of several centuries makes it, perhaps, a little surprising to the modern sensibility that Camden's initial instructions prescribed that the ancient historiographer to whom the Camden Professor should devote his energies was Florus: 'I desire that he [sc. the Professor] should read L. Annus Florus to the youth to the point which seems good to him.'[17] Florus (another whom we have encountered briefly in the course of this study)[18] wrote an *Abridgement of all the Wars for 700 Years*, which, as the title suggests, ferociously condensed Roman history (mainly in its martial aspects) into two books of narrative. In other words, a historical epitome was originally prescribed as one of the cornerstones of the Chair's activities.

Camden, it is worth stressing, did subsequently qualify and explain his intentions:

> I do hereby signify, that it ever was and is my intention, that
> (according to the practice of such professors in all the Universities
> beyond the seas) he should read a civil history, and therein make such
> observations, as might be most useful and profitable for the younger
> students of the University, to direct and instruct them in the
> knowledge and use of history, antiquity and times past.[19]

It is possible that the original choice of Florus as a preferred text had been suggested by Camden's reading in the works of his friends.[20] Nonetheless, it is salutary to note how a work of summary history which would not feature highly in most people's lists of the most significant pieces of historiography produced in the ancient world turns up thus in an important document for the evolution of Renaissance pedagogy. Nor was this the result of simple ignorance. It is worth remembering that Camden himself was conversant with both Tacitus and Polybius. One of his most striking similes for the importance of truth in history is ultimately derived from the latter: 'Which truth to take from history, is nothing else but, as it were, to pluck out the eyes of the beautifulest creature in the world.'[21]

Writing on the fringes of what one might consider 'mainstream' historiography is, then, worth keeping under attention. What, however, can we say about such 'para-historical' production in antiquity. Was its relationship with more familiar forms of historiography as complicated as that which we have been obtaining in the modern world?

Such an enquiry, moreover, entails a further question. This study has explored at some length some key questions about the ways in which ancient historiography functions, processes which the 'action of the swan' goes some distance towards occluding.[22] It has examined the broad array of techniques for handling, processing and organizing data in the historical output of the ancient world – and a spread of different attitudes to the relationship between that data and a finished work of history.

There remains, however, a fundamental issue. Our analysis of how historiography *works* has been illuminating. It has shed only incidental light, however, on exactly what history-writing *is* and what it is *for*. Some clues emerged in the previous chapter, where we observed historians having to make decisions about issues (where their texts should begin and where they should end, how they were appropriately to be organized) which have obvious implications for what sort of shape a history should ideally be.

Further investigation, then, is required. How did ancient authors decide what made for a well-formed historiographical narrative? What formal characteristics or subject matter did a text need, in their opinion, to qualify as 'proper' history? And what was the relationship between 'proper' history and the alternative ways of processing the past whose modern analogues we have just encountered?

Some Definitions

Historiography, like many phenomena ancient and modern, often found itself being defined in terms of contrasts with other things. A particularly famous example of this tendency occurs at the start of Plutarch's biography of Alexander the Great, where the author makes the following statement of generic differentiation:

> For we are writing not histories, but Lives, and by no means is virtue or vice clearly delineated in deeds of the greatest note; rather, a little thing or a saying or a joke has captured character better than battles with titanic casualties, the mightiest confrontations, or the sieges of cities.[23]

The ramifications of Plutarch's reasoning here are interesting, particularly if one comes at his text with a generalized sense, derived from the historiography of the modern world, that biography is simply a particular manifestation of history-writing. Plutarch, by contrast, couches his defence of what he is about in the *Life of Alexander* in terms of what he claims to be a clear distinction between biography and historiography: 'we are writing not histories, but Lives'. Hence, since part of what biography is about is the capturing of character, it is appropriate for him to include such matters as 'a little thing or a saying or a joke'.

The unspoken but clear implication of this is that 'a little thing or a saying or a joke' would *not* be appropriate to record in detail if Plutarch were writing a history rather than a biography. Moreover, the list of things which are in fact inferior to these apparent trivia in the matter of delineating character ('battles with titanic casualties, the mightiest confrontations, or the sieges of cities') suggests strongly that these are the sorts of things Plutarch would be foregrounding if he *were* writing an actual history. He is not saying, of course, that his *Life of Alexander* will not treat such matters; it is hard to imagine a viable narrative of Alexander's life that would not. But Plutarch's priorities, inasmuch as he is a biographer rather than a history-writer, are nevertheless differently organized.

The implicit inseparability of historiography from a focus on battles and sieges and suchlike which we find in this passage tallies with some of the other ruminations on appropriate content which we encounter in the texts of the ancient historians themselves. A notable example is to be found in the complaints of Tacitus as to the intractability of his own subject matter in the fourth book of the *Annals*. Historians of the Roman Republic (he avers) had the advantage of exciting themes:

> I am aware that most of what I have reported and am going to report
> seems perhaps small and slight, but let no one compare our annals
> with the writing of those who represented the old deeds of the
> Roman people. They recorded huge wars, the sacks of cities, the rout
> and capture of kings, or, if they did turn their attention to domestic
> affairs, the disagreements of consuls with tribunes, agrarian and grain
> legislation, the struggles of the people and the *optimates* with free
> digression. Our toil is cramped and inglorious: there was a sterile and
> somewhat troubled peace, the state of a miserable city and a leader
> with no appetite to extend empire.[24]

Once more, we find this insistence on the contribution of 'huge wars, the sacks of cities, the rout and capture of kings' to historiography. Tacitus also notes (again, by way of contrast to the materials with which he asserts that *he* has to work) other key topics. He alludes, with apparent yearning, to the exciting clashes of domestic politics ('the disagreements of consuls with tribunes, agrarian and grain legislation, the struggles of the people and the *optimates*') which Plutarch did not mention (although, of course, 'domestic politics' would in any event have been a tricky category to apply to Alexander, who spent most of his life on campaign).

These two passages suggest a working definition of 'proper' historiography which seems, at first blush, to accord pretty well with the emphases of most extant works of history from the ancient world. 'Histories' are not just narratives which set out past or contemporary events with a certain coherence of structure and a certain element of analysis; they are narratives of the past with special emphasis on the great themes of politics and war. The prevalence of military narratives and political action in classical historiography will already be readily apparent from the subject matter of the texts on which we have spent most of our attention: Thucydides's declaration of his intent to write the history of the (emphatically singular) Peloponnesian War; the narratives of Polybius and Livy, and Cassius Dio and Appian, describing the rise of the Romans to world hegemony and (in the last-named particularly) their energetic internal dissensions *en route*; and Sallust's accounts of war in Africa and civil unrest in Italy. Nor is Tacitus entirely ingenuous in his claims for the apparent pettiness of what he is forced to offer instead. Quite apart from the element of 'author theatre' that so often attends upon a historian's claims that his work is dry or meagre or bitty, or difficult or unrewarding,[25] it is not, in fact, true to say that the *Annals* altogether lack the thematic elements of which Tacitus here regrets the dearth.[26] Certainly his *Histories* have room for conflict, bloodshed and politicking aplenty.

Closer scrutiny, however, reveals a somewhat more complicated picture. In order to see it, it is necessary to suspend for a time a particular reading strategy that is not infrequently used by modern students of the ancient world. This is the practice of, as it were, 'cherry-picking'.

As I have noted earlier in this study, this is a book about writing ancient history, in more ages and senses than one, and it is also a book about the importance of making decisions. The decisions which classical historiographers made as they processed the past for display in their narratives are only a part of this, albeit a very important one. It is important to remember the decisions which later students of these historians then make as they too try (perhaps only in the privacy of their own heads) to write ancient history. How do we account for this particular feature of a text? What grounds do we have for preferring this text, at a particular point, to another one? Indeed (to anticipate the subject of the final chapter), what *version* of a given text are we going to accept?[27]

Now, a particularly common and useful technique for processing historiographical texts is the practice of excerpting. One extracts the bits of text one requires for one's purposes and sets aside the rest. As on numerous occasions in the course of this study, there is a continuity of sorts here between ancient and modern practice. When Pliny the Elder (himself, as we have already seen, a considerable historiographer) was about to demonstrate one of the possible downsides of authorial autopsy in his rescue mission *cum* fact-finding expedition to the erupting Vesuvius in 79 CE, his nephew bowed out on the grounds that he was busy making excerpts from Livy.[28] The younger Pliny's goals were stylistic, but excerpts on the grounds of interesting subject matter were likewise a possibility, continuing into Late Antiquity and beyond. A fair amount of our knowledge of Polybius is derived from thematic collections of excerpts compiled under the Byzantine Emperor Constantine VII Porphyrogenitus in the tenth century CE.[29]

These practices have continued into the modern world. Studies of classical history often base their arguments upon particular snippets of text from the ancient historians. Since footnoting and citation are now the norm ('the action of the swan' having for the most part experienced its swansong), it is usually possible for the reader to chase up these snippets and subject them to his or her own perusal.

Excerpting is a natural consequence of the need, when making an enquiry, to sort out the significant from the irrelevant. However, the cutting up and rearranging of texts in this fashion carries with it an unfortunate side-effect. Passages of the ancient historians which, for one reason or another, are not relevant to the sort of questions that people routinely want to ask about the ancient world can easily slip under the modern radar. If, for example, one's main concern is to unravel the political and military history of antiquity, one will tend to spend one's time looking at the snippets of the ancient historians which deal with those topics. This can easily slide into a belief that such topics were all that held the interest of classical historiography, because one never looks at the other bits. It is an especial hazard with voluminous historians who cover a vast chronological span at tremendous length and so do not necessarily invite a comprehensive reading with open arms.

The hazards of cherry-picking are, in fact, the flip side of the problems posed to the modern student by narrative suppression and omission in ancient history-writing, which was examined in the previous chapter.[30] Just as there is a temptation to be lulled by the 'blanks' of classical historiography – to assume that what we are not being told cannot have been very important – so there is an equal danger in failing to spot elements in the ancient history-writers which do not seem immediately germane to the task of historical enquiry in hand. It is all too easy for elements of the unexpected to fall between the cracks of modern scrutiny, simply because one is not necessarily expecting to see them. Historiography is by no means the only department of ancient literature where this is a hazard, of course. For example, the characterization of Homer as inaugurating 'martial epic' and (or so it is averred) an unrelenting focus on deeds of war, or at the very least, of valorous action needs to acknowledge, if it is to do full justice to the thematic complexity of the work, that this is also a poet capable of spending four lines on how to mix a posset and 27 lines on how to build a raft.[31]

Once one looks at the history-writing of the classical world with this sort of attention, things become rather more complicated than a simple succession of grand narratives of politics and war. The works of the historiographers suddenly look much more plural and various. One has to deal with the phenomenon of Thucydides on fashions in clothes[32] or Xenophon on honey that drives the eater mad: those who 'ate only a little were like people who were exceedingly drunk, whereas those who ate a lot were like madmen, or people dying'.[33] Then there is Polybius on the distribution patterns of livestock in Corsica[34] and pig-management in Italy,[35] Tacitus on the alleged reappearance of the mythical Phoenix[36] and Theopompus on the sexual habits of the Etruscans:

> Theopompus in the 43rd book of his *Histories* says that it is customary
> with the Etruscans to share their women in common; the women
> bestow great care on their bodies and often exercise even with men,
> sometimes also with one another, for it is no disgrace for women to
> show themselves naked.[37]

Considerations of context are important here, of course. Thucydides does not discourse on costume history when he is in full narrative flow in the middle of his history; his remarks on it are actually part of the so-called archaeology in which he briefly surveys earlier Greek history before commencing the story of the Peloponnesian War. Xenophon does not talk about the 'mad honey' out of simple botanical interest. Rather, he records its properties because they proved almost catastrophic for some members of his expedition. Polybius turns from his grand narrative to an everyday story of country folk because it affords him another opportunity to lord it over Timaeus (who, he claims, had got all these details wrong). The text of Theopompus is, as we have already mentioned, very fragmentary, and the processes by which historical 'fragments' have been transmitted to the present day not only rob them of their immediate context but, as we shall see in the final chapter,[38] can make it perilous to assume that any particular fragment is necessarily representative of its author's oeuvre.

Proportion is another important factor. The extent to which historiographers were prepared to admit treatments of material divorced from their martial and political themes into their histories varied widely. This should not surprise us. We have noted a like spectrum of usage in the deployment of other possibilities available to the ancient narrative historian, most notably speeches; in Herodian, in fact there seems to be a correlation between the frequency of speeches in particular stretches of text and the frequency of digressions in the same places.[39] In Thucydides, material that is not central to his themes is allowed an appearance comparatively rarely.[40] Although (as previously noted) there are considerable methodological issues involved in assessing issues of proportion with regard to a fragmentary historian, enough of the fragments of Theopompus are concerned with the manners and mores of foreign peoples and related material to make it clear that his emphases were probably rather different.

It is worth noting, too, that variegation of material was explicitly recognized as a possible narrative strategy by the historiographers of antiquity. This phenomenon is usually known in modern scholarship as the 'digression', although ancient names for it are slightly different.[41] As ever, Polybius has some remarks on how the strategy might work in practice:[42]

> I would appeal to the testimony of Nature herself, who in the case of
> any of the senses never elects to go on persistently with the same
> allurements, but is ever fond of change and desires to meet with the
> same things after an interval and a difference ... the same holds good

as regards the sense of sight. For it is quite incapable of gazing
constantly at one object, but requires variety and change to captivate
it. But this is especially true as regards the intellect. For hard workers
find a sort of rest in change of the subjects which absorb and interest
them. And this, I think, is why the most thoughtful of ancient writers
were in the habit of giving their readers a rest in the way I say, some
of them employing digressions dealing with myth or story and others
digressions on matters of fact.[43]

Polybius goes on to claim that his own means of organizing a narrative so
that the theatre of operations changes so often liberates him from the
need to secure variety by such means. In fact, this is part of what is essentially a counter-argument to those who might object, such as Dionysius
of Halicarnassus or Appian,[44] to a historical narrative where the sequence
of events in one region is suspended while the narrator deals with simultaneous happenings elsewhere:

I am not unaware that some people will find fault with this work on
the ground that my narrative of events is imperfect and disconnected.
For example, after undertaking to give an account of the siege of
Carthage I leave that in suspense and interrupting myself pass to the
affairs of Greece, and next to those of Macedonia, Syria and other
countries, while students desire continuous narrative and long to
learn the issue of the matter I first set my hand to.[45]

As a formal device, nonetheless, the digression continues to show vitality
throughout the ages of classical historiography. Herodian, writing in the
third century CE, includes disquisitions on the freezing of the Danube
and the conditions for farming in North Africa.[46]

Even when all these considerations have been taken on board, however, the occasional admission of unusual material and themes into the
texts of what one is accustomed to consider political and military historians remains notable. Interest in social structures and the habits of
foreign peoples is fairly easy for the modern reader to get a handle on,
especially where the peoples form an important element of the narrative
themselves or the social structures are relevant to the functioning of the
political units that feature in the history. Thus, Polybius's much-discussed

analysis of the nature of the Roman constitution,[47] which is the centre-piece of Book Six of his work, is carefully positioned by the author at the point in the narrative where Rome is poised for world domination and forms an integral part of the overarching plan to explain 'how *and thanks to what kind of constitution*' Rome had reached the state where this was possible.[48] The martial colouring is important elsewhere in Book Six, which also contains an invaluable extended account of Roman army organization and castrametation.[49] In similar vein, if somewhat less well known, is the description of the constitution of the fourth-century BCE Boeotian Confederacy which the 'Oxyrhynchus historian' works into its account of a conflict between Thebes and Phocis.[50]

Dissertations on the weird and wonderful are perhaps a little harder to digest: local variations on well-known myths; the alleged sites of miracu-lous or legendary happenings; bizarre freaks of nature; interesting concinnities or incongruities of place and time and situation. The irrup-tion of such matters into what one might think of as more conventional historiography may give the modern reader pause for thought. Such irruptions were, however, by no means the only examples of such 'borderline' or 'fringe' historiography in the ancient world. It is worth taking a moment to investigate these alternate means of processing and deploying the past in classical antiquity.

Doing the Polis *in Different Voices*

We have already noted a few of the many modes of engaging with the his-torical past that obtain in the modern world. Investigation soon reveals that there was an equal plurality of approach in classical antiquity. Moreover, some of the forms that were in operation then were not so very dissimilar to what is practised now.

Historical fiction (to take the most obvious example) was one such category of 'past-processing' in the ancient world. As in the modern, it seems to have covered a broad spectrum of approaches to the historical data available to the author.[51] A notable instance is the novel *Chaereas and Callirhoe*. This was written in Greek by an individual named Chariton at an indeterminate date not later than the middle of the second century CE; the novel is attested on papyri from that date, but how much earlier than that it was originally composed remains unclear.[52] This (like most ancient Greek novels) is a love story concerning the travails of the eponymous hero and heroine. For our purposes, however, it is interesting because of the ways in which the author goes to some trouble to inveigle his story into the cracks of prior historiography.[53] The heroine, Callirhoe, is said to be the daughter of the distinguished Syracusan general Hermocrates. Hermocrates is a very important figure in Thucydides's account of Sicilian affairs; it is this prominence which some scholars have seen as informing Chariton's choice of Callirhoe's father here.[54] In fact, Chariton even slyly glances at the success of such historiography, by means of his frequent allusions to how the fame of the Sicilian statesman and what he has achieved against the Athenians has spread throughout the world.[55] Hermocrates's position in history and historiography is made clear from his first introduction, and at one point Callirhoe notes the contrast between her father's success and her own helplessness: ' "Father," she said, "in this very sea you defeated three hundred Athenian warships; a tiny boat has carried off your daughter, and you do nothing to help me". ' Other historical and historiographical allusions also shimmer through the narrative. The hero's siege of Tyre seems to contain reminiscences and echoes of accounts of Alexander the Great's historical investment of the same city.[56]

Chariton's novel, as it were, bounces off the sides of historical narrative. In other works from the ancient world, the engagement with history takes a rather different form. Xenophon's *Cyropaedia* (the *Education of Cyrus*), for example, presents itself as an account of the Emperor Cyrus I the Great, but its glaring contradictions with the rest of the extant tradition about Cyrus, its detailed narration of the twists and turns of its protagonist's life and social interactions (complete with a sketchy romantic sub-plot in the story of Panthea and Abradatas), and its explicit pedagogical and didactic agenda, have generally led post-classical readers to bracket it more closely with the ancient novels than with 'proper' historiography. Gibbon, in a lapidary formulation, used it to illustrate the polarity between fiction and history: 'The *Cyropaedia* is vague and languid; the *Anabasis* circumstantial and animated. Such is the eternal difference between fiction and truth.'[57] Cicero (who took a rosier view of the work) commented on its usefulness as a protreptic to his brother Quintus, claiming that it was the habitual reading of Scipio Aemilianus.[58]

A still tighter and more enigmatic engagement with the past appears in a text which we have already cited. This is the so-called *Augustan History*, a set of biographies of the later Roman emperors purporting to have been composed by several authors, which quotes a superficially breathtaking array of documents, material evidence and other writers. On inspection, as we have seen in an earlier chapter,[59] the manifold inconsistencies and implausibilities of these works, and the suspicious absence of reference to the sources which these biographies claim to cite in such loving detail anywhere else in the texts that have come down to us from the ancient world, soon impel the hypothesis that they are an elaborate pastiche or instance of literary forgery.

The *Historia Augusta* illuminates, in fact, another way in which the modern reader's evaluation of the literary productions of the ancient world is complicated by the 'action of the swan'. It has been demonstrated earlier in this work that Greco-Roman antiquity did not universally fail to perceive distinctions between history and fiction.[60] However, the general reluctance of ancient texts to advertise consistently the exact nature of their alleged relationship to supporting data (a tendency to which the *Historia Augusta* is an ironic exception) can make it difficult to determine, in a given case, with what sort of a text one is dealing. Moreover, the cases where we can penetrate this veil with a reasonable amount of certainty have already indicated a whole gamut of different possibilities. Ancient historians and other classical authors who engage in one way or another with the past negotiate their relationship to prior data in very different ways and mostly do not demonstrate a Polybian clarity about how they are doing it.

The problem becomes particularly acute when one is dealing with texts such as the ancient novels and other prose fables. Not every author displays the engaging frankness of Lucian's narrator at the beginning of his fantastic tale of bizarre adventures and lunar exploration, the ironically titled *True Story*: ' ... I am much more sensible about it than others are, for I will say one thing that is true, and that is that I am a liar ... My subject, then, is things I have neither seen nor experienced nor heard tell of from anybody else.'[61]

Lucian's ironies, moreover, illustrate the ways in which ancient historical fiction complicates its relationship to historiography by swiping some of its characteristic techniques and manoeuvres. Lucian is carefully insistent that he is talking about things he has *not* seen or experienced and about which he has received no oral reports. Despite the absence of consistent citation practices in antiquity, we have already seen the important role that claims based upon personal experience and the accounts of others could lay in authenticating the historical narratives of the classical world.[62] The appeal to convincing testimony, to alleged data 'outside' the narrative itself, to autopsy, is a technique which we can see being deployed at numerous points in the novels of antiquity (not to mention, as we have already seen, the *Historia Augusta*). So, for example, the narrator of Longus's romance *Daphnis and Chloe* bases his narrative on the explication of a series of pictures he observed while out hunting, the 'historical' significance of which is duly explained to him by an obliging local exegete:

> On Lesbos, while hunting, in a grove of the Nymphs, I saw the most beautiful sight I have ever seen, a depiction of an image, a history of love (*historian erotos*) ... I looked and I wondered, and a desire seized me to respond to the painting in writing. I found someone to interpret the picture, and have laboured hard to create four books.[63]

The most elaborately extreme example of this passion for 'documentation' seems to have arisen in the 24-book-long *Incredible Things Beyond Thule* of Antonius Diogenes, now known only from a few fragments and the rather bewildering epitome in the *Library* of the Byzantine patriarch Photius.[64] The main narrative of this purported to have been written on tablets by its hero, Deinias, and found in his grave during the course of that popular episode, Alexander the Great's Siege of Tyre.

Of course, where so much non-fictional documentation and source material from the ancient world has disappeared, it is by no means always straightforward to spot where parody or historical romance ends and historiography 'proper' begins. Or, to put it in a less bipolar fashion, where the broad spectrum of techniques and attitudes to evidence we have discerned in our survey of approaches to processing the past is concerned, it is not necessarily obvious *where* a text from antiquity should be placed in that spectrum. Our situation with regard to some ancient texts, particularly those which lack much in the way of surrounding context, can be uncomfortably like that of Plato, the fictional future historian whose

acquaintance we made in Chapter 1 and whose big problem as an inter-
preter is his inability to determine the basic assumptions and 'ground
rules' which underline the ancient nineteenth-century literature he is
trying to explicate.[65]

Again, Lucian supplies a helpful example here. The narrator of *True
Story*, as we have already seen, lays great stress on the fact that he is a liar
and his story is a tissue of fabrications. This explicit emphasis, he notes,
stands in sterling contrast to the practice of some other authors
he could (and sometimes does) name:

> My readers will be attracted not merely by the novelty of the subject,
> the appeal of the general design, and the conviction and verisimilitude
> with which I compound elaborate prevarications, but also by the
> humorous allusions in every part of my story to various poets,
> historians and philosophers of former times who have concocted long,
> fantastic yarns – writers I should mention by name did I not think
> their identities would be obvious to you as you read. For instance,
> Ctesias of Cnidos, the son of Ctesiochus, wrote an account of India
> and its customs; he had neither himself seen nor heard from any
> reliable source the things he wrote about.[66]

Lucian's initial target here is an interesting one.[67] Ctesias, a Greek
doctor at the court of the Persian Emperor Artaxerxes II in the late fifth
century BCE, wrote in addition to the *Indika* ('Account of India', which
Lucian mentions)[68] a 23-book account of 'Persian affairs' (*Persika*) and a
geographical treatise (the *Periodos*). All of Ctesias's works have disappeared except for fragments: we know, for example, that he claimed to
have consulted the royal records of the Persian emperors,[69] and to have
personally seen a manticore sent to the Persian Emperor from India, a
beast the size of a man, with two or three rows of teeth in each jaw, the
claws of a lion, the face of a man, the voice of a trumpet and the speed
of a deer.[70] Since the work of Ctesias himself has mostly disappeared, the
task of working out what the ground rules for *his* text were becomes
rather difficult. Was he a mendacious historiographer or a historical
romancer, or someone in between?[71]

The ways in which Ctesias is read (and upbraided) by Lucian and
Plutarch suggest that they at least saw him more in the former light, as a

historian who was a conscious and deliberate liar. Since Ctesias himself accused both Hellanicus and Herodotus of lying, he was in any event reaping the whirlwind.[72] With even more obscurely attested texts, we do not always have the benefit of access to their ancient reception. At this point, determining the nature of a composition, and of its author's intentions in releasing it into the world, becomes even more complex than is usual in the handling of ancient texts. It is in many cases by no means always clear whether a text that seems at odds with what we can reconstruct of ancient historical reality is in fact purporting to give a representation of that reality and lying (like mendacious history), constructing its own more-or-less independent fictitious reality (like some instances of the novel), or is elegantly insinuating its fictions in between the cracks of conventional historiography, while dropping hints to the informed reader about what it is doing. This last alternative perhaps best fits what is going on with the *Historia Augusta* and also with many examples of the flourishing ancient genre of 'pseudepigraphica', the construction of fictional letters supposedly written by important historical personages. For example, the most (in)famous of such letters from antiquity, those attributed to the proverbially cruel Sicilian tyrant Phalaris of Agrigentum, display a scrupulous concern about ensuring that their fictions remain as consistent as possible with the 'real' historical record: thus, when the fictional 'Phalaris' of the letters importunes the great poet Stesichorus to write a sort of poem which the historical Stesichorus is not known ever to have written, he is careful to indicate his awareness that he is asking for something unprecedented (and so unlikely to be mirrored in the historical record).[73] The intention of the unknown writer was most probably here not to gull people into *genuinely* thinking that the letters were by Phalaris, although in the post-classical era there have certainly been readers who bought into the illusion.[74] Rather, the intent might well have been for readers to observe the cleverness with which the known facts about Phalaris and his age were accommodated or even 'explained' by the fictional text,[75] or the neatness with which events might suggest a particular sally of wit or 'reality-improvement'. *Punch's* 'peccavi' had its ancient counterparts, indeed.

Once again, then, the combination of the action of the swan (which we have already examined)[76] and the imperfect preservation to the modern day of ancient texts (which will be the subject of the final chapter)

presents the twenty-first-century reader with certain interpretative difficulties in dealing with certain works. It is prudent to remember that
there are certainly texts which survive from antiquity of which the
intended relationship to historical data is not just debatable at particular
passage but radically ambiguous in its very conception. There are big
problems in working out what game someone was playing when time has
effaced the touchlines and stolen the goalposts.

Other Histories

Historical fiction, whatever its exact flavour, was by no means the only
alternative to narratives of politics and war which was possible in the
ancient world. We have extensive, if mostly fragmentary, evidence for
historical output of a complexion not dissimilar to that shown by the historiography that has been our main concern throughout this study, but
focussed on subjects rather different from the exalted military and political emphases which Plutarch and Tacitus seem to be enjoining.
Biography, indeed, is an obvious example. Plutarch and Suetonius are the
two exponents of this mode of engagement with the past whom we have
already encountered, but they were by no means unique in practising it,
even if the works of most of the other practitioners of the form survive
only in fragments. Apart from Plutarch and Suetonius, whose works we
have already cited at several points, the main example of an ancient
biographer whose works survive substantially intact is the Roman first-
century BCE writer Cornelius Nepos. There are also collections of
Lives of the Philosophers by Diogenes Laertius and *Lives of the Sophists* by
Flavius Philostratus.

Works centred on the life of an individual were not the only other
alternatives. Another one, for which the evidence is now entirely fragmentary, was the phenomenon of 'local histories', works about the internal history of a city state. Not unexpectedly, the local histories which are
usually most discussed are those of Athens, as produced by the so-called
Atthidographers,[77] but accounts of other cities there certainly were.[78]
Apart from these, the topics of enquiry which are usually most interesting to the student of historiography might be described as ethnography
(the study of a particular people, often including details of its societal

practices and territories), chronography (the detailed study of chronologies, often based upon the calibration of different calendars) and genealogy/mythography (pretty much what its name suggests).[79]

It is important to stress that this is a very partial list of the possible avenues of investigation which antiquity took in its variant approaches to writing about human affairs. A full enumeration of the possibilities would require a much longer book than this. A further note of caution is needed. The categories mentioned in the previous paragraph have a heuristic usefulness and are deployed sometimes in scholarly discussion as if they are to be considered discrete and uncontroversial 'sub-genres' of ancient history-writing which were acknowledged as such in antiquity. However, we should avoid confusing modern classifications for classical orthodoxies. For example, although many ancient authors talk about peoples and societal practices in a broadly similar fashion which one might call 'ethnography', it is in fact difficult to find a consistent and distinctive ancient terminology which identifies 'ethnography' as a discrete practice.[80]

I am concentrating on these broad categories (themselves susceptible, like the grand narratives we have already encountered, to much overlap and internal variation of practice and technique) for two main reasons. The first is simply to stress the profusion of different ways of investigating and representing the human past in the ancient world. The extant classical historiographers on whom accounts like this perforce concentrate were only a part of a much bigger and more variegated picture.

The other, as suggested by this chapter's opening case study of Sir Charles Napier, is to explore the productive interrelationships between these different modes of 'past-processing' in the ancient world. We saw in the case of the nineteenth-century general how different modes of historical production – orthodox history, biography, caricature, even songs – ended up cross-fertilizing each other. Did a similar situation obtain in antiquity?

Scholarship, when faced with the profusion of different historiographical modes in the classical world, has often tried to weld them together into a model of organic development. One broad category of history-writing (it is asserted) gradually develops into another; a third springs into being as a counterblast to the second. The progenitors of such models were already at work in Greco-Roman antiquity itself. We have already seen Cicero's (not particularly satisfactory) explanation for the growth of historiography in Rome.[81] One might also instance the disquisition by Dionysius of Halicarnassus, near the beginning of the treatise *On Thucydides* from which we have already quoted,[82] on the growth of Greek history-writing. Dionysius is talking about historiographers before Thucydides:

> These men chose their subjects on similar principles and did not differ greatly in ability. Some wrote Greek history, others that of foreign lands, without any connexion but divided up by single tribes and cities and published separately. They all had the same aim: to make generally known the traditions of the past as they found them preserved in local monuments and religious and secular records in the various tribal and urban centres without adding to or subtracting from them ... But Herodotus of Halicarnassus, who was born shortly before the Persian War and survived into the Peloponnesian War, enlarged the scope and added to the splendour of the subject. He chose not to record the history of one city or of a single nation, but to gather together accounts of many different events which occurred in Europe and Asia and assemble them into a single comprehensive work.[83]

Dionysius is in line with the trend to see Herodotus as a key figure here. Certainly the obvious formal characteristics of Herodotus's work lead to the temptation to see him as straddling or fusing different modes of historiographical production. To a much greater extent than the other authors who have been the principal topic of our study, he produces at length the detailed analyses of the manners and customs of other peoples which are often seen as the defining characteristic of ethnography. Hence the scholarly inclination to view him as occupying a key position in this developmental model of how the different forms of historical production in antiquity arose.

While Herodotus is usually pivotal in such theories, not all have plotted the development in the same way as Dionysius. Felix Jacoby, whose life's work of editing the fragments of all the imperfectly preserved historians writing in Greek will concern us in the final chapter,[84] briskly dismissed Dionysius's theory and promptly substituted one of his own. According to Jacoby, Herodotus started as an ethnographer in a more-or-less settled format that had been established by writers before him, but inaugurated the subsequently dominant tradition of grand political and military history as a result of the impact upon him of the intellectual climate of Athens. Local histories (Jacoby asserted) then arose as a localized counterbalance to Herodotus's grand-scale work, providing city states with the more bespoke historical narrative which Herodotus's universalizing approach denied them.[85]

There is certainly reason to take the exact evidential basis of Dionysius's assertions with a pinch of salt. We have already seen in the case of Cicero that the 'developmental' narratives of the rise of historiography which we encounter in the classical authors are not necessarily reliable, especially when they are obviously geared to culminate at a particular point. Cicero was intent on establishing how historiography *ought* to be written on the basis of the alleged deficiencies of what had gone before, while Dionysius is mapping out a royal road that ultimately leads to Thucydides.

On the other hand, Jacoby's own model of how historiography developed is itself less than encumbered with much in the way of evidential support. In fact, there are a fair few data (such as, for example, indications of 'city histories' existing before the acme of Herodotus) which seem to tell against it and which he therefore has to explain away. The evidence for historical production in the era before and contemporary with Herodotus and Thucydides is fragmentary and sparse, but, such as it is, it does not seem to support a sweeping account of historiographical genres blossoming, with organic inevitability, into different ones.[86]

Speculation along such lines is, perhaps, to be expected. A possible side-effect of it, however, is something which we should strenuously avoid. This is the temptation to compartmentalize unduly the various processes of historiographical production in the ancient world: by assuming, for example, that once ethnography fulfilled its biological imperative by putting Herodotus into a position from which he could inaugurate 'proper' historiography, the two modes of historical production detached completely and no longer had any impact on each other.

The testimony of the ancient texts themselves, it has to be admitted, are more than a little responsible for fostering such a delusion. It will already have emerged from this study that few subjects were as dear to the pen of many historiographers as the superiority of their own flavour of history-writing to the unworthy alternatives. We have viewed at length Polybius's stated objections to the form of the so-called historical 'monograph' in contrast to his own more universalizing mode of history.[87] It should therefore be unsurprising that he sometimes gives evidence of looking on other alternatives with a like sniffiness. Timaeus's enthusiasm for chronographic investigations meets with derision: 'this is the author who compares the dates of the ephors with those of the kings in Lacedaemon, and the lists of Athenian archons and priestesses of Hera at Argos with those of the victors at Olympia, and who convicts cities of inaccuracy in these records'.[88] It is worth noting that the point of this passage is to point up an alleged fraud by an author who makes a great deal of unwavering accuracy; it is not an attack on chronography per se. Nonetheless, there is certainly here (as in the reference to Timaeus and epigraphy just afterwards) an element of derision concerning the activity itself as well. Moreover, Polybius exhibits strong disapproval of the notion that meaningful historiography can be centred on the biographical account of a single individual, however distinguished. Hence his strictures on Theopompus's decision to write his *History of Philip*, centred on the person of Philip II of Macedon:

> Again, no one could approve of the general scheme of this writer. Having set himself the task of writing the history of Greece from the point at which Thucydides leaves off, just when he was approaching the battle of Leuctra and the most brilliant period of Greek history, he abandoned Greece and her efforts, and changing his plan decided to write the history of Philip. Surely it would have been much more dignified and fairer to include Philip's achievements in the history of Greece than to include the history of Greece in that of Philip.[89]

From another perspective, we have also seen the discrimination Plutarch makes at the beginning of his *Life of Alexander* between what is appropriate to biography and what to history.[90]

Once again, however, this is a case where the disparity between ancient declaration and ancient practice needs a little probing. This study has already remarked upon the fact that Polybius himself appears to have swallowed his objections to the form of the historical monograph sufficiently to write one on Scipio Aemilianus's conduct of the Numantine War in his old age.[91]

A more pertinent point, however, is the evidence of the ongoing impact of 'divergent' modes of historiographical production upon works of political and military history conceived upon the largest of scales which can be garnered from looking at the texts themselves. The *Roman History* of Appian constituted, as we have already noted, an exploration of Roman wars and internal politics of impressive scope, a piece of political and military historiography of the most obvious kind. Even if one leaves aside, however, its unusual structural organization, it is hard to ignore the points at which Appian echoes and evokes the emphases and techniques of other, less well known modes of engagement with the past. His narrative of the Roman *Civil Wars*, for example, is interrupted, after the death of Julius Caesar on the Ides of March, by an extended formal comparison of the personal characteristics and fortunes of the deceased Dictator and Alexander the Great: an exercise more reminiscent of the paired comparisons in Plutarch's biographies, the *Parallel Lives*, than of what we might have considered 'orthodox' historiography. Book Four of his *Civil Wars*, by contrast, presents its account of the Roman proscriptions under the second Triumvirate as a sequence of exemplary stories, including discrete vignettes of loyal slaves and faithful wives. This too evokes a form of past-processing popular under the Roman Empire, in which the particular notable deeds or sayings of individuals were collected together as models of virtue and examples worthy of emulation (or, alternatively, as instances of reprehensible vice).[92] The exemplary use of the proscriptions and the comparison of Caesar and Alexander are both large set-pieces and are delimited within the larger text of the *Roman History* quite carefully by Appian as narrator. He is equally capable, however, of flickering over into such unusual emphases unannounced and at a moment's notice. Thus, in his description of the behaviour of the last king of Pontus, Mithradates, in attacking Romans in Asia from a position in Europe, Appian carefully notes the paradoxical nature of such a sally,[93] and how well it would fit into the category of matters delineated in the catalogues of weird and wonderful happenings which were another stalwart of engagement with the past in the classical world.[94] To judge from the (admittedly somewhat treacherous) evidence of titles, histories which engaged still more closely with the genre of catalogues of surprising matters were to be found elsewhere in antiquity as well.[95] Appian's text, then, while at first blush an unexceptionable example of straightforward political and military historiography, proves on closer inspection to be multiform and various, aping at various points the themes and rhythms of those other forms of historical production which it sometimes suited ancient authors to claim were entirely distinct.

The limits of historiography, then, in the ancient world as in the modern, were actually by no means easy to delineate.[96] In antiquity, as in later times, what is striking is the variety of ways in which literary activity could engage with the human past, and how these different modes of engagement went on interacting with one another. This chapter has only scratched the surface of the variant possibilities. It would take a volume many times the size of this to do justice, for example, to the ancient traditions of encyclopaedias,[97] of learned commentaries on historically significant texts,[98] of speeches supposed to have been delivered on historical occasions or by historical individuals.

What emerges too is the necessity, if one is to achieve a complete sense of history-making as a human activity, of paying attention to the nooks and crannies of historiographical texts. It is understandable that the grand narratives of politics and war continue to be the target of most modern scrutiny. It requires, however, comparatively little digging beneath the smooth surface presented by much historiography to find a strange and diverting world of other concealed narratives: necromancers, sinful animals and kings who ate their wives.[99]

This chapter has also had to face in a particularly acute form a problem to which we have alluded throughout this study. The assessment of classical historiography is an enterprise hugely complicated by the disappearance of so much material from the ancient world and the problems concerned with determining how representative what remains may be of what there once was. It is the examination of this issue, the long and hazardous path between the writing of a work of ancient history and its arrival in the twenty-first century, which forms the topic of our final chapter.

8

TEXTS AND TRANSLATIONS: THE TRANSMISSION OF ANCIENT HISTORY

> *If Queen Elizabeth had been a Ptolemy history would have been quite dif-*
> *ferent ... But instead, the Egyptian noodle made carnal embrace with the*
> *enemy who burned the great library of Alexandria without so much as a*
> *fine for all that is overdue. Oh, Septimus! — can you bear it? All the lost*
> *plays of the Athenians! Two hundred at least by Aeschylus, Sophocles,*
> *Euripides — thousands of poems — Aristotle's own library brought to Egypt*
> *by the noodle's ancestors! How can we sleep for grief?*
>
> Tom Stoppard, *Arcadia*, Act I, Scene III

The schoolgirl Thomasina's speech against Cleopatra in the first act of Stoppard's play *Arcadia* is interesting historiographically on two fronts. The first, which is of relevance to the subject matter of the previous chapter, is its rhetorical indulgence in counterfactual history: speculation on what *would* have happened if given historical circumstances had been (in the case of Thomasina's scenario, inordinately) different. This sort of thought experiment has acquired a fair amount of attention in recent historiography; it should not surprise anyone who has reached this point in the present study that the ancients were active in that arena as well.

The second interesting subject which Thomasina broaches (and one that would go on interesting Stoppard in his subsequent dramaturgy)[1] is that of textual transmission. What we can read today is only a frac-tion of the literary production of the ancient world. All the rest has been lost.

165

In most cases, the disappearance of ancient literature occurred under conditions less exciting than the torching of the Great Library of Alexandria. Before the advent of printing, histories, like all other texts, had to be written and subsequently copied by hand – a laborious and cumbersome undertaking. For a work of historiography to survive to the point where you the reader can go out and buy a copy of it, it is necessary that a copy should survive until it was possible for a printed edition to be put into circulation. Because of the effort involved in copying books, and the uncertain fate of manuscripts between the classical world and the Renaissance, this survival was by no means guaranteed.

Even if a text did thus survive as far as the birth of printing, there remained another vexing issue. People who try to copy things tend to make mistakes in doing so. Moreover, someone who is copying a manuscript will also be copying the mistakes of the people who copied it before him. This is famously the basis of the game known variously as 'Chinese Whispers' or 'Russian Scandal', in which one player whispers a message to a second, who in turn whispers to a third and so on, until at last a (usually hideously garbled) version is announced and compared with the original. Copying manuscripts is not quite as bad as this, since one gets more than a single look at what one is copying. But the principle of cumulative error remains comparable.

Students of ancient history-writing are posed, then, with a twofold problem. On the one hand, as we have repeatedly seen in this study, assessments of the character of classical historiography and exercises in historical enquiry face the problem that so much relevant material has disappeared. This is not simply an issue of not having enough data, although that is certainly a very important part of the challenge. A more insidious difficulty, which, again, has already been examined in Chapter 6,[2] is the way in which the character and shape of the data we do possess may tempt us into ill-founded conjectures. To reiterate an obvious and crude example, the mere fact that there is a great deal of extant historiography about a certain topic does not guarantee per se the actual importance of that topic. It will therefore be useful for us to examine the various strategies by which students of ancient history-writing can compensate for the disappearance of such a large quantity of pertinent sources.

On the other hand, we face the problem that the texts which *have* survived to the present day have rarely done so in exactly the form in which they left the pens of their authors. The whisper game that transmits texts from classical antiquity to the twenty-first century often leaves them somewhat garbled and transmuted in the process. As a result, the student of ancient history-writing has to deal with yet another round of decision-making in his or her response to the classical texts. How does one decide, under circumstances where textual garbling may have taken place, what the author is most likely to have written? Moreover, since we have become aware of many possible models of explanation for apparently unusual or anomalous features within a historical text, how do we adjudicate between the different possibilities? While textual criticism is a discipline too complex to handle in all but the most summary form in these pages, it is a consideration which the critical reader of ancient history-writing cannot reasonably ignore.

Mapping the Absences: Testimonies and Fragments

So, if there is no complete extant copy of the text of an ancient historian, what options are available for determining its nature?

Suppose a pernicious but tidy-minded literary holocaust obliterated every copy of the Greek text of a historian we actually possess in a more-or-less complete state. 'Completeness' is a rather relative term here, since it is usually more accurate to say that we have a substantial quantity of a historian than that we have the 'complete text'. For these purposes, however, let us use the text of Thucydides as an example, despite the issues of its probably unfinished state. If every Greek copy of Thucydides disappeared from the face of the Earth, by what means would we be able to reconstruct it?

If a full text disappears from history, it nevertheless often leaves traces in other texts that still remain. We would still have all the authors who *quoted* Thucydides, as well as those who mentioned, paraphrased or explicitly contradicted him. Many of these references would be in the sort of texts one would expect: other histories, scholarly commentaries and such like. But some bits of Thucydides would persist in some rather more unusual contexts. One of these has been fleetingly mentioned above, a quotation in Alasdair Gray's 2007 novel *Old Men in Love*. We join a Greek class at Lampeter in the nineteenth century:

'Thucydides now describes the sporting customs of the Spartans. Will you translate Mr Rees? Egoom-no-they-san tay protoy kai – ?'

With much hesitation Rees said, 'They were the first also who … stripped themselves and … pulling off their clothes in public, anointed themselves with fat for, for athletic exercises. Whereas … formerly … even in the Olympic Games the wrestlers used to fight wearing … exontes, exontes … '

"Skirts," said the tutor, 'Girdles. Belts.'

Hurriedly Rees muttered, ' … used to fight with belts round their loins which shows that the primitive Greeks lived like the barbarians of the present day.'

'Yes,' said the tutor urbanely, 'The custom of sporting nudity was started by Orsippus of Megara, who accidentally lost his girdle in the Olympic stadium and consequently won the race. Greek notions of barbarism, you see, were in some matters the reverse of ours … '[3]

This passage demonstrates in a nutshell some of the characteristic difficulties of reconstructing the works of lost historians from later allusions to them in other texts. Suppose we try to extract from this passage of the novel, without reference to other data, what Thucydides actually wrote. The most obvious consideration for trying to recoup the original passage of Thucydides from Gray's use of it is that it has of course been translated into English, although there are a few snatches of phonetically (and in one case, misleadingly) rendered original Greek.[4] Apart from these, the best that the seeker after original Thucydides can retrieve from this passage is thus a translation.

Even in terms of translation, however, the seeker soon encounters a methodological problem. How much of this passage is actually a direct translation of Thucydides? It is not hard to compensate for Rees's stops and starts in stitching together a continuous passage. What, however, do we make of the tutor's reply? Is the sentence beginning 'The custom of sporting nudity … ' the tutor's rendition of the part of Thucydides that comes next, or is it his own independent gloss on what Thucydides is saying? Where does citation end and commentary begin?

By way of comparison, here is a translation of how the relevant passage of Thucydides appears in the actual Greek text:

> They also set the example of contending naked, publicly stripping and anointing themselves with oil in their gymnastic exercises. Formerly, even in the Olympic contests, the athletes who contended wore belts across their middles; and it is but a few years since that the practice ceased. To this day among some of the barbarians, especially in Asia, when prizes for boxing and wrestling are offered, belts are worn by the combatants. And there are many other points in which a likeness might be shown between the life of the Hellenic world of old and the barbarian of today.[5]

Some obvious points emerge. In the first place, it becomes clear that the tutor's sentence about Orsippus of Megara *was*, in fact, his own gloss and not a continuation of Thucydides. One also notes that there is a stretch in the original which Rees simply missed out ('and it is but a few years since that the practice ceased. To this day among some of the barbarians, especially in Asia, when prizes for boxing and wrestling are offered, belts are worn by the combatants').

Another, more subtle consideration is that Rees's translation, while not exactly inaccurate, removes some ambiguities which were present in the Greek. Rees suggests that the emphasis of the whole of the passage is explicitly on combat sports. He says that the '*wrestlers* used to *fight*', whereas the passage above talks about the '*athletes* who *contended*'. The latter is in fact closer to the Greek: Thucydides talks of *athlētai* rather than simply wrestlers and uses the verb *agōnizesthai*, which *can* refer to combat but can equally refer to simple competition. I should add that the comparison between translations is not, in fact, always to Rees's discredit: his version makes it clear (as the published one by Richard Crawley given above does not) that Thucydides used the word *aidoia* (loins or genitals) to describe the positioning of the belts. Crawley coyly opted for 'middles' instead.

There is a larger issue as well. It was noted in a previous chapter that this passage of Thucydides is in fact an unusual departure from the historian's usual narrative emphases.[6] For the vast majority of his text, Thucydides displays little interest in such societal and cultural details as the history of nudity at the Olympics. This snippet is in fact lodged very firmly in a larger discussion about early Greek history. If, however, the text of Thucydides had disappeared and this passage, preserved in this novel, was all that remained, what inappropriate conclusions might have been drawn about the nature of Thucydides's general interests as a historian? Might we have incautiously assumed that this sort of cultural history was a matter of constant interest to him? The mere fact a particular passage of a work has been preserved in no way guarantees that that passage is representative of the work as a whole.

In the case of Thucydides, we are fortunate enough to have the full Greek text against which to check its appropriation in other works. In the case of many of the historians of the classical past, we are much less lucky. Students of ancient history-writing interested in such figures, named earlier in this study as Theopompus, Timaeus, Ephorus and Asinius Pollio, often have to proceed along much the same lines as we have just done in the thought-experiment of reconstructing a passage of Thucydides from Alasdair Gray's novel.

Moreover, such an enterprise involves all the hazards which our experiment so graphically demonstrated. It can be hard to tell, in such exercises, where what looks like a rendering of a passage from a historian is accurate citation or a paraphrase. If it is a paraphrase, there is often little assurance of how accurate it is, or what might have been left out. It can likewise be exceedingly difficult to determine where the citation of an earlier text begins and where it ends (remember the ambiguity of the sentence about Orsippus of Megara).[7]

Above all, one has to bear in mind that authors quote, paraphrase or allude to texts for their own purposes. These purposes rarely include the convenience of textual archaeologists. Gray, for example, has very good reasons for choosing and treating the passage of Thucydides in the style he does. Rees is being deftly characterized as a halting translator. Moreover, this particular passage, while not particularly representative of Thucydides's work as a whole, is ideally fitted for the use to which Gray puts it in his narrative, starting off a discussion about the 'depravity of the Greeks' in the reading class which enables the central character of this part of the novel to get on a high horse about his religious conscience on matters of morality. Gray also neatly weaves together the various strands of his complex novel through the use of Thucydides at this point: another storyline within it concerns Athens at the time of the Peloponnesian War (Thucydides's own theme, of course), while the tutor's later instruction to his students to 'translate what Thucydides says about early cities, piracy and the *rise of capital*' [my italics] links into the economic historiography which also forms one of its strands.[8] Authors have their own agenda in the use of earlier writers and are under no obligation to ensure that these cohere with the agenda of those primarily concerned with disinterring such writers.

These textual manipulations are, in some cases, very obvious in the ancient world. For example, what seems at first a surprisingly high proportion of the surviving allusions, paraphrases and citations to the lost historians of the classical past appears to be about food, drink and social eating. This is not, however, evidence for a general gastronomic bias in the historiography of antiquity. The explanation for this emphasis lies in the fact that one of the most allusive classical texts to have survived, and so one of the most useful for the purpose of reconstructing lost authors, is the *Deipnosophistae* ('Philosophers at the Dinner-Table'), written by Athenaeus of Naucratis at the end of the second or beginning of the third century CE. Athenaeus's work, as its title suggests, is set at a learned banquet. This enables the author to construct a monumental treasure-house of allusions to all manner of things connected with food, drink or revelry. Given that Athenaeus cites around 1250 authors, it is not surprising that his particular emphases lead to a certain tilting in the nature of the citations of lost authors across the range of literary activity in the ancient world.[9] In addition, and more subtly, he displays a notable tendency to adapt them or reshape them to suit his particular argumentative context.[10]

Not all such textual manipulations announce themselves quite so obviously as Athenaeus's convivial predilections, however. Again, the example of *Old Men in Love* is worth bearing in mind here. The discrete elision of some transitional material, the instances of debatable translation, would not be discernible if we could not check what was going on against the full text of Thucydides. Indeed, we have already seen how the précis of Book Three of that historian, on which Dionysius of Halicarnassus spends a lot of time in his treatise on him, presents a version of Thucydides's narrative that slightly but notably skews the emphases of the earlier historiographer's actual narrative,[11] even though

Dionysius (beyond his desire to demonstrate the 'bittiness' of Thucydides's narrative) has no particular axe to grind in composing it. All of this suggests that one should not be unduly sanguine about the likelihood of extracting large authentic chunks (what classicists sometimes call the *ipsissima verba*) of the text of a vanished historian.

This due scepticism is worth keeping in mind when one approaches the great monuments of scholarly labours to assemble material relating to the works of vanished classical historians such as *Die Fragmente der griechischen Historiker* ('Fragments of the Greek Historians'), which was the lifework of Felix Jacoby, or the *Historicorum Romanorum Reliquiae* ('Remains of the Roman Historians') of H. Peter.[12] These volumes fulfil a titanic labour in gathering together the places in extant classical literature at which otherwise lost historians leave their traces, in the way Thucydides leaves his traces on *Old Men in Love*, and organize them into coherent patterns. There is, however, a particular difficulty with their format and indeed the sort of picture which the word 'fragment' (the usual term for citations of this sort) tends to convey to the incautious reader.[13]

A fragment sounds very much like a discrete piece, small and jagged perhaps, but definite in its outlines, of an original whole. In fact, as we have already seen, the relationship between the version of a passage from a lost historian which appears in a later text and what that historian originally wrote can vary from full and exact quotation to vague paraphrase, and the exact limits of its extent within the later text may well be open to conjecture. This is particularly important to remember in dealing with *Die Fragmente der griechischen Historiker*, where 'fragments' are routinely delimited from the surrounding text by typographical conventions, even when the scope of the fragment is debatable. Moreover, presentation of these fragments without their full surrounding context in the later author can sometimes obscure the reasons why that author is citing or alluding to the historian in question, or why he refers to that particular passage rather than another one. The particular imperatives which the author might have to reshape or distort the reference thus become less than clear. To continue with the analogy, Alasdair Gray's reasons for fixing upon that particular bit of Thucydides are much less apparent if one cannot immediately determine what place the scene in which it appears occupies in the plot of the larger novel. Works like those of Peter and Jacoby are very useful in the task of puzzling out the natures of ancient historiography, but one should always bear in mind the methodological limits on what they attempt to achieve.[14]

In fact, many of the important lessons one has to take on board about the use of historiographical fragments as a student of ancient history-writing are not dissimilar to those we observed in Chapter 6, dealing with issues of scale, omission and proportion in the extant historians.[15] Above all, it is crucial not to allow the survival of particular data in a particular form to blind us to the fact that these data are not necessarily representative of what has been lost. Moreover, those who transmitted this data had their own priorities in doing so.

Some consequences of this observation are fairly obvious, although scholarship has not in all cases perhaps taken them on board as consistently as one would like. In particular, the polemical context in which Polybius quotes so many of his predecessors, a circumstance which we have already noted,[16] makes it dangerous to assume that he is necessarily being entirely fair in his representation of their achievement. It is probably going too far to attribute his strictures entirely to personal animosity and one-upmanship, since his censure does often base itself upon methodological principles which are demonstrably important throughout his work. On the other hand, there is at least one notable case where the passage of an earlier historian which he is criticizing is still sufficiently lucid for us to see that his detailed objections to it are, to a great extent, captious and nit-picking.[17] We have also observed the occasions on which Polybius's own practice seems less than consistent with the principles he espouses.[18] These considerations mean that we should pause before swallowing too readily his pictures of his predecessors, influential though these have been in determining scholarly theories about their nature.[19]

The reputations of Polybius's targets have, perhaps, suffered through the circumstances of their transmission. It is possible, however, that there are other historians, the obliteration of whose texts represented an exceptionally shrewd posthumous career move. Where there is nothing to read, there is nothing to criticize, which has enabled some lost historians to acquire an effortless reputation as paragons of historiographical method on the basis of works which we are now unable to examine. It is worth bearing in mind, when one reads the glowing account of Gaius Asinius Pollio as a historiographer at the beginning of Syme's *The Roman Revolution*,[20] how scanty the evidence is for what quality of historian

Pollio actually was. What Pollio's remains *do* attest is his fondness for criticizing and censuring the accounts of others.[21] This, as Polybius was well aware, is often a sure-fire means of projecting an image of independence and so obtaining an easy fame:

> Perhaps, therefore, some might wonder how, being such as I have proved him to be, he meets with such acceptance and credit from certain people. The reason of this is that, as throughout his whole work he is so lavish with fault-finding and abuse, they do not form their estimate of him from his own treatment of history and his own statements, but from the accusations he brings against others ... it is very easy to find fault with others, but it is difficult to behave faultlessly oneself, and one notices as a rule that those who are readiest to blame others err most in the conduct of their own life.[22]

There are perils in accepting too readily that the extant historians whose texts we can analyse represent some sort of declension from the lost perfections of those whose texts we cannot.[23]

Lost in Translation

The case of Rees and his efforts to master Thucydides brings into sharp focus the issues that attend upon disentangling remnants of lost texts from later ones which cite them. It also, however, illuminated another important issue. It was not merely the case that Rees's account of Thucydides lopped off parts of the original text. It also, as we saw, *translated* a portion of the text in a fashion which, while not entirely inaccurate, did not quite render an original nuance of the Greek: a sentence which in Thucydides's original refers loosely to 'athletes' was rendered as though it referred narrowly to 'wrestlers'. Moreover, and rather more disturbingly, comparison with a translation of Thucydides that had actually been published as such revealed an instance where the published translator bashfully renders a Thucydidean reference to genitalia as the bland and misleading 'middles'.

The labour of understanding ancient history-writing rests, as we have stressed, on an often invisible foundation of decision-making. At one end of this lies the decisions of the authors in how they organized their narratives, responded to data and arrived at notions of what to include or omit. At the other end lies our own decisions as we evaluate these texts, making working hypotheses to explain their characteristics and weighing them in the light of the other data at our *own* disposal. This chapter, however, is largely concerned with the decision-making of the (often anonymous) intermediaries who lie in between: those who decided which texts from the ancient world they were going to pass on to future generations and in what form this transmission was going to take place.

If we are reading these texts in translation, another layer of decision-making intervenes: the decisions of the translator as to how the original Greek or Latin is to be rendered into a modern language. As the example of *Old Men in Love* and Crawley's translation of Thucydides indicate, this is not always a process which occurs without a hitch.

Translations are not necessarily accurate. Sometimes they fall prey to simple inadvertence. Sometimes a version in another language simply cannot do justice to the implications of the original. Sometimes, too, translations, like texts that cite fragments, are documents of the cultural milieu that produces them. Crawley's bashfulness about Thucydidean genitals, for example, is an interesting sidelight on attitudes to the body in the Victorian England in which he was writing.

The issue of translation in understanding ancient historiography is one which this study has mostly elided. In the interests of reaching as large an audience as possible, all the texts which I have discussed have been provided in translation. Only on a few occasions have I indicated places where differences of translation make a material impact upon the discussion of a passage.[24] This decision should not obscure the very real consideration, however, that interpretation of classical historiography which is founded upon translations can, at important points, run into considerable difficulties. Moreover, not all of these announce themselves as explicitly as the more opaque theoretical passages of Thucydides. Crawley's rather misleading moment of prudery, for example, occurs in a fairly straightforward passage. Translation, then, must always be considered as another possible route by which the student can find his or her response to ancient history-writing being influenced without his or her awareness.[25]

Careless Whispers

Issues of translation and fragmentation, however, are only part of the story where the transmission of classical historiography is concerned. As we saw above, there is also the issue of the Russian Scandal or Chinese Whispers effect, the principle of cumulative error, which has impacted upon the texts that have come down to us from the ancient world. There is a temptation to contrast the Greek text we now possess of a writer such as, say, Xenophon, seemingly ample and complete, with the parlous state of an Asinius Pollio or the unavoidable distortions of a translation. In fact, the text of Xenophon which we use stands every bit as much on a foundation of myriad acts of decision-making as the assembled fragments of a Theopompus or an Ephorus.

As we have already noted, texts which reach us as copies of copies of copies tend to become at least a little garbled in the process. Antiquity itself was well aware of this. Those who are inclined placidly to assume that textual corruption (as the 'garbling' process is known) takes centuries to do its wicked work would be well-advised to look at Polybius's censure of Timaeus for criticizing Ephorus over what he should have recognized as a scribal error.[26] How, then, can we reconstruct a text that is as close as possible to the 'autograph' (which, in this context, denotes the version of the text that left the hand of the original author)?

Textual criticism is, as we have noted, a business too complicated to handle in detail here, but some words are in order as to its basic procedures. As one might expect, a lot can be done by comparing, where possible, alternative manuscripts of the same text. However, where through paucity of manuscripts no such comparison is possible, or where a garbling started so early in the transmission of the text that all extant manuscripts bear its mark, the editor is often impelled either to indicate that the passage is irretrievably corrupt or to remedy the situation by suggesting a restoration (so-called conjectural emendation).

From our present perspective, of course, the possibility of textual garbling, as we have hinted before,[27] raises an interesting problem of method. How does one *tell* that a text has become corrupt? If one is fortunate, it will be because the text has become simple gibberish. However, any simple experiment with fast typing on a word processor that provides a spell and grammar check will confirm that not every mistake that gets made in transferring something from one medium to another is so considerate as to advertise its status as a mistake by being misspelt or impossible grammatically. Indeed, one special category of textual corruption which is important (and irritating) to readers of ancient historiography is the phenomenon of *interpolation*, when material which was not originally in the text is added to it by a third party. By definition, this sort of corruption is unlikely to be obvious gibberish (unless it too has become corrupted in turn, of course).

As a result, textual criticism must also keep an eye out for instances of notable incongruity or peculiarity within the work to which it is applied. Here, however, we face the particular problem that there are often several possible explanations for a particular textual peculiarity. Does an odd word appear at a particular point because a scribe inserted it by mistake? Or was the word used by the author's source material and not changed by the author? Or is the author using the unusual word simply for its dramatic effect? Here, as so often in thinking about ancient history, it is necessary to weigh the local plausibilities of different explanatory models.

To give an example of how such considerations weigh upon us as we assess ancient historians, one might look at the problem of apparent factual errors in the text of a historian. This, in fact, revisits Polybius's argument with Timaeus over the merits of Ephorus. Does the appearance within the text of a historian of a particular number, which our other evidence (or simple considerations of logic and plausibility) indicates to be false, show that the historian made a mistake or was using a mistaken source, or merely that a copyist perpetrated an error?

Once again, considerations of relative likelihood will apply. Some sorts of textual corruption are more common, or more easily explained, than others. In similar vein, other data at our disposal as to the likelihood of particular mistakes being made at particular points, or by people using particular sources, will affect our assessment as to the most plausible explanation for any particular moment of textual difficulty. Nonetheless, the possibility of textual interference is something which should always be kept in mind. The texts of even the most substantially extant ancient historians are not necessarily as solid and reassuring as their bulk on a bookshelf may suggest.

The chapters that preceded this took the autonomy of the texts with which they dealt, perhaps, somewhat for granted. However, a study like this, which bases itself upon the examination of historiographical texts, must at some point acknowledge that the units with which it deals have their own issues as regards reliability. Again, the mere fact of the existence of vagaries in transmission, whether from textual corruptions or the inadequacies of translations, does not entail an easy scepticism about the possibility, in the modern world, of writing ancient history. But it does alert us, once more, to the necessity for unfailing vigilance and flexibility in our explanatory models as we engage with the historiography of the classical world.

CONCLUSION

'And if you ask all those who hav gone before i am not sure whether they would agree that it is worth it. But it is too late now.'

G. Willans and R. Searle, 'Lessons and how to avoid them: 2. History', from *Down with Skool!*

This introduction to classical historiography has been constructed along lines that are, perhaps, somewhat unorthodox. There has been, for example, no chronological survey of ancient historians. The Royal Road from Herodotus to Procopius has not been traversed anew.

This is because introductions to the history-writing of the ancient world written in the standard format run the risk of gliding too smoothly over certain assumptions which I wanted to explore. In particular, they often start with certain, rather fixed notions of what history meant (or should have meant) in antiquity and therefore how its practitioners worked (or should have worked). These notions might be derived from the practice of Thucydides or the theoretical pronouncements of Cicero, but they do not always grapple with the problem of how legitimate it is to generalize that practice or those pronouncements across the totality of ancient historiographical production.

I have therefore found it useful to try to keep the focus of this study on the particular conditions imposed by the nature of our evidence for ancient history-writing. Hence the occasional recourse as an instructive analogy to the figure of Plato, the fictional historian of Earth's future.

Plato's dearth of evidence with regard to what we would consider the present or the recent past mirrors our own evidential situation with regard to the ancient world. Like us, Plato is driven to construct explanatory models and hypotheses to explain the nature of the texts at his disposal. In Plato's case, we can see the various ways in which (for good reasons) he gets things wrong. These observations clarify the basis of our own theories and inferences about how historiography worked in the ancient world. This does not, of course, justify radical scepticism about the viability of any enquiry into the history of the ancient world. The fact that a hypothesis may be wrong is no reason not to hypothesize.

The study has also demonstrated how writers can exploit narrative structures and the ways in which they organize data to assist the particular picture they want to convey. This book is itself, of course, no exception. One of the things I wanted to stress in this analysis was the apparent *plurality* of ways of writing history in the ancient world, a plurality to which the theoretical statements on the subject in antiquity, useful though they can be, do not really do justice. In fact, the evidence suggests that historiographers in the Greco-Roman world had widely varying notions of such important matters as a historian's relationship to his data, what matters and modes of explanation were appropriate to history and how legitimate it was to engage in speculative historical reconstruction. Hence my decision to eschew a chronological treatment of historiography, which carries with it, as we have already discussed, the temptation to try to unify history-writing into an organic, developmental stemma. Instead, my mode of presentation, which assembles the historiographers of antiquity and (for the most part) puts them together synchronically for comparison and contrast, tends to bring out the divergences, the arguments, the contrasting approaches which seem to characterize the processing of the past in the ancient world.

This insistence helps to explain, too, another feature of the book. Throughout I have attempted to illustrate aspects of historical activity in the ancient world by reference to the history-writing of subsequent ages. This is an approach that bears the risk, of course, of minimizing historical difference and suggesting that 'they were just like us really'. Nonetheless, this was a risk that I felt worth taking, since it helped to demonstrate the plurality of historiographical approaches in the Greco-Roman world as well as its successors, and that there is more affinity between some practices prevalent in ancient history-writing and its later cousins than contemporary rhetoric has always suggested. Ancient historiography is not always as ancient, or modern historiography as modern, as is often supposed.

The other consequence of my analogies to later ages of historiography has, I hope, been an emphasis on historiography as an important and ongoing human activity. Again, this is a rhetorical manoeuvre with all sorts of ideological baggage attached (notably notions of the primacy of the author and the autonomy of the individual), but one that I feel is worth making. Historiography can be hard work, as I hope the foregoing chapters on the problems of handling data and structuring a narrative have made clear, but work that repays the effort. This is worth bearing in mind when we join the authors of antiquity as, in our contemplations and analyses of texts and data and hypotheses that explain the relationships between them, we all make our own contribution to the writing of ancient history.

NOTES

Chapter 1

1   The writing of history is often known as 'historiography', a useful term which makes it clear that one is talking about the characteristics of 'histories' composed as texts rather than the historical process itself. In what follows, history-writing and historiography are treated as synonymous.

2   Writers of history in Greco-Roman antiquity were (as far as we know) almost always male. Hornblower, Simon, 'Introduction', in S. Hornblower (ed), *Greek Historiography* (Oxford, 1994), pp.1–72, at p.34, summarizes some of the exceptions. The first well-known extant example of a history written in Greek or Latin by a woman is the *Alexiad*, which the Byzantine princess Anna Comnena composed in the middle of the twelfth century CE.

3   For more on titulature in ancient texts and its consequences in the special case of Tacitus's *From the Death of the Divine Augustus*, see Oliver, Revilo P., 'The first Medicean MS of Tacitus and the titulature of ancient books', *Transactions and Proceedings of the American Philological Association* 82 (1951), pp.232–61, especially pp.243–8.

4   *The Annals of Imperial Rome – Tacitus, Translated with an Introduction by Michael Grant* (London, 1963).

5   On this point, see Goodyear, Frank R. D. (ed), *The Annals of Tacitus: Vol. 1 (Annals 1. 1–54)* (Cambridge, 1972), pp.85–7.

6   For more on the relationship between manuscripts and the texts which a modern reader uses, see pp.165–78 below.

7   Sallust, *Bellum Catilinae* 4.3.

8   Sallust, *Bellum Catilinae* 24.2.

9   Appian, *Preface* to the *Roman History*, 1.

10 Gibbon, Edward, *The History of the Decline and Fall of the Roman Empire* (J. B. Bury, ed) (London, 1896–1900), Vol. 4, p.211. This phrase is often misquoted as 'the *decent* obscurity ... '. For more on the reception of Procopius's work, see Cameron, Averil, *Procopius and the Sixth Century* (Berkeley, 1985), p.49.

11 Tartt, Donna, *The Secret History* (London, 1993).

12 Xenophon refers to an account of the expedition by 'Themistogenes' in the course of one of his other works (Xenophon *Hellenica* 3.1.2). The Byzantine encyclopaedia called the *Suda* has an entry which suggests Themistogenes was a separate person, but this is widely believed to be just a hypothesis on the basis of earlier references.

13 Plutarch, *Moralia* 345. For more on this question, see Rood, Tim, 'Pan-Hellenism and self-presentation: Xenophon's speeches', in Robin Lane Fox (ed), *The Long March: Xenophon and the Ten Thousand* (New Haven and London, 2004), pp.305–29, at p.322.

14 Arrian, *History of Alexander* 1.12.5. On the effect of Arrian's anonymity here, see Marincola, John, 'Some suggestions on the proem and "second preface" of Arrian's *Anabasis*', *Journal of Hellenic Studies* 109 (1989), pp.186–9, at pp.188, 189.

15 Appian, *Proem* 62.

16 See Moles, John L., 'The interpretation of the "second preface" in Arrian's *Anabasis*', *Journal of Hellenic Studies* 105 (1985), pp.162–8.

17 Taylor, Alan J. P., *The Struggle for Mastery in Europe 1848–1918* (Oxford, 1954), pp.158, 159.

18 Taylor, *Struggle*, p.158, note 4.

19 Taylor, *Struggle*, pp.571, 572.

20 Thucydides 4.70.1.

21 Tacitus, *Annals* 1.8.6–7. For more on this passage, see Pitcher, Luke V., 'The Roman Historians after Livy', in M. Griffin (ed), *A Companion to Julius Caesar* (Oxford, 2009), pp.268–76, at p.268.

22 See Marincola, John, *Greek Historians* (Cambridge, 2001), p.40 with note 90.

23 See Lang, Mabel, 'Participially expressed motivation in Thucydides', *Mnemosyne* 48 (1995), pp.48–65, and Hornblower, Simon, *A Commentary on Thucydides: Vol. 2: Books IV–V.24* (Oxford, 1996), pp.48, 49.

24 For analysis of the circumstances in which ancient historians *do* tend to mention their sources, see Marincola, John, *Authority and Tradition in Ancient Historiography* (Cambridge, 1997), pp.80–6.

25 Kantorowicz, Ernst H., *Kaiser Friedrich der Zweite* (Berlin, 1927). On this controversy, see Grafton, Anthony, *The Footnote: A Curious History* (London, 1997), pp.19–22.

26 Macaulay, Thomas Babington, *The History of England from the Accession of James the Second*, Everyman edition (London, 1906), Vol. 3, pp.602, 603.

27 On such examples of 'counter-factual' reasoning in history, see p.165 below.

28 Macaulay, *History*, Vol. 3, pp.233f.

29 Herodotus, *Preface*.

30 See Pelling, Christopher, 'Epilogue', in C. S. Kraus (ed), *The Limits of Historiography: Genre and Narrative in Ancient Historical Texts* (Leiden, 1999), pp.325–60, at p.326 note 2: 'a work does not change genre if it is subsequently demonstrated to be less accurate than the author wished'.

31 O'Brian, Patrick, *The Ionian Mission*, paperback edition (London, 2003), pp.43, 44.

32 On this point about 'horizons of interpretation', see also Pelling, 'Epilogue', 328f.

33 On the anticipated limits of licence in historical fiction, Sidebottom, Harry, 'Herodian's historical methods and understanding of history', *Aufstieg und Niedergang der römischen Welt* II.34.4 (Berlin and New York, 1998), pp.2775–836, at p.2829 is acute (although O'Brian's surname is there consistently misspelt). For more on the Aubrey-Maturin novels and history, see Roger, Nicholas, 'History as fiction in the novels of Patrick O'Brian', in R. S. O. Tomlin (ed), *History and Fiction: Six Essays celebrating the Centenary of Sir Ronald Syme* (London, 2005), pp.86–99.

34 O'Brian, Patrick, *The Mauritius Command*, paperback edition (London, 2002), p.xiii.

35 Ackroyd, Peter, *The Plato Papers: A Novel* (London, 1999).

36 Ackroyd, *The Plato Papers*, pp.5, 6.

37 Ackroyd, *The Plato Papers*, prefatory material. Compare the first sentence of Thucydides (1.1): 'Thucydides, an Athenian, wrote about the war of the Peloponnesians and the Athenians, how they fought each other, from the very moment it began, thinking that it would be great and more worthy of relation than what had happened before.' In the light of what we have

already noted about the gender of classical historians (above, note 2), it is possibly pointed that Myander turns out to be female.

38 For further details, see Homeyer, Helene, *Lukian: Wie man Geschichte schreiben soll* (Munich, 1965), pp.46, 47.

39 These texts can be consulted in Bowen, Anthony J. (ed), *Plutarch: On the Malice of Herodotus* (Warminster, 1992) [Greek text facing translation; and notes], and Usher, Stephen (ed) *Dionysius of Halicarnassus: Critical Essays*, Vol. 1 (London, 1974), pp.456–633 [Greek text facing translation].

40 For an examination of some of the issues which *On Thucydides* highlights, see pp.127–8 below.

41 Marincola: *Greek Historians*, p.6.

42 A convenient text and translation of this work, with accompanying commentary, can be found in MacLeod, Matthew D. (ed), *Lucian: A Selection* (Warminster, 1991), pp.198–247. As MacLeod notes (283), it is 'the only monograph on the theory of historiography to have survived from classical literature'. On some of the issues concerned with its interpretation, see Greenwood, Emily, *Thucydides and the Shaping of History* (London, 2006), pp.113–17.

43 Aristotle *Poetics* 9, 1451a36–b11. For discussions of this passage, see in particular de Ste. Croix, Geoffrey E. M., 'Aristotle on history and poetry (*Poetics* 9, 1451a36–b11)', in B. Levick (ed), *The Ancient Historian and his Materials: Essays in Honour of C. E. Stevens on his Seventieth Birthday* (London, 1975), pp.45–58; Walbank, Frank W., *Polybius* (Berkeley, Los Angeles and London, 1972), pp.34–40; and Marincola, *Greek Historians*, pp.6, 7, note 18.

44 Wilkins, Augustus S. (ed), *M. Tullii Ciceronis De Oratore Libri Tres – Liber I* (Oxford, 1879), p.6.

45 Cicero, *De Oratore* 2.36.

46 Cicero, *De Oratore* 2.51–4.

47 Cicero, *De Oratore* 2.55–8.

48 Important discussions include: Petzold, Karl-Ernst, 'Cicero und Historie', *Chiron* 2 (1972), pp.253–76; Brunt, Peter A., 'Cicero and historiography', in P. A. Brunt, *Studies in Greek History and Thought* (Oxford, 1993), pp.181–209; Woodman, Anthony J., *Rhetoric in Classical Historiography: Four Studies* (London, 1988), pp.78–101; Fantham, Elaine, *The Roman World of Cicero's De Oratore* (Oxford, 2004), pp.147–52; and Fox, Matthew, *Cicero's Philosophy of History* (Oxford, 2007), pp.134–41.

49 Cicero, *De Oratore* 2.62–3, as translated at Woodman, *Rhetoric*, p.80.

50 Above, pp.7–10.

51 Cicero, *De Oratore* 2.62.

52 Cicero, *Rhetorica ad Herennium* 1.15; translation adapted from Woodman, *Rhetoric* (London and Sydney, 1988), p.85.

53 Compare Cicero, *De Inventione* 1.29, along with the discussion at Woodman, *Rhetoric*, p.85.

54 Russell, Donald A., 'Rhetoric and criticism', *Greece and Rome* 14 (1967), pp.130–44, at p.135.

55 Cicero, *De Inventione* 1.9, 'Inventio est excogitatio rerum verarum aut veri similium, quae causam probabilem reddant'. Woodman, *Rhetoric*, p.87, renders this as 'the *devising* of matter true or lifelike which will make a case appear convincing'. However, 'devising' carries connotations in English of creation or making up which I have preferred to avoid in this context, since the creative element in *inventio* should not be overstated (see above).

56 Cicero, *De Inventione* 1.46, 'Probabile autem est id, quod fere solet fieri aut quod in opinione positum est aut quod habet in se ad haec quandam similitudinem, sive id falsum est sive verum'. Translation from Woodman, *Rhetoric*, p.87.

57 Woodman, *Rhetoric*, p.87.

58 Below, pp.103–9.

59 This refers to the phenomenon that later Roman historians seem to have been able to compose much longer accounts of early Rome than earlier ones, suggesting either an unusual access of new data, wholesale fabrication or expanded scale of treatment. For the view that wholesale fabrication is at issue, see Badian, Ernst, 'The early historians', in T. A. Dorey (ed), *Latin Historians*, pp.1–38, at pp.11–13. For a critique of this view, see Cornell, Tim J., 'The formation of the historical tradition of early Rome', in I. S. Moxon, J. D. Smart and A. J. Woodman (eds), *Past Perspectives: Studies in Greek and Roman Historical Writing* (Cambridge, 1986), pp.67–86.

60 Cicero, *De Oratore* 2.62, 'Nam quis nescit primam esse historiae legem, ne quid falsi dicere audeat? Deinde ne quid veri non audeat? Ne quae suspicio gratiae sit in scribendo? Ne quae simultatis?' Translation from Woodman, *Rhetoric*, p.80. On the subject of what exactly 'bias' might have meant to ancient historians, Luce, Torrey J., 'Ancient views on the causes of bias in historical writing', *Classical Philology* 84/1 (1989) pp.16–31, is illuminating.

61 Woodman; *Rhetoric*, 87.

62 Tacitus, *Annals* 1.1. Compare also Sallust, *Bellum Catilinae* (translated by S. A. Handford): 'a task for which I felt myself the better qualified inasmuch as I was unprejudiced by the hopes and fears of the party man'. Lucian, *How History Ought To Be Written*, also repeatedly notes the perils of partiality to proper history; see Marincola, *Authority and Tradition*, p.160.

63 So, for example, the discussion at Woodman, *Rhetoric*, p.87, moves from the proposition 'Antonius' first pair of rhetorical questions, dealing with *falsum* and *verum*, are *explained* [my italics] by his second pair, which deal with *gratia* and *simultas*', to the claim 'Thus Cicero here sees truth *only* [my italics] in terms of impartiality'.

64 Cicero, *Letters to his Friends* 5.12. For interpretations of this text and examinations of its relationship to the passage in *De Oratore*, see Shackleton Bailey, David R. (ed), *Cicero: Epistulae ad Familiares*, Vol. 1, (Cambridge, 1977), ad. loc.; Woodman, *Rhetoric*, pp.70–7; and Fox, *Cicero's Philosophy of History*, pp.256–63.

65 Lucian, *How History Ought To Be Written* 24 (translated by M. D. MacLeod). As noted at MacLeod *Lucian*, p.295, the two Macedonian colonies in Syria called Europus were actually on the non-Mesopotamian bank of the Euphrates, as was Samosata.

66 Velleius Paterculus 1.7.

67 Dionysius of Halicarnassus, *Roman Antiquities* 4.7, with Forsythe, Gary, *The Historian L. Calpurnius Piso Frugi and the Roman Annalistic Tradition* (Lanham, New York and London, 1994), pp.227–30. Timaeus of Tauromenium (on whom more below) seems to have criticized the earlier historian Ephorus for muddling the regnal dates of the elder Dionysius (Polybius 12.4a.3).

68 Plutarch complains (in his *Life of Solon* 27.1) that 'some scholars fancy that they have disproved on chronological grounds' the idea that the Athenian lawgiver met the Lydian king Croesus, as described by Herodotus. For analysis of this passage and the truth-claims of ancient biography, see Pelling, Christopher, 'Truth and fiction in Plutarch's lives', in Christopher Pelling, *Plutarch and History: Eighteen Studies* (London, 2002), pp.143–70, at pp.143, 144.

69 Polybius 12.7.6. For other nuanced discussions of different sorts of untruth in antiquity, see Wiseman, Timothy P., 'Lying historians: Seven types of mendacity', in C. Gill and T. P. Wiseman (eds), *Lies and Fiction in the Ancient World* (Austin, 1993), pp.122–46, p.127.

70 For studies of the factors which determine Polybius's relations with his predecessors, see Walbank, *Polybius*; and Schepens, Guido and Bollansée, Jan (eds), *The Shadow of Polybius: Intertextuality as a Research Tool in Greek Historiography* (Leiden, 2004).

71 Woodman: *Rhetoric*, pp.87, 88.

72 Compare. Moles, John L., 'Truth and untruth in Herodotus and Thucydides', in C. Gill and T. P. Wiseman (eds), *Lies and Fiction in the Ancient World* (Austin, 1993), pp.88–121, at p.118, on the theory of 'truth as impartiality': 'the theory does not actually engage with ... the many passages where truth is seen not in terms of prejudice but of solid historical criteria such as eye-witness testimony or its absence, paucity or excess of evidence, conflict of sources, carelessness, chronological inaccuracy, dramatic exaggeration and so on'.

73 For more on the phenomenon of 'universal history', see pp.115–6 below.

74 Diodorus 1.4.1.

75 See Stylianou, P. J., *A Historical Commentary on Diodorus Siculus Book 15* (Oxford, 1998), p.21 with note 55.

76 Diodorus 2.3.2.

77 Diodorus 73.23.5. For such claims, see also Marincola, *Authority and Tradition*, pp.151, 152.

78 Polybius 12.25.d. For more on Polybius and his criticism of Timaeus, see pp.105–6 below.

79 Polybius 12.4.3.

80 Polybius 12.25e.

81 On the perils of working back from ancient historiographical treatises to ancient historiographical practice, see also Marincola, *Authority and Tradition*, p.2.

82 Below, pp.124–5.

Chapter 2

1 Compare Pelling, Christopher, 'Epilogue', in C. S. Kraus (ed), *The Limits of Historiography: Genre and Narrative in Ancient Historical Texts* (Leiden, 1999), pp.325–60, at p.328.

2 For a nicely judicious awareness of the need to define one's terms carefully when comparing earlier and modern historiography, see Collinson, Patrick,

'One of us? William Camden and the making of history', *Transactions of the Royal Historical Society* Sixth Series, 8 (1998), pp.139–63, at p.141. See also Wiseman, Timothy P., 'Lying historians: Seven types of mendacity', in C. Gill and T. P. Wiseman (eds), *Lies and Fiction in the Ancient World* (Austin, 1993), pp.122–46, p.125.

3 Chapter 1, pp.6–8.

4 Grafton, Anthony, *The Footnote: A Curious History* (London, 1997), p.34. Grafton slyly points up the more complicated character of the history of historiography by introducing this tongue-in-cheek claim with an adapted mannerism of the rather different historian Macaulay, on whom see pp.9–10 above. For a more obvious use of this trick, compare Browning, Andrew, 'Lord Macaulay, 1800–59', *Historical Journal* 2 (1959), pp.149–60, at p.150.

5 Grafton, *The Footnote*, p.44, translating von Ranke, Leopold, *Geschichten der romanischen und germanischen Völker von 1494 bis 1514, Zur Kritik neuerer Geschichtschreiber* (Leipzig and Berlin, 1824), p.v.

6 A comprehensive treatment of debates on historiographical theory in the modern age is beyond the scope of the present work. However, representative works include: Butterfield, Herbert, *The Whig Interpretation of History* (London, 1931); Collingwood, Robin G., *The Idea of History* (Oxford, 1946); Bloch, Marc, *The Historian's Craft* (Manchester, 1954); Carr, Edward H., *What is History?* (Basingstoke, 1961); Elton, Geoffrey R., *The Practice of History* (Sydney, 1967); White, Hayden, *Metahistory: The Historical Imagination in Nineteenth-Century Europe* (Baltimore, 1973); Momigliano, Arnaldo D., 'The rhetoric of history and the history of rhetoric: On Hayden White's tropes', in A. D. Momigliano, *Settimo contributo alla storia degli studi classici e del mondo antico* (Roma, 1984) pp.49–59; and Evans, Richard J., *In Defence of History* (London, 1997).

7 Chapter 1, pp.11–13.

8 Smalley, Beryl, *The Study of the Bible in the Middle Ages* (Oxford, 1941).

9 Namier, Lewis, *The Structure of Politics at the Accession of George III* (London, 1957).

10 Braudel, Fernand, *The Mediterranean and the Mediterranean World in the Age of Philip II (La Méditerrannée et le Monde Méditerrannéen à l'époque de Philippe II)*, second edition, two volumes (London and New York, 1966, 1973). On Braudel and his contemporaries, see Burke, Peter, *The French Historical Revolution: The 'Annales' School, 1929–89* (Stanford, 1990).

11 Sellar, Walter C. and Yeatman, Robert J., *1066 and all that: A Memorable History of England: Comprising, all the Parts You Can Remember Including One Hundred and Three Good Things, Five Bad Kings, and Two Genuine Dates* (London, 1930); Pile, Stephen, *The Book of Heroic Failures: Official Handbook of the Not Terribly Good Club of Great Britain* (London, 1979). See pp.141–2 below.

12 Langlois, Charles and Seignobos, Charles, *Introduction to the Study of History (Introduction aux Études Historiques)*, translated by G. G. Berry (London, 1898).

13 Chapter 1, pp.13–14.

14 Langlois and Seignobos, *Introduction*, p.319 (my italics).

15 Langlois and Seignobos, *Introduction*, pp.46–7, note 1.

16 Langlois and Seignobos, *Introduction*, p.316.

17 Chapter 1, pp.19–21.

18 (Of Herodotus) 'The secrets of his workshop are not yet all out' (Arnaldo D. Momigliano, quoted at Carolyn Dewald and John Marincola (eds), *The Cambridge Companion to Herodotus* (Cambridge, 2006), p.xiii).

19 Chapter 1, pp.5–14.

20 A point well made by Hornblower, Simon, *A Commentary on Thucydides – Vol. I: Books I–III* (Oxford, c.1991), p.59, which also points up the interesting contrast we have already seen: 'Methodological prefaces of any kind, discussing how one has arrived at the truth, are rare in the historians of antiquity (the opening of Arrian's *Anabasis* is an exception for which he too rarely gets credit); though writers of oratorical or other *treatises* (Cicero, Lucian) talk about the "laws of history" etc.' For the pronouncements of Thucydides and Arrian, see pp.107–8 and 73–5, respectively, below.

21 On the prestige of the single source, see pp.23–4 and, in a different context, pp.124–5.

22 For an example in the field of classical scholarship, witness Nigel Wilson's unpicking of the claims made for the evidential basis of the Oxford Classical Text of Homer (Wilson, N. G., 'Thomas William Allen, 1862–1950', *Proceedings of the British Academy* 76 (1990), pp.311–19).

23 See below, pp.71–2.

24 For a nuanced treatment of a possible case, see Trevor-Roper, Hugh, *A Hidden Life: The Enigma of Sir Edmund Backhouse* (London, 1976), pp.274, 275, examining Backhouse's claims in his memoirs to have had sexual intercourse with Lord Rosebery (who was Prime Minister at the time). Note

too the case of Goodwin Wharton, who combined the typical public life of a seventeenth-century Whig grandee with a memoir in which he recorded his fathering of 106 children by the same woman and marriage to the queen of a fairy kingdom (Clark, J. Kent, *Goodwin Wharton*, Oxford, 1984).

25 *FGrHist* 90 F 96, with Yarrow, Liv, *Historiography at the End of the Republic: Provincial Perspectives on Roman Rule* (Oxford, 2005), p.80. On deliberate mendacity in the ancient historians, see also Moles, John L., 'Truth and untruth in Herodotus and Thucydides', in C. Gill and T. P. Wiseman (eds), *Lies and Fiction in the Ancient World* (Austin, 1993), pp.88–121, at p.115; and Wiseman, 'Lying historians', p.141.

26 For a deft analysis of this work and how it fits into discussions of veracity in antiquity, see Wiseman, 'Lying historians', pp.124–5.

27 *Historia Augusta: Quadrigae Tyrannorum* 2.1.

28 *Historia Augusta: Vita Hadriani*. On this document, see Syme, Ronald, *Ammianus and the Historia Augusta* (Oxford, 1968), pp.60–5; and Schmid, Wolfgang, *Historia-Augusta-Colloquium 1964/5* (Bonn, 1966), pp.153ff.

29 For a modern parallel to this detailed documentation of imaginary sources, compare Trevor-Roper, *A Hidden Life*, p.269.

30 On the excessive paranoia which the *Historia Augusta*'s citation habits can instil in analysing the historiography of the Roman Empire, see also the remarks at Sidebottom, Harry, 'Herodian's historical methods and understanding of history', *Aufstieg und Niedergang der römischen Welt* II.34.4 (Berlin and New York, 1998), pp.2775–836, p.2786.

31 Lloyd-Jones, Hugh, 'Wagner' in Hugh Lloyd-Jones, *Blood for the Ghosts: Classical Influences in the Nineteenth and Twentieth Centuries* (London, 1982), pp.126–42, at p.137, paraphrasing Wagner, Richard, *Die Kunst und die Revolution* (Leipzig, 1849).

32 This was never written, despite the urgings of Grotius's friend De Thou. See Worden, Blair, 'Hugh Redwald Trevor-Roper 1914–2003', *Proceedings of the British Academy* 150 (2007), pp.247–84, at pp.283–4.

33 On this undertaking, see Trevor-Roper, Hugh, 'Gibbon's last project' in David Womersley (ed), *Edward Gibbon: Bicentenary Essays, Studies on Voltaire and the Eighteenth Century* 355 (Oxford, 1997), pp.405–19.

34 For Lord Acton's 'History of liberty', see Watson, George, *Lord Acton's History of Liberty: A Study of his Library with an Edited Text of his History of Liberty Notes* (Aldershot, 1994). All that was actually produced was a pair of published lectures. For Momigliano's projected *Liberty and Peace in the*

Ancient World, see Brown, Peter, 'Arnaldo Dante Momigliano 1908–1987', *Proceedings of the British Academy* 74 (1988), pp.405–42, at p.416; and Murray, Oswyn, 'Arnaldo Momigliano in England', *History and Theory*, 30/4, Beiheft 30, *The Presence of the Historian: Essays in Memory of Arnaldo Momigliano* (December, 1991), pp.49–64, at p.53.

35 'In the last 30 years of his life Butterfield never wrote another monograph. Many enterprises were left unfinished, especially his projected history of diplomacy, the longer study on Acton, and the biography of Temperley' (Simms, Brendan, 'Butterfield, Sir Herbert (1900–1979)', *Oxford Dictionary of National Biography* (Oxford, 2004) http://www.oxforddnb.com/view/article/30888, accessed 16 July 2008).

36 This was projected as an opus of 300,000 words but eventually produced three essays and unpublished material instead. See Worden: *Trevor-Roper*, pp.264, 265. Worden also notes Trevor-Roper's other unfinished or unattempted works, which included books on the Duke of Marlborough and the France of Louis XIV, along with *A History of the English Ruling Classes*.

37 Gomme, Arnold W., *A Historical Commentary on Thucydides – Volume I: Introduction and Commentary on Book I* (Oxford 1945), p.v; Walbank, Frank W., *Historical Commentary on Polybius – Volume II: Commentary on Books VII–XVIII* (Oxford, 1967), p.v; Hornblower, Simon, Preface to the 1997 paperback edition of *A Commentary on Thucydides – Vol. I: Books I–III* (Oxford, *c*.1991), p.v.

38 Compare Carr, Edward H., *A History of Soviet Russia 12: Foundation of a Planned Economy 1926–1929* (London, 1976), Vol. 3, Part 1, p.vii.

39 On Baronio, also known by the Latinized form of his name, Baronius, see Pullapilly, Cyriac K., *Caesar Baronius: Counter-reformation Historian* (Notre Dame, 1975). Baronio's own account of the genesis of his work can be found in the *Annales Ecclesiastici* under AD 57, § 162. In light of what we have already seen about the play with anonymity in the works of the ancient historians (Chapter 1, p.5 above), it is interesting that this account omits Baronio's own name.

40 Diodorus 1.3.2–3.

41 Polybius 3.5.7.

42 Herodotus 9.122. For Herodotus as a completed text, see in particular Dewald, Carolyn, 'Pickled heroes, wanton kings, and gnomic founding fathers: Reading the end of Herodotus' histories', in D. H. Roberts, F. M. Dunn and D. Fowler (eds), *Classical Closure: Reading the End in Greek and*

Latin Literature (Princeton, 1997), pp.62–82. For an (unconvincing) attempt to demonstrate that the text is unfinished, see Asheri, David, Lloyd, Alan B. and Corcella, Aldo, *A Commentary on Herodotus I-IV* (Oxford, 2007), pp.11, 12.

43 Thucydides 8.109.1. For discussion, see Gomme, Arnold W., Andrewes, Antony and Dover, Kenneth J., *A Historical Commentary on Thucydides – Vol. V: Book VIII* (Oxford, 1981), p.358, with their Appendix 1 'Indications of incompleteness', pp.361–83.

44 Konishi, Haruo, 'Thucydides' history as a finished piece', *Liverpool Classical Monthly* 12 (1987), pp.5–7 (not, however, very convincing).

45 Based on the description of it as 'histories from the beginning of the civil wars, when truth first disappeared, down almost to the day of his own death', in the extant fragments of the biography of Seneca written by his son (Seneca, fr. 99 Haase). For further discussion, see Griffin, Miriam, 'The Elder Seneca and Spain', *Journal of Roman Studies* 62 (1972), pp.1–19, at pp.9–11.

46 Tacitus, *Histories* 1.1 (translated by W. H. Fyfe).

47 For such an interpretation of the third-century CE historian Herodian, see Sidebottom, 'Herodian's historical methods', p.2813, note 183. Compare Hidber, Thomas, 'Zeit und Erzählperspektive in Herodians Geschichtswerk', in M. Zimmerman (ed), *Geschichtsschreibung und politischer Wandel im 3. Jh. N. Chr.* (Stuttgart, 1999), pp.145–67.

48 See Gomme, Andrewes and Dover, *Thucydides Book VIII*, Appendix 2, 'Strata of composition'. For issues relating to this strategy, and further bibliography, see Marincola, John, *Greek Historians* (Cambridge, 2001), p.69.

49 Polybius 1.1.5 (translated by W. R. Paton).

50 Polybius 3.4.4–6; again (translated by W. R. Paton).

51 p.185 n37.

52 For reflections on Thucydides's situation here, see Gomme, Andrewes and Dover, *Thucydides Book VIII*, p.384. For more general remarks on the issues where events may 'unwind' with the production of the text, see Henderson, John, 'Livy and the invention of history', in John Henderson, *Fighting for Rome: Poets and Caesars, History and Civil War* (Cambridge, 1998), pp.301–19.

53 Above, p.32. As Henderson, 'Livy', p.303, puts it: 'Books that mean to be gargantuan must calculate their chances of coming to fruition.'

54 Gibbon, Edward, *The Miscellaneous Works of Edward Gibbon, Esq: With Memoirs of His Life and Writings*, John Holroyd Sheffield (ed) (Dublin, 1796), p.107.

Notes

55 Carr, Edward H., *A History of Soviet Russia 14: Foundation of a Planned Economy 1926–1929* (London, 1978), Vol. 3, Part 1, p.viii.

56 Livy 31.1.5. It is notable that Edward Gibbon quoted this passage as the epigraph on the title page of Vol. I of his own similarly monumental *History of the Decline and Fall of the Roman Empire*. See Kelly, Christopher, 'A grand tour: Reading Gibbon's "Decline and Fall" ', *Greece and Rome* 44 (1997), pp.39–58, at pp.48–9.

57 Below, pp.38–9.

58 Most familiar now, perhaps, from the title of White, *Metahistory*, but actually older in this sense. The forthcoming volume on meta-poetics by Ingo Gildenhard and Andrew Zissos promises a cultural history of this prefix in modern times.

59 p.26.

60 Grafton, *The Footnote*, p.44, translating von Ranke, *Geschichten*, p.36.

61 Lucian, *How History Ought to be Written* 2 (translated by K. Kilburn).

62 On polemic as a means of self-definition in ancient historiography, see also Marincola, John, *Authority and Tradition in Ancient Historiography* (Cambridge, 1997), pp.218–36.

63 Walbank, Frank W., 'The two-way shadow: Polybius among the fragments', in G. Schepens and J. Bollansée (eds), *The Shadow of Polybius: Intertextuality as a Research Tool in Greek Historiography – Proceedings of the International Colloquium Leuven, 21–2 September 2001* (Leiden, 2004), pp.1–18, at pp.3–6; and Luce, Torrey J., 'Ancient Views on the Causes of Bias in Historical Writing', *Classical Philology* 84/1 (1989) pp.16–31, at pp.23–5, give useful discussions of cases where Greek historians criticize their predecessors.

64 Polybius 12.7.5 (translated by W. R. Paton).

65 On Polybius and Phylarchus see, besides the works quoted in note 67 below, Schepens, Guido, 'Polybius' criticism of Phylarchus', and Haegemans, Karen and Kosmetatou, Elizabeth, 'Aratus and the Achaean background of Polybius', both in G. Schepens and, J. Bollansée (eds), *The Shadow of Polybius: Intertextuality as a Research Tool in Greek Historiography – Proceedings of the International Colloquium Leuven, 21–2 September 2001* (Leiden, 2004), pp.123–39 and pp.141–64, respectively. As I noted in my review of the volume (http://ccat.sas.upenn.edu/bmcr/2007/2007-08-62.html, accessed on 02.11.08), some of their claims about allusion in Polybius are a trifle suspect, however.

66 Polybius 33.1.5.

67 Extensive general analyses of Polybius's possible motivations in criticizing other historians may be found in Walbank, Frank W., 'Polemic in Polybius', *Journal of Roman Studies* 52 (1962), pp.1–12 (Walbank, F. W., *Selected Papers: Studies in Greek and Roman History and Historiography* (Cambridge, 1985), pp.262–79) and Walbank: 'The two-way shadow', at pp.12–18.

68 Above, p.32.

69 Polybius 3.4.7. Compare, for example, Walbank: 'The two-way shadow', at p.3: 'I am now inclined to think that methodological reasons and moral judgements weighed more strongly in Polybius' discourse than I once believed to be the case.'

70 Tacitus, *Histories* 1.1 (translated by W. H. Fyfe).

71 Tacitus, *Annals* 1.1.

72 For further discussion of the discrepancy, see Chilver, Guy E. F., *A Historical Commentary on Tacitus' Histories I and II* (Oxford, 1979), pp.33–5.

73 Tacitus, *Histories* 1.1 (translated by W. H. Fyfe).

74 The question of which historians are supposed to be on which list has exercised scholars considerably. As Goodyear, *The Annals of Tacitus*, p.95 observes, Livy, Pollio, Cremutius Cordus, the elder Seneca, T. Labienus, Aufidius Bassus and Velleius Paterculus have all been suggested as *decora ingenia*. See also Weber, Wilhelm, *Princeps: Studien zur Geschichte des Augustus* (Stuttgart, 1936), p.2.

75 Cassius Dio 43.25.1 (translated by E. Cary). For further treatment of this, see Pitcher, Luke V., 'The Roman historians after Livy', in Miriam Griffin (ed), *A Companion to Julius Caesar* (Oxford, 2009), pp.268–76, at p.270.

76 Syme, Ronald, *Tacitus* (Oxford, 1958), Preface; Syme, Ronald, *The Augustan Aristocracy* (Oxford, 1986), p.v. On claims of effort and toil in the classical historiographers, see also Marincola, *Authority and Tradition*, pp.148–58. Outside classical historiography, cf. Carr, Edward H., *A History of Soviet Russia 14: Foundations of a Planned Economy 1926–1929* (London, 1978), Vol. 3, Part 3, p.viii: 'Had I realized at that time the formidable dimensions of the task, I might not have been rash enough to undertake it.'

77 Homer, *Iliad* 2.485–93. On the relevance of the 'inability of the epic narrator to remember — or even to get to know — all he needs to tell' to ancient historiography, see Kraus, Christina S., 'Caesar's account of the Battle of Massilia (*BC* 1.34–2.22): Some historiographical and narratological

approaches', in John Marincola (ed), *A Companion to Greek and Roman Historiography* (Malden, MA and Oxford, 2007), pp.371–8, at p.373.

78 Livy *Proem* 4 (translated by B. O. Foster).

79 This work is sometimes called the *History of the Empire after Marcus*. However, Whittaker, C. Richard (ed), *Herodian I: Books I–IV* (Cambridge, 1969), p.2 note 1, notes that 'the title is variously recorded in the MSS ... but it is uncertain whether any of the titles are authentic'. For issues relating to the titulature of ancient historiography, see Chapter 1 pp.2–5.

80 Herodian 1.1–3 (translated by C. R. Whittaker).

81 Thucydides 1.22.4: On the phrase in its original context, see Flory, Stewart, 'The meaning of *to mē muthōdes* (1.22.4) and the usefulness of Thucydides' *History*', *Classical Journal* 85 (1990), pp.193–208.

82 For example, the defence of his practices of revision in the Addendum to the Preface of Syme: *The Augustan Aristocracy* ('Of what avail is this tardy knowledge? Where error is irretrievable, repentance is useless!'), is a quotation from Edward Gibbon's annotated revisions in the first volume of his *History of the Decline and Fall of the Roman Empire*. On these annotations, see also Jackson, H. J., *Marginalia: Readers Writing in Books* (New Haven and London, 2001), pp.98–9. Syme also took Gibbon's *A Vindication of Some Passages in the Fifteenth and Sixteenth Chapters of The History of the Decline and Fall of the Roman Empire* (London, 1779), as the formal model for Syme, Ronald, *The Historia Augusta: A Call of Clarity* (Bonn, 1971).

83 Whittaker, *Herodian*, p.3 note 2, observes that 'the whole of this critique of contemporary historiography has a strongly conventional flavour' and notes the Thucydidean parallel.

84 Thucydides 1.22.2. On Thucydides and *akribeia*, see also Hornblower, Simon, *Thucydides* (London,1987), p.37.

85 Herodian 1.1.4: 'there have never been such earthquakes and plagues ...' Compare Thucydides 1.23.2–3.

86 Polybius 7.7.1 (translated by W. R. Paton). Compare Thucydides 1.21.2, and see Walbank, F. W., *Polybius* (Berkeley, Los Angeles and London, 1972), p.41.

87 Polybius 29.12.10.

88 This instance is taken from Rhodes, Peter J., 'In defence of the Greek Historians', *Greece and Rome* 41 (1994), pp.156–71, at p.156 and pp.157, 158. As Rhodes puts it (p.158): 'The fact that a passage is a *topos*, that it says what is conventionally said in a particular situation, and perhaps expresses

it in a conventional way, does not exclude the possibility that it is an authentic report, or that what is stated is true.'

89 For Herodian's failings in this regard, see Whittaker, *Herodian*, xxxix–xliii.

90 See Whittaker, *Herodian*, xlv–liii; and Sidebottom, 'Herodian's historical methods', p.2813.

91 Even Polybius conceded that historiography could also give pleasure: see Walbank, Frank W., 'Profit or amusement: Some thoughts on the motives of Hellenistic historians', in H. Verdin, G. Schepens and E. deKeyser (eds), *Purposes of History: Studies in Greek Historiography from the 4th to the 2nd Centuries BC* (Leuven, 1990), pp.253–66.

92 For the complex relationship between Herodian's preface and the subsequent text, see also Sidebottom, 'Herodian's historical methods', pp.2778–80.

93 Herodian 1.6.1, 1.6.2 (translated by C. R. Whittaker). See also Pitcher, Luke V., 'Herodian' in I. de Jong (ed). *Space in Ancient Greek Literature* (forthcoming).

94 Herodian 1.15.2 (translated by C. R. Whittaker).

95 Herodian 1.15.8 (translated by C. R. Whittaker).

96 Herodian 1.3.1 (translated by C. R. Whittaker).

97 Herodian 1.3.2–4. Sidebottom, 'Herodian's historical methods', pp.2805, 2806 notes Marcus's insistence on the understanding of history here.

98 For further examples and discussion of such individual, see Krebs, Christopher and Grethlein, Jonas, 'Introduction', in C. Krebs and J. Grethlein (eds), *The Historian's Plupast* (in press).

99 Livy 21.38.3–5.

Chapter 3

1 von Ranke, Leopold, 'Deutsche Geschichte im Zeitalter der Reformation', in P. Joachimsen et al. (eds), Vol. 1 (Munich, 1925–6), p.6. Translation from Grafton, Anthony, *The Footnote: A Curious History* (London, 1997), p.51.

2 Chapter 2, pp.26–7.

3 Chapter 1, pp.5–14.

4 Chapter 2, pp.37–8.

5 Chapter 1, p.22.

6 Polybius 12.4c4–5 (translated by W. R. Paton).

Notes

7   Polybius 12.25e (translated by W. R. Paton).

8   Polybius 12.11.2 (translated by W. R. Paton).

9   Polybius 3.33.17–18, 56.1–4, with Walbank, Frank W., *Polybius* (Berkeley, Los Angeles and London, 1972), p.82.

10 Herodotus 1.51. Rhodes, Peter J., 'Documents and the Greek historians', in John Marincola (ed), *A Companion to Greek and Roman Historiography* (Malden, MA, and Oxford, 2007), pp.56–66, at p.57, notes that this passage shows Herodotus's awareness of the possibility of forgery.

11 Velleius Paterculus 2.25.4.

12 Velleius Paterculus 2.61.3. For the usage of such material in Velleius, see Gowing, Alain M., *Empire and Memory: The Representation of the Roman Republic in Imperial Culture* (Cambridge, 2005), p.42; and Pitcher, Luke V., 'The stones of blood: Family, monumentality, and memory in Velleius's second century', in E. Cowan (ed), *Velleius Paterculus* (Swansea, in press).

13 'Charters and Grants of Kings and Great Personages, Letters, Consultations in the Council-Chamber, Embassadours Instructions and Epistles, I carefully turned over and over ... ' (MacCaffrey, Wallace T. (ed), *William Camden: The History of the Most Renowned and Victorious Princess Elizabeth Late Queen of England: Selected Chapters* (Chicago and London, 1970), p.3). For the qualities of this research, see Collinson, Patrick, 'One of us? William Camden and the making of history', *Transactions of the Royal Historical Society*, Sixth Series, 8 (1998), pp.139–63, at pp.157f.

14 Tucci, Ugo, 'Ranke and the Venetian document market', in G. G. Iggers and J. Powell (eds), *Leopold von Ranke and the Shaping of the Historical Discipline* (Syracuse, 1990), pp.99–107.

15 Haslam, Jonathan, 'Carr, Edward Hallett (1892–1982)', *Oxford Dictionary of National Biography* (Oxford, September 2004), online edn [http://www.oxforddnb.com/view/article/30902, accessed 30 July 2008].

16 Compare, e.g., the picture of the great Tudor historian Sir Geoffrey Elton in Collinson, Patrick, 'Elton, Sir Geoffrey Rudolph (1921–94)', *Oxford Dictionary of National Biography*, (Oxford, 2004) [http://www.oxforddnb.com/view/article/54946, accessed 30 July 2008]: 'Elton went behind *Letters and Papers* to the original documents in the Public Record Office, where he worked steadily, almost every day, for a couple of years, for a daily five hours, before emerging to travel up to Lord's [cricket ground].' The cultural history of the relationship between modern historiography

and cricket remains to be written: compare Murray, Oswyn, 'Arnaldo Momigliano in England', *History and Theory*, 30/4 (1991), Beiheft 30: *The Presence of the Historian: Essays in Memory of Arnaldo Momigliano* (December, 1991), pp.49–64, at p.50.

17 Chapter 1, pp.6–8.

18 Taylor, Alan J. P., *The Struggle for Mastery in Europe 1848–1918* (Oxford, 1954), p.569.

19 Grafton, *The Footnote*, p.50.

20 Compare Arnaldo Momigliano, ap. Murray: 'Arnaldo Momigliano in England', p.49, note 2, on the difficulties of using Moscow libraries in the middle of the twentieth century.

21 For a study of Roman Egypt utilizing its still extant documentary riches, see Capponi, Livia, *Augustan Egypt: The Creation of a Roman Province* (New York, 2005).

22 For the ramifications of fluctuation in the supply of writing materials, see Reynolds, Leighton D. and Wilson, Nigel G., *Scribes and Scholars: A Guide to the Transmission of Greek and Latin Literature*, 3rd edn (Oxford, 1991), p.3.

23 Polybius 16.15.8.

24 See the discussion at Walbank, *Polybius*, p.83. Polybius did, however, claim to have access to a letter from Scipio Africanus to Philip V (Polybius 10.9.3) and also to one from Scipio Nasica to an unnamed Hellenistic monarch (Polybius 29.14.3).

25 Marincola, John, *Authority and Tradition in Ancient Historiography* (Cambridge, 1997), p.103, notes the rarity of claims to the use of archives in classical historiography. On archives in general, see Brosius, Maria (ed) *Ancient Archives and Archival Traditions: Concepts of Record-Keeping in the Ancient World* (Oxford, 2003).

26 Culham, Phyllis, 'Archives and alternatives in Republican Rome', *Classical Philology* 84 (1989), pp.100–15, and Purcell, Nicholas, 'Atrium Libertatis', in *Proceedings of the British School at Rome 61* (1993), pp.125–55, at pp.135–42, take a minimalist view. For a contrast, see Rhodes, Peter J., 'Public documents in the Greek states: Archives and inscriptions, Part II', in *Greece and Rome*, Second Series, 48/2 (October, 2001), pp.136–53, at pp.147, 148.

27 Chapter 1, pp.15–16.

28 Cicero, *De Oratore* 2.51f (translated by J. May and J. Wisse).

29 Cato the Elder, in Peter, H., *Historicum Romanorum Reliquiae* (Stuttgart, 1906–14), F77. For further issues relating to the *Annales Maximi*, see also Cornell, Tim J., 'The formation of the historical tradition of early Rome', in I. S. Moxon, J. D. Smart and A. J. Woodman (eds), *Past Perspectives: Studies in Greek and Roman Historical Writing* (Cambridge, 1986), pp.67–86, at pp.73, 74; and Beck, Hermann, 'The early Roman tradition', in John Marincola (ed), *A Companion to Greek and Roman Historiography* (Malden, MA and Oxford, 2007), pp.259–65, at p.261.

30 The pioneering study here is Rawson, Elizabeth, 'Prodigy lists and the use of the *Annales Maximi*', *Classical Quarterly*, New Series, 21/1 (May 1971), pp.158–69.

31 Cassius Dio 53.19.1–4.

32 It is interesting to compare here the 'fog' which descends on attempts to write Soviet history after the Spring of 1929; see Carr, Edward H. and Davies, Robert W., *A History of Soviet Russia 9: Foundations of a Planned Economy 1926–1929* (London, 1969), Vol. 1, Part 1, p.xii.

33 See below, pp.73–8.

34 Suetonius, *Divus Julius* 20.1.

35 Suetonius, *Augustus* 36.1.

36 See Suetonius, *Tiberius* 73; and Cassius Dio 57.23.2.

37 Tacitus, *Annals* 15.74.3.

38 Suetonius, *Augustus* 5.1, while talking about the attempt of C. Laetorius to mitigate a charge of adultery.

39 Mommsen, Theodor, *Römisches Staatsrecht* (Leipzig, 1887–8), Vol. 3, p.1021, note 1, claims that the passages mentioned in the two preceding notes are the only explicit citations of the *Acta* in classical texts, but this claim ignores their extensive use by the commentator on Cicero, Asconius (Asconius 19C, 31C, 44C, 47C, 49C). See also Lewis, R. Geoffrey, *Asconius: Commentaries on Speeches by Cicero* (Oxford, 2006), p.xvi.

40 See, for example, Syme, Ronald, ''Tacitus: Some sources of his information', *Journal of Roman Studies* 72 (1982), pp.68–82, at pp.73–6 [arguing for extensive use]. Goodyear, Frank R. D., *Tacitus – Greece and Rome New Surveys* (Cambridge, 1970), p.26, is more cautious.

41 Above, pp.51–2. This will have been in ink on a whitewashed board. For Roman practices of this sort, Rhodes: 'Public documents in the Greek states', p.145, is illuminating.

42 As, for example, Rhodes, 'Documents and the Greek historians', p.56: 'For the purposes of this chapter I take a document to be "something written, inscribed, engraved, etc., which provides information or serves as a record, *esp.* an official paper" (*New Shorter Oxford English Dictionary*, I.719b, definition 3).'

43 *FGrHist* 342. Our belief that this collection was at least eight books long is based upon the fact that 'book eight' of it is cited by later authors (FF 5–8). For further discussion, see Rhodes, 'Documents and the Greek historians', p.64.

44 Chapter 2, pp.34–9.

45 For an interesting case, see Beard, Mary, 'Writing and ritual. A study of diversity and expansion in the *Arval Acta*', *Proceedings of the British School at Rome* 53 (1985), pp.114–62.

46 For a discussion of the motivations behind inscriptional activity in the ancient world, see the Introduction to Rhodes, Peter J. and Osborne, Robin (eds), *Greek Historical Inscriptions, 404–323 BC* (Oxford, 2003).

47 The most recent edition of the Tribute Lists is *Inscriptiones Graecae* I³, 259–60, 71, 77, 100. The standard treatment of them remains Meritt, Benjamin D., Wade-Gery, Henry T. and McGregor, Malcolm F., *The Athenian Tribute Lists*, four volumes (1939–53).

48 For travel and the ancient historian, see below, p.64.

49 For more on the *Tabula Bembina* and the texts it preserves, see Crawford, Michael H. (ed), *Roman Statutes*, two volumes, (London, 1996), no. 2; Lintott, Andrew W., *Judicial reform and land reform in the Roman Republic: a new edition, with translation and commentary, of the laws from Urbino* (Cambridge, 1992).

50 Cassius Dio 39.21.1–2.

51 Above, p.49.

52 On this, see Badian, Ernst, *From Plataea to Potidaea: Studies in the History and Historiography of the Pentecontaetia* (Baltimore and London, 1993), Chapter 1, which also gives an introduction to the copious bibliography on this subject.

53 *FGrHist* 115 F 154.

54 Athenaeus 6.234 d.

55 Thucydides 6.54.6–7. For a full discussion, see Rhodes, 'Documents and the Greek historians', p.60.

56 For texts of these inscriptions, the so-called *Tabula Siarensis* and the *Senatus Consultum de Cn. Pisone Patre*, see González, Julian, 'Tabula Siarensis, Fortunales Siarenses, and the Municipia Ciuium Romanorum', *Zeitschrift*

für Papyrologie und Epigraphik 55 (1984), pp.55–100, with the translation at Sherk, Robert K., *The Roman Empire: Augustus to Hadrian* (Cambridge, 1988), no. 36 and Eck, Werner, Caballos, Antonio and Fernández, Fernando, *Das Senatus Consultum de Cn. Pisone Patre* (Munich, 1996). For an analysis of the relationship between these inscriptions and the works of Tacitus, see Kraus, Christina S. and Woodman, Anthony. J., *Latin Historians* (Cambridge, 1997), pp.99–102.

57 On textual problems in the classical historians, see pp.176–8 below.

58 See Chapter 1, pp.13–14.

59 See above, pp.47 and 49.

60 So Walbank, Frank W., 'The two-way shadow: Polybius among the fragments', in. G. Schepens and J. Bollansée (eds), *The Shadow of Polybius: Intertextuality as a Research Tool in Greek Historiography – Proceedings of the International Colloquium Leuven, 21–2 September 2001* (Leiden, 2004), pp.1–18, at p.12.

61 *FGrHist* 566 T 6–8.

62 Chapter 2, p.32.

63 For discussion of Polybius's date of birth, see Walbank, *Polybius*, p.6, note 26.

64 An exception is the first-century CE author Apion (*FGrHist* 616), who asserted that he had called up Homer's ghost, but did not publish the interview (Pliny the Elder *Natural History* 30.6.18). Somewhat more reputably, a vision of the dead Nero Drusus impelled the Elder Pliny to write his histories (Pliny the Younger *Letters* 3.5.4). On this, see Ash, Rhiannon. '"Aliud Est Enim Epistulam, Aliud Historiam ... Scribere"' (Epistles 6.16.22): Pliny the historian?', *Arethusa* 36/2 (2003), pp.211–25, at pp.223, 224.

65 Jacoby, Felix, 'Über die Entwicklung der griechischen Historiographie', *Klio* 9 (1909), pp.80–123. It has never really caught on, because of its rather limited compass and lack of relation to the actual diversity of historical production in the ancient world. Compare Humphreys, Sally C., 'Fragments, fetishes, and philosophies: Towards a history of Greek historiography after Thucydides', in G. W. Most (ed), *Collecting Fragments. Fragmente sammeln* (Göttingen 1997), pp.207–24, at p.208.

66 For Cephalion (*FGrHist* 93), see Photius *Bibliotheca* 34 a 16. See also Bowie, Ewen L., 'The Greeks and their past in the Second Sophistic', in *Past and Present* 46 (1970), pp.3–41, at pp.12, 13.

67 Ammianus's history began with the reign of Nerva in 96–8 CE, and reached its climax with the Battle of Adrianople on 9 August 378. For

more on Ammianus's history and, in particular, his distribution of material, see pp.122–3 below.

68 Bowra, C. Maurice, *Memories 1898–1939* (London, 1966), p.138.

69 Particularly common is the claim that one distinguished individual saw in old age a youth who would himself go on to be distinguished. On this topic, see Pitcher, Luke V., 'Narrative technique in the lives of the Ten Orators', *Classical Quarterly* 55 (2005), pp.217–34, at p.224.

70 In fact, gerontology even produced compilation tribute albums. Notable here is the *Makrobioi* ('Big Lives') attributed to Lucian, which collected famous cases of longevity. Polybius appears in it as a historical notable himself, having allegedly died at the age of 82 after falling off a horse (Pseudo-Lucian *Makrobioi* 23).

71 Syme, Ronald, *The Roman Revolution* (Oxford, 1939), p.1. As Syme explains in a footnote, M. Junius Silanus, the grandson of Augustus's granddaughter Julia, was born in 14 CE, the year of Augustus's death (Pliny the Elder *Natural History* 7.58).

72 'The greatest of the Roman historians began his *Annals* with the accession to the Principate of Tiberius, stepson and son by adoption of Augustus, consort in his powers' (Syme, *Roman Revolution*, p.1). The last words are a direct appropriation of 'filius, collega imperii, consors tribuniciae potestatis' at Tacitus *Annals* 1.3. See also Chapter 2, pp.38–9 above.

73 Tacitus, *Annals* 1.3.

74 In Tacitus's original Latin, the rhetorical question takes the form 'quotus quisque *reliquus* qui rem publicam vidisset?' It is unlikely to be coincidental that the first time the word 'reliquus' ('left') is used of an individual in the *Annals*, it is of Augustus. See further O'Gorman, Ellen, 'On Not Writing About Augustus: Tacitus' Annals Book 1', *MD* 35 (1995), pp.91–114, at pp.104–8.

75 Chapter 1, pp.4–5.

76 Appian, *Pun.* 636–7.

77 On this passage, see further Pitcher, Luke V., 'War stories: The uses of the Plupast in Appian', in C. Krebs and J. Grethlein (eds), *The Historian's Plupast* (in press).

78 Plato, *Laches* (translated by Benjamin Jowett).

79 Compare Shakespeare, *Henry V* 4.3.44–50.

80 Compare Plutarch, *Life of Nicias* 12.1.

81 See Chapter 2, p.45.

Notes

82   Polybius 3.48.12.

83   Polybius 29.8.10.

84   As Pelling, Christopher, *Plutarch: Life of Antony* (Cambridge, 1988), p.196, observes: 'the splendid touch reminds us that the gathering of oral traditions could have its longueurs'.

85   Polybius 12.28 a. 9–10. See the discussion at Walbank: *Polybius*, pp.73, 74. Also useful are the remarks in Schepens, Guido, 'Some aspects of source-theory in Greek historiography', *Ancient Society* 6 (1975), pp.257–74, at 268–72 and Sacks, Kenneth, *Polybius on the Writing of History* (Berkeley, 1981), pp.203–9. For speculations on Polybius's own informants, see Gelzer, Matthias, 'Über die Arbeitsweise des Polybios', in M. Gelzer, *Kleine Schriften*, Vol. 3 (1964), p.173.

86   See Plutarch, *Life of Demetrius* 28–9. For issues relating to the numbers in ancient historiographical texts, see pp.66–7 below.

87   Polybius 3.107f. For discussion, see Lazenby, John, *Hannibal's War: a Military History of the Second Punic War* (Norman, 1998).

88   E.g., Poseidon at Homer *Iliad* 13.10–12. This mountain is in fact visible from the plain of Troy. See Janko, Richard, *The Iliad: A Commentary*, Vol. 4 (Cambridge, 1990–93), on this passage. Lucian, *How History Ought to Be Written*, 49, equates the ideal perspective of the historian with Homer's godly audience.

89   Lucretius, *De Rerum Natura* 2.5–6: 'It is also sweet to watch great contests of war drawn up through the fields at no personal risk.' On this passage, see also Fowler, Don, *Lucretius on Atomic Motion. A Commentary on De Rerum Natura, Book Two, Lines 1–332* (Oxford, 2002) pp.28–32.

90   An interesting exception happened in the career of Scipio Aemilianus, who seems to have commented on a battle in his youth that he had the same perspective on it as Homer's gods, and how much of a contrast that was to the ones he fought later (Appian, *Pun.* 327).

91   Plutarch, *Life of Caesar* 48. Before the ubiquity of television, visionaries and psychics continued to be pressed into service by authors who wanted to organize an overview of a battle through a spectator: compare the Pope in G. K. Chesterton's *Lepanto* and the hermit's mirror in Lewis, C. S., *The Horse and His Boy* (London, 1954).

92   Marincola: *Authority and Tradition*, pp.68, 69, neatly quotes Euripides *Suppliant Women* 846–56 and Thucydides 7.44.1 to illustrate the problems here. In Rhodes, Peter J., 'In Defence of the Greek historians', *Greece and*

Rome 41 (1994), pp.156–71, at p.168, both the examples of uncertainty over the course of events (the battle of Salamis and contemporary conflicts in Iraq) are drawn from military engagements.

93 For an account of this breakdown in communications, see Appian, *Civil Wars* 4.472f.

94 Woodman, Anthony J., *Rhetoric in Classical Historiography: Four Studies* (London and Sydney, 1988), pp.17–19, makes illuminating use of twentieth-century accounts of wars to show how presence at important historical happenings by no means guarantees accuracy of insight.

95 Compare, for example, Strabo 15.1.9 on the conflict of testimony over events in the career of Alexander the Great (on which see also pp.73–5 below).

96 On such issues, the history of 'Fermi problems' is revealing. See now Weinstein, Lawrence and Adam, John A., *Guesstimation: Solving the World's Problems on the Back of a Cocktail Napkin* (Princeton, 2008). Compare also Thucydides 5.68.2, where the historian notes the various factors (including secrecy and boastfulness), which make it hard for him to guarantee numbers at the Battle of Mantinea.

97 On autopsy in the ancient historians, see in particular Schepens, Guido, *L' 'Autopsie' dans la Méthode des Historiens Grecs du V Siècle Avant J.-C.* (Brussels, 1980).

98 For an accessible introduction to this work, see Lane Fox, Robin, 'Introduction', in Robin Lane Fox (ed), *The Long March: Xenophon and the Ten Thousand* (New Haven and London, 2004), pp.1–46.

99 Above, Introduction.

100 Thucydides 4.104.4f.

101 Thucydides 5.26.5.

102 Thucydides 2.48.3.

103 Polybius 38.21.1–22. On this famous moment, see Astin, Alan E., *Scipio Aemilianus* (Oxford, 1967), pp.282–7.

104 Cassius Dio 80.1–5.

105 For an analysis of these exploits, see Marincola: *Authority and Tradition*, pp.201–4.

106 Polybius claims to have crossed the Alps to follow in the footsteps of Hannibal at Polybius 3.48.12.

107 So Fehling, Detlev, *Herodotus and His 'Sources': Citation, Invention and Narrative Art* (Leeds, 1989), p.243.

Notes

108 Langlois, Charles and Seignobos, Charles, *Introduction to the Study of History (Introduction aux Études Historiques)*, translated by G. G. Berry (London, 1898), p.125 with p.126 on 'Froude's disease' (i.e., chronic inaccuracy). An irony is that this criticism is itself inaccurate.

109 Fowler, Robert, 'Herodotos and his contemporaries', *Journal of Hellenic Studies* 116 (1996), pp.62–87, at p.81 note 125, produces a nice example from personal experience: 'Fehling makes little allowance for the distortions of memory ... I recently revisited Kenilworth and was amazed to discover that someone had put up two 400-year-old buildings in my absence.'

110 Above, pp.50–4.

111 Cicero *Brutus* 62.

112 Livy 8.40.2.

113 See Degrassi, Attilio, *Inscriptiones Latinae liberae rei publicae* (Firenze, 1963), no. 309–10. For further treatment of such familial records, see Wiseman, Timothy P., 'The prehistory of Roman historiography', in John Marincola (ed), *A Companion to Greek and Roman Historiography* (Malden MA and Oxford, 2007), pp.67–75, at pp.71–3.

114 Herodotus 2.23.

115 Thucydides 1.10.3. Compare also 1.3.3. For Thucydides' attitude and argumentation here, see Howie, James G., 'Thukydides' Einstellung zur Vergangenheit: Zuhörerschaft und Wissenschaft in der Archäologie', *Klio* 66 (1984), 502-32.

116 Appian, *Civil Wars* 5.483. Compare Homer, *Odyssey* 12.260f. Hornblower, Simon, 'Introduction', in S. Hornblower (ed), *Greek Historiography* (Oxford, 1994), pp.1–72, at p.65, sees such expressions as implying 'a rather modern and academic study of Homer', but this means of talking about particular episodes in Homer's epics was common in antiquity. See Taplin, Oliver, *Homeric Soundings: the Shaping of the Iliad* (Oxford, 1992), p.286.

117 See Chapter 1, p.22. For Polybius's views on the relative importance of different modes of historical enquiry, see Levene, David S., 'Polybius on "seeing" and "hearing": 12.27', *Classical Quarterly* 55.2 (2005), pp.627–9.

118 Below, pp.72–91.

119 Below, pp.165–81.

120 Polybius 12.4a, translated by W. R. Paton.

121 Lane Fox, Robin, 'Sex, gender and the other in Xenophon's *Anabasis*', in Robin Lane Fox (ed), *The Long March: Xenophon and the Ten Thousand* (New

Haven and London, 2004), pp.184–214, at pp.205–6, has some interesting remarks on the 'language problem' as it appears in Xenophon's *Anabasis* and Polybius. See also Caesar *Gallic Wars* 1.19.3 and 1.47.4.

122 Herodotus 1.139. See also Harrison, Thomas, 'Herodotus' conception of foreign languages', *Histos* 2 (1998), at http://www.dur.ac.uk/Classics/histos/1998/harrison.html (accessed 4 April 2008).

123 Chapter 2, p.36.

124 Polybius 39.1.10–12. Walbank: 'The two-way shadow', p.17 observes that this was 'perhaps a common-place among non-Greek authors which was not to be taken too seriously'.

125 Plutarch, *Life of Demosthenes* 2. However, 'the statement in *Demosthenes* occurs in the context of Plutarch's explanation of his inability to compare the style of the speeches of Demosthenes and Cicero. It does not follow that he did not know enough Latin to read historical sources for himself.' (John Briscoe, in a review of C. P. Jones, *Plutarch and Rome* (Oxford, 1971), *Classical Review* 24 (1974), pp.202–4, at p.203).

Chapter 4

1   So, most famously, Horace, *Odes* 3.30.1–2.

2   Above, pp.14–24.

3   For the influence, see Grafton, Anthony, *The Footnote: A Curious History* (London 1997), p.58 with note 47, who notes that there was an element of misunderstanding here.

4   Nissen, Heinrich, *Kritische Untersuchungen über die Quellen der vierten und fünften Dekade des Livius* (Berlin, 1863), p.77.

5   Nissen: *Kritische Untersuchungen*, pp.70–9.

6   I am indebted for this observation of the inevitable obsolescence that afflicts metaphors from the world of Information Technology to the late Peter Derow.

7   So, for example, Collinson, Patrick, 'One of us? William Camden and the making of history', *Transactions of the Royal Historical Society*, Sixth Series, 8 (1998), pp.139–63, at p.149. Collinson does go on to note, however, that 'Tacitus had the talent to transform many of the passages which he ingested.'

8   Above, pp.5–11, 47–8.

9   Chapter 2, p.28.

10   Arrian, *History of Alexander* 1.1.1–3, translated by P. A. Brunt.

Notes

11 Ptolemy we have already met (above, pp.vii–ix, 63). Aristobulus (*FGrHist* 139) was a minor officer who served in Alexander's army, and wrote a history of the king's reign in his old age.

12 However, Bosworth, A. Brian, *A Historical Commentary on Arrian's History of Alexander*, volume 1 (Oxford, 1980), p.43 notes that Arrian 'does not state outright that there is no falsehood in Ptolemy's history; he merely suggests that he would have been eager to avoid the disgrace inherent in a detected lie'. For Arrian's penchant for the works of Xenophon, see Brunt, Peter A. (ed), *Arrian: History of Alexander and Indica I* (Cambridge, Massachusetts and London, 1976), pp.xiii–xiv.

13 Compare Bosworth: *Historical Commentary*, p.31; Brunt, Peter A. (ed), *Arrian: History of Alexander and Indica II* (Cambridge, Massachusetts and London, 1983), p.546.

14 Brunt, *Arrian II*, pp.545–6.

15 For an analysis of Arrian's criteria of credibility, see Brunt, *Arrian II*, pp.551, 552.

16 Brunt, *Arrian I*, p.xxxi records some scepticism, while acknowledging its subjectivity. He does, however, concede that 'there is probably some interweaving of Pt.[olemy] and Ar.[istobulus]' (Brunt, *Arrian II*, p.544). Contrast Bosworth on such passages as Arrian's account of Alexander's visit to the Siwah oasis (*History of Alexander* 3.3.3–6): 'there are passages ... which juxtapose material from Ptolemy and Aristobulus in a way that suggests that material from the two authors was blended in a composite narrative' (Bosworth, *Historical Commentary*, p.17).

17 Not always on good grounds, however. For example, Bosworth criticizes Arrian's 'remarkable lapse' in saying (*History of Alexander* 3.22.4) that Darius was among the first to flee dishonourably 'at Arbela', even though he notes at 6.11.5 that 'Arbela is six hundred stades distant from the place where Darius and Alexander fought their last battle' (Bosworth: *Historical Commentary*, p.348). However, Arrian also notes at 6.11.5 that Arbela was the well-known (albeit misleading) name for that battle, and it would impart an unnecessary piece of fussy pedantry if he dragged the correction into the elegant necrology for Darius at 3.22.4.

18 Arrian, *History of Alexander* 2.3.8, 3.3.6, 6.11.2, 7.14.2.

19 Arrian, *History of Alexander* 4.14.3, translated by P. A. Brunt. The fact that Arrian picks this particular case of divergence to make one of his most explicit complaints about the difficulty of reconciling sources is

particularly ironic when one considers that he is talking about the death of a historian.

20 Arrian, *History of Alexander* 5.14.5.

21 For discussions of Arrian's treatment of his sources in the *History of Alexander*, see Brunt, *Arrian II*, pp.544f.; and Bosworth, *Historical Commentary*, pp.16f.

22 p.201, n39.

23 Asconius 31C (translated by R. Geoffrey Lewis). Fenestella was a historian of the first century BCE whose history of Rome in at least 22 books covered events down to 57 BCE. Asconius usually quotes him to disagree with him (R. Geoffrey Lewis, *Asconius: Commentaries on Speeches by Cicero* (Oxford, 2006), p.xvii).

24 On the form of Asconius's work, see Lewis, *Asconius*, pp.xiv–xv. To his list of examples of other instructive works addressed to sons, add the *Controversiae* of the elder Seneca, which the author claims to have been extorted from him, so that his sons could hear about the declaimers of his lifetime (Seneca the Elder, *Controversiae*, 1.1). For more on 'historical' production in the ancient world beyond straight narrative history, see pp.158–63 below.

25 Pliny the Younger, *Letters* 5.8.12, translated by Betty Radice (with the correction of some punctuation in the original).

26 See Chapter 1, pp.13–14.

27 Benson, Edward F., *As We Were: A Victorian Peep-Show* (London, 1985), p.135. On Headlam, see Arnott, W. Geoffrey, 'Walter Headlam: Achiever or Non-Achiever?', in H. D. Jocelyn (ed), *Aspects of Nineteenth-Century British Classical Scholarship*, Liverpool Classical Papers No. 5 (Liverpool, 1996), with the review of Robert B. Todd in *Bryn Mawr Classical Review* (http://ccat.sas.upenn.edu/bmcr/1996/96.07.18.html, gathered on 5 August 2008).

28 Yeats, W. B., *Four Years* (Churchtown, Dundrum, 1921), p.40.

29 See Stylianou, P. J., *A Historical Commentary on Diodorus Siculus Book 15* (Oxford, 1998). For the ways in which such an analysis of dependence on a lost source can be conducted, and their limitations, see pp.79–91 below.

30 Most memorably, perhaps, by A. E. Housman (although his target was those looking for a single source of the poet Juvenal): 'And to the sister science of *Quellenforschung* I am equally a stranger: I cannot assure you, as

some other writer will assure you before long, that the satires of Juvenal are all copied from the satires of Turnus' (Housman, A. E., *D. Ivnii Ivvenalis Saturae* (London, 1905), p.xxviii).

31 Compare, e.g., C. Richard Whittaker (ed), *Herodian I: Books I–IV* (Cambridge, 1969, p.lxii) on the digressions of Herodian: 'Baaz' attempt [E. Baaz, *De Herodiani fontibus et auctoritate*, Diss. (Berlin, 1909), p.11f.] to prove that Herodian's source for all his digressions was the Augustan writer, Verrius Flaccus, is based on no other evidence than that much of what the historian says is similar to information in Ovid, who was known to have drawn on Flaccus ... there is absolutely nothing to show that this was the sole source of Herodian's information or that the historian had not himself read Ovid.'

32 Walbank, Frank W., *Polybius* (Berkeley, Los Angeles, and London, 1972), p.76, responding to von Scala, Rudolph, *Die Studien des Polybios* (Stuttgart, 1890). In fact, as Walbank notes (pp.81–3), the source-criticism of Polybius is often 'largely a matter of guess-work; and where one can attempt some sort of source analysis ... the result is so complicated as to suggest that Polybius' sources and how he used them are alike problems without an answer'. See also Bosworth, *Historical Commentary*, p.18, on Arrian.

33 Chapter 3, p.53.

34 Appian, *Civil Wars* 2.346. For another example of the tendency to quote authorities explicitly on the numbers of casualties at big battles, compare Livy's reference to Fabius Pictor's numbers for the dead at the battle of Lake Trasimene (Livy 22.6.8-12; 22.7.2).

35 See Grafton, *The Footnote*, pp.13, 14, quoting Thomasius, Jacob, *praeses, Dissertatio Philosophica de plagio literario*, resp. Joh. Michael Reinelius (Leipzig, 1692), §251, §252.

36 Above, p.80.

37 See below, p.83.

38 For more on Pollio and his relationship to the text of Appian, see Pitcher, Luke V., 'The Roman Historians after Livy', in Miriam Griffin (ed), *A Companion to Julius Caesar* (Oxford, 2009), pp.268–76, at p.269, and p.81 below. For general issues relating to Pollio and other lost historians, see pp.173–4 below.

39 See Chapter 3, p.75.

40 Brunt, *Arrian II*, p.546, is sceptical on this count.

41 See Chapter 3, p.51.

42 Appian, *Civil Wars* 2.35; Plutarch, *Life of Julius Caesar* 32.4; Suetonius, *Divus Julius* 32. Contrast Caesar's own words 'he set out with his legions to Ariminum' (*Civil Wars* 1.8.1). Caesar's account 'suppresses his illegal crossing of the river entirely' (Morgan, Llewelyn, 'The Autopsy of Gaius Asinius Pollio', *Journal of Roman Studies* 90 (2000), pp.51–69, at 58).

43 Suetonius, *Divus Julius* 56.4. Pollio's expression of independence does not, of course, mean that his account was in fact necessarily as independent of Caesar's at all points as he implies; see p.80 above, and note also Morgan, 'Autopsy', at pp.59f.

44 Above, pp.74–5.

45 Compare Chapter 3 pp.63–4 above.

46 Appian, *Ann.* 116.

47 So Hahn, István, 'Appian und seine Quellen', in G. Wirth (ed), *Romanitas-Christianitas: Untersuchungen zur Geschichte der Römischen Kaiserzeit* (Berlin, 1982), pp.251–76.

48 The case is laid out by Leidl, Christoph, 'Appians "Annibaike": Aufbau-Darstellungstendenzen-Quellen', *Aufstieg und Niedergang der Römischen Welt* 2.34.1 (Berlin, 1972–), pp.428–62, at pp.449–53. Pictor (whose version of events is preserved at Polybius 3.8.1–4) seems to have put the blame for the Second Punic War on the planned coup of Hasdrubal, which led to a campaign in Spain waged without the endorsement of Carthage. Appian, by contrast, is much more interested in Hamilcar, and suggests at *Iber.* 22 that Carthage was soon won over to Hasdrubal's Spanish policy. Moreover, Appian's numbers for the casualties at the Battle of Lake Trasimene (20,000 dead and 10,000 taken prisoner, according to *Ann.* 41) do not cohere with those of Pictor (see note 34 above).

49 Appian, *Pun.* 629 ' … Scipio said, looking at Polybius the writer, whether willingly, or because this word slipped out, "there will come a day when holy Ilios will perish and Priam and the people of Priam of the good ashen spear." And when Polybius asked him frankly (for he was his teacher) what the speech meant, he said that he had taken care not to name his fatherland, over which, knowing the way mortal affairs turn out, he was now afraid.' It is unlikely that Polybius would have relished being called a *logopoios* (cf. p.41 above, on Polybius's pointed distancing of himself from *logographoi*); one wonders whether the description might therefore bear a hint of Appianic malice.

50 For detailed discussion of some discrepancies between Polybius and Appian (mostly focussed on Roman activities in Spain), see Richardson, John S., *Appian: Wars of the Romans in Iberia, with an Introduction, Translation and Commentary* (Warminster, 2000), pp.4, 5, with his commentary on *Iber.* 14–15, 27–29, 36, 43, 51, 57, 74, 76 and 96. For a discussion of Appian's own possible sources here, see Scullard, Howard H., *Scipio Africanus in the Second Punic War* (Cambridge, 1932), pp.1, 2 and 26.

51 As, for example, at Richardson, *Appian*, p.174 (cf. also p.4), on the note that Rutilius Rufus, whose presence in Spain as a tribune in Spain during the Numantine War Appian records at *Iber.* 382, 'wrote a history of these exploits': 'the note of Appian suggests that he (or, perhaps more likely, his sources) used Rutilius for the events of the Numantine War'.

52 The most famous example of this is probably the appearance of Cremutius Cordus in Tacitus (*Annals* 4.34f.). For 'meta-history', see Chapter 2, p.34. For the appearance of historians within a historical text as a *mise en abyme* for historical reflection, see Krebs, Christopher and Grethlein, Jonas, 'Introduction', in C. Krebs and J. Grethlein (eds), *The Historian's Plupast* (forthcoming).

53 For more on this topic, see pp.167–74 below.

54 Appian, *Civil Wars* 2.500; Cassius Dio 44.21.4. See also Pitcher, 'Caesar', p.269.

55 One such problem emerges in the relationship between Herodian and Cassius Dio. For a discussion of the issues, see Sidebottom, Harry, 'Herodian's Historical Methods and Understanding of history', *Aufstieg und Niedergang der römischen Welt* II.34.4 (Berlin and New York, 1998), pp.2775–836, at pp.2780–92.

56 For discussion of such a case involving Dionysius of Halicarnassus and Nicolaus of Damascus, see, for example, Yarrow, Liv., *Historiography at the End of the Republic: Provincial Perspectives on Roman Rule* (Oxford, 2005), p.171.

57 See below, pp.176–8.

58 See below, pp.167–74.

59 Chapter 3, pp.63–4.

60 Chapter 3, p.49.

61 Chapter 2, pp.39–44.

62 Herodian 1.2.5, translated by C. R. Whittaker.

63   So Whittaker, *Herodian*, p.xxxiii. However, see p.86 and note 68 below.

64   Appian, *Civil Wars* 3.268f.

65   See Trevor-Roper, Hugh, *A Hidden Life: The Enigma of Sir Edmund Backhouse* (London 1976), pp.259–60, and Chapter 2, pp.28–30.

66   See Lovecraft, H. P., *History of the Necronomicon* (West Warwick, RI., 1980).

67   Lucian, *How History Ought to Be Written* 51 (translated by K. Kilburn). 'Phidias' is an allusion to the famous classical sculptor. For further reflections on vividness in classical historiography, see Walker, Andrew, '*Enargeia* and the Spectator in Greek historiography', *Transactions of the American Philological Association* 123 (1993), pp.353–77 and Pitcher, Luke V., 'War Stories: The Uses of the Plupast in Appian', in C. Krebs and J. Grethlein (eds), *The Historian's Plupast* (forthcoming).

68   Whittaker, *Herodian*, p.xxiv and Sidebottom: 'Herodian's historical methods', p.2789, expose the deficiencies of 'vividness' as a criterion for reliability in Herodian. For Appian, compare Hutchinson, Gregory O., *Cicero's Correspondence: A Literary Study* (Oxford, 1998), pp.84, 85.

69   On this, and Civil War historiography in general, see 'The American Civil War', in Kate McLoughlin (ed), *The Cambridge Companion to British and American War Writing* (Cambridge, 2009). For a classic study of the conflict in context, Wilson, Edmund, *Patriotic Gore: Studies in the Literature of the American Civil War* (London, 1962) is still worth reading. See also the meditation upon notions of authenticity and realism, in which the example of Stephen Crane is pressed into service, on the opening page of David Lodge's novel *Author, Author* (London, 2004).

70   Polybius 9.1.1 (translated by W. R. Paton). Compare also Polybius 14.1a.5: 'As I wish to give such an account of the facts as their importance deserves, I have not comprised the events of two years into one book as was my practice in previous cases.' For a detailed examination of Polybius's disposition of events between the books of his history, see Walbank, *Polybius*, pp.108–17, with the chart on p.129.

71   Lucian, *How History Ought to be Written* 28 (translated by K. Kilman).

72   For the arguments over the authenticity of the people Lucian satirizes in *How History Ought to be Written*, see Macleod, Matthew D., *Lucian: A Selection* (Warminster, *c.*1991), pp.284–6.

73   Sallust, *Bellum Catilinae* 51–2 (the debate involving the Younger Cato and Julius Caesar in the Senate, to decide the fate of the Catilinarian conspirators). See also below, pp.103–4.

74 Sallust, *Bellum Catilinae* 25 (on Sempronia).

75 Jaeger, Mary, 'Guiding metaphor and narrative point of view in Livy's *Ab Vrbe Condita*', in C. S. Kraus (ed), *The Limits of Historiography: Genre and Narrative in Ancient Historical Texts* (Leiden, 1999), pp.169–95, at p.184, note 41.

76 On this text, see, above all, Hollis, Adrian S. (ed), *Hecale* (Oxford, 1990).

77 Contrast, Lucian *How History Ought to be Written* 57.

78 A point well made (in relation to a rather different question of data-availability) by Cornell, Tim J., 'The formation of the historical tradition of Early Rome', in I. S. Moxon, J. D. Smart and A. J. Woodman (eds), *Past Perspectives: Studies in Greek and Roman Historical Writing* (Cambridge, 1986), pp.67–86, at p.81.

79 On this point, see Pelling, Christopher, *Literary Texts and the Greek Historian* (London, 2000), p.34, on 'doing a Poirot': 'the fallacy is that the detective needs to show, not just that this story could explain the evidence, but that this is the only story that could ... If a logical causal chain goes forward from the reconstructed crime to the evidence, it need not follow that we can follow that chain backwards from the evidence to the crime: for any number of alternative chains might explain precisely the same evidence.'

80 Lucian, *How History Ought to be Written* 16 (of an anonymous, and possibly fictitious historian): 'after beginning in Ionic, for some reason I can't fathom he suddenly changed to the vernacular' (translated by K. Kilburn). For attested fluctuations in the lexis of Xenophon, see Reynolds, Leighton D. and Wilson, Nigel G., *Scribes and Scholars: A Guide to the Transmission of Greek and Latin Literature*, third edition (Oxford, 1991), p.48.

81 For example, Thucydides is praised for using the Homeric word *perirrutos* ('sea-girt') to describe Sicily (Thucydides 4.64.3) at Demetrius *De Elocutione* 113.

82 Below, pp.176–8.

83 For an example of the complex methodological problems which assail scholars handling writers who composed in unusual dialects of Greek, see Bowie, Angus M. (ed), *Herodotus: Histories. Book VIII* (Cambridge, 2007), pp.22–7. Donald Lateiner's review of this work in the *Bryn Mawr Classical Review* (http://ccat.sas.upenn.edu/bmcr/2008/2008-07-34.html#t3; accessed on 9 August 2008) illustrates how competing models of explanation can apply to such questions as linguistic variation within a text.

84 See Chapter 3, pp.73–4.

85 Reynolds and Wilson, *Scribes and Scholars*, p.231.

86 Diodorus, for example, does indeed seem to reproduce the emphases of his sources (down to the level of vocabulary and authorial comment) quite extensively. For his use of Hieronymus of Cardia, a lost Hellenistic historian covering the period from the death of Alexander to at least the death of Pyrrhus in 272, in books 18–20 of his *Universal History*, see Hornblower, Jane, *Hieronymus of Cardia* (Oxford, 1981). However, Diodorus, too, gives evidence of his own authorial agenda; for a discussion of these, see the analysis in Sacks, Kenneth S., *Diodorus Siculus and the First Century* (Princeton, NJ, *c*.1990).

87 E.g., Velleius Paterculus vs. Cato the Elder on the foundation date of Capua. See Chapter 1, p.20.

88 E.g., Arrian on his decisions about using Ptolemy and Aristobulus to write the history of Alexander (Chapter 3, pp.73–4). For further discussion amongst the ancient historians on the evaluation of sources, see Marincola, John, *Authority and Tradition in Ancient Historiography* (Cambridge, 1997), pp.280–6, and pp.95–6 below.

89 So Polybius polemicizing against Timaeus, on which see Chapter 3, pp.61–2.

90 See below, pp.154–7.

91 See Chapter 1, pp.1–5.

Chapter 5

1 *Bradley's Arnold Latin Prose Composition*, for example, claims to be founded on the usage of 'Caesar ... Cicero (in his speeches) ... [and] Livy' (p.302). It is actually, as its treatment of gerundival phrases in -orum, -arum makes clear (p.219), much more narrowly focussed on Caesarean usage than on the other two. On Xenophon, compare Lane Fox, Robin, 'Introduction', in Robin Lane Fox (ed), *The Long March: Xenophon and the Ten Thousand* (New Haven and London, 2004), pp.1–46, at p.5.

2 Adams, James N., 'The vocabulary of the later decades of Livy', *Antichthon* 8 (1974), pp.54–62.

3 See, for example, Momigliano, Arnaldo D., 'The first political commentary on Tacitus', *Journal of Roman Studies* 37 (1947), pp.91–101; Morford, Mark, 'Tacitean *Prudentia* and the doctrines of Justus Lipsius'; Kelley, Donald, 'The *Germania* in the Renaissance and Reformation'; Weinbrot, Howard,

'Some uses of Tacitism in eighteenth-century Britain', all in T. J. Luce and A. J. Woodman (eds), *Tacitus and the Tacitean Tradition* (Princeton, 1993); and Krebs, Christopher, *Tacitus' Germania from Humanism to National Socialism* (New York, 2009). For the subsequent fortunes of Xenophon's *Anabasis*, see Rood, Tim, *The Sea! The Sea! The Shout of the Ten Thousand in the Modern Imagination* (London, 2004). For the impact of classical historiography on the subsequent literature of war, see Pitcher, Luke V., 'Classical war literature', in Kate McLoughlin (ed), *The Cambridge Companion to British and American War Writing* (Cambridge, 2009), pp.71–80.

4   Most famously, perhaps, in the use of Herodotus in Ondaatje, Michael, *The English Patient* (London, 1992). On this, see Jackson, H. J., *Marginalia: Readers Writing in Books* (New Haven and London, 2001), pp.179–81. Note also Peter Ackroyd's reworking of the opening of Thucydides at the start of *The Plato Papers* (London, 1999), on which see Chapter 1, pp.13–14.

5   Macaulay, Thomas Babington, *The Letters of Thomas Babington Macaulay*, Thomas Pinney (ed), six volumes (Cambridge, 1974–81), III, pp.153–4. See also Williams, Wynne, 'Reading Greek like a man of the world: Macaulay and the classical languages', *Greece and Rome* 40 (1993), pp.201–16, pp.208f. It is worth noting (as Williams does) that stylistic criteria were certainly not Macaulay's only concern in reading the classical historians. Compare his remarks on Polybius: 'I detest his style. Yet dearly as I love Livy, I would give the 3rd and 4th decades of Livy for Polybius' lost books' (*Letters* III, 211).

6   Compare pp.44–5 above.

7   See Chapter 2, pp.25–6.

8   For its application in Polybius, see Walbank, Frank W., 'Polemic in Polybius', *Journal of Roman Studies* 52 (1962), pp.1–12, at pp.5, 6; Walbank, Frank W., 'The two-way shadow: Polybius among the fragments', in G. Schepens and J. Bollansée (eds), *The Shadow of Polybius: Intertextuality as a Research Tool in Greek Historiography – Proceedings of the International Colloquium Leuven, 21–22 September 2001* (Leiden, 2004), pp.1–18, at p.11.

9   Tacitus, *Histories* 2.37 (translated by W. H. Fyfe).

10   Augustus had adopted Tiberius in 4 CE.

11   Tacitus, *Annals* 1.6.

12   As usual (compare Chapter 4, pp.71–2), there is no certainty as to the exact identities of these sources. See Ash, Rhiannon (ed), *Tacitus: Histories 2*

(Cambridge, 2007), pp.177–8. Compare also Damon, Cynthia, *Tacitus: Histories 1* (Cambridge, 2003), p.23.

13　See also Pitcher, Luke V., 'Characterisation in ancient historiography', in John Marincola (ed), *A Companion to Greek and Roman Historiography* (Malden, MA, and Oxford, 2007), pp.102–17, especially pp.103, 104.

14　Contrast Miller, Norma P. (ed), *Tacitus: Annals Book 1* (London, 1992), pp.115, 116: 'it [sc. Augustus's plan to have Agrippa killed] is not in fact difficult to credit, if Augustus thought Tiberius the more suitable successor'.

15　Taylor, Alan J. P., *The Struggle for Mastery in Europe 1848–1918* (Oxford, 1954), pp.158, 159.

16　See Chapter 1, pp.6–7.

17　Taylor, *The Struggle for Mastery*, p.159.

18　So, for example, Woodman, Anthony J., *Rhetoric in Classical Historiography: Four Studies* (London and Sydney, 1988), pp.87, 88. Woodman does, however, note the use of models in social and economic history (p.88). On this, see also note 28 below.

19　Above, pp.25–7.

20　Compare also Rhodes, Peter J., 'In defence of the Greek historians', *Greece and Rome* 41 (1994), pp.156–71, at pp.168, 169: 'Those who claim that ancient historians were not like modern historians sometimes fail to do justice to the variety of modern writers on history. There is a very wide spectrum from serious scholars, who try to investigate and verify and document everything, to historical novelists and journalists and derivative writers who base their work largely on one or two earlier accounts; from those who try to be impartial to those who are openly partisan; from those who think it a virtue to write what is hard to read to those who think that a text which is good to read is more important than a text which is reliable.'

21　Euclid, *Elements* 1.47. Compare Loomis, Elisha Scott, *The Pythagorean Proposition*, second edition (Washington, DC, 1968), which contains 367 proofs of the eponymous proposition (including Garfield's original one). For the early history of the proposition, Heath, Thomas, *A History of Greek Mathematics*, two volumes (Oxford, 1921), Vol. 1, p.144 remains the standard treatment.

22　Euclid, *Elements* 9.20. See also Hardy, Godfrey H., *A Mathematician's Apology* (Cambridge, 1940), § 12.

23　Cf. Wilson, Robert A., *Everything is Under Control: Conspiracies, Cults, and Cover-Ups* (London, 1999), p.246.

Notes

24 So Rhodes, 'Defence', pp.156–71, at p.168 (discussing the nature of historical knowledge in relation to A. J. Ayer's *Language, Truth, and Logic*): 'for many purposes the fact that Ayer's total certainty cannot be achieved is a fact which we should remember but by which we need not be discouraged.'

25 For a more nuanced account of Bayle, and the contribution to historiographical technique of his vast and perennially baffling *Dictionnaire historique et critique* (third edition, Rotterdam, 1697), see Grafton, Anthony, *The Footnote: A Curious History* (London, 1997), pp.195–200.

26 For Plato, see Chapter 1, pp.13–14.

27 See Chapter 4, pp.87–9.

28 Hopkins, Keith, 'Taxes and trade in the Roman Empire (200 B.C.–A.D. 400)', *Journal of Roman Studies* 70 (1980), pp.101–25, at p.101.

29 See Chapter 3, p.52.

30 Syme, Ronald, *The Augustan Aristocracy* (Oxford, 1986), p.112. On the role of inference and assumption in this work, see Wiseman, Timothy P., 'Late Syme: A study in historiography', in T. P. Wiseman, *Roman Drama and Roman History* (Exeter, 1998), pp.135–52, at p.146.

31 Once more, Wiseman, 'Late Syme', p.147, is instructive: 'Even where evidence does exist, Syme is prepared to reject it. In 2 BC, for instance, "Caesar Augustus was imposing a tight regime. After the catastrophe of Julia, he appointed for the first time commanders of the Praetorian Guard." After; but Dio puts it before, "surely in error".' The quotation is taken from Syme, *The Augustan Aristocracy*, p.113.

32 Motion, Andrew, *Wainewright the Poisoner: The True Confessions of a Charming and Ingenious Criminal* (London, 2000), p.xvii.

33 Motion, *Wainewright the Poisoner*, p.xix. Compare also the remarks at Wiseman, 'Late Syme', p.150.

34 Again, Rhodes, 'Defence', p.168 is a useful corrective: 'different kinds of investigation have their own procedures and their own degrees of certainty … We have more evidence, and better evidence for some times and places than for other times and places; and some levels of question are more capable of being answered with certainty than others.'

35 So, for example, Syme, *The Augustan Aristocracy*, p.409, does note that the author's theory of enmity between Tiberius and Paullus Fabius Maximus is not, in fact, attested by any extant author. See also Wiseman, 'Late Syme', p.146.

36 Motion, *Wainewright the Poisoner*, pp.xv–xix.

37 See Chapter 1, p.9.

38 Ellmann, Richard, *Oscar Wilde* (London, 1987), p.429.

39 Ellmann, *Oscar Wilde*, p.89. The narrative looks forward as well as back: Ellmann builds on Wilde's imputed perception of prison in this passage later when he is confronted by the reality of detention in Pentonville (p.454).

40 For another extended study of this phenomenon, based this time upon the portrait of Florence Nightingale in Strachey, Lytton, *Eminent Victorians* (London, 1918) and on modern biographies of Martin Luther, Bismarck and Hugh Gaitskill, see Pelling, Christopher, 'Childhood and personality in Greek biography', in Christopher Pelling (ed), *Characterization and Individuality in Greek Literature* (Oxford, 1990), pp.213–44, at p.244. Sidebottom, Harry, 'Herodian's historical methods and understanding of history', *Aufstieg und Niedergang der römischen Welt* II.34.4 (Berlin and New York, 1998), pp.2775–836, at p.2822, notes the implications of this methodology for our readings of ancient historiography.

41 Compare also Hornblower, Simon, 'Narratology and narrative techniques in Thucydides', in Simon Hornblower (ed), *Greek Historiography* (Oxford, 1994), pp.131–66, at p.137, citing Ehrman, John, *The Younger Pitt*, three volumes (London 1969–96), and Woodward, Bob and Bernstein, Carl, *Final Days* (New York, 1977), as modern examples.

42 The bibliography on speeches in ancient historiography is vast, and what follows here is only a summary account. The most useful and accessible introductions, with substantial bibliographies, remain Walbank, Frank W., 'Speeches in Greek historians' (third Myres Memorial Lecture: Oxford, 1965) (Walbank, F. W., *Selected Papers: Studies in Greek and Roman History and Historiography* (Cambridge, 1985), pp.242–61), and Marincola, John, 'Speeches in Classical historiography', in John Marincola (ed), *A Companion to Greek and Roman Historiography* (Malden, MA, and Oxford, 2007), pp.118–32.

43 The phenomenon was not limited, in the ancient world, to Greco-Roman historiography: see Schaeberg, David, 'Social pleasures in Early Chinese historiography and philosophy', in C. S. Kraus (ed), *The Limits of Historiography: Genre and Narrative in Ancient Historical Texts* (Leiden, 1999), pp.1–26, for a discussion of speeches in the Chinese *Zuo Tradition* and *Legends of the States*.

44 Lobur, John A., '*Festinatio* (haste), *brevitas* (concision), and the generation of imperial ideology in Velleius Paterculus', *Transactions of the American Philological Association* 137 (2007), pp.211–30.

45   Appian, *Iber.* 412. Appian also sets up this unusual display of loquacity by emphasizing that this summary came at the end of a 'long and verbose speech about the bravery of the Numantians', which he does not give.

46   Thucydides 2.35–46.

47   Appian, *Civil Wars* 2.299–302 (Pompeius); 2.303–310 (Caesar).

48   Sallust, *Bellum Catilinae* 51–52. See Chapter 4, p.87. This proportion, moreover, does not include the other speeches in the work, Catiline's initial address to his conspirators (Sallust, *Bellum Catilinae* 20), and his exhortation to his troops before the battle in which he died (58). The percentages here make the arguments at Syme, Ronald, *Sallust* (Berkeley, 1964), p.197, for alleged eschewing of some speeches in Sallust's *Histories* ('Sallust is an economical writer, averse from rhetoric'), distinctly ropey.

49   Sallust, *Bellum Iugurthinum* 10, 14, 31, 85, 102 and 110. Kraus, Christina S., 'Jugurthine disorder', in C. S. Kraus (ed), *The Limits of Historiography: Genre and Narrative in Ancient Historical Texts* (Leiden, 1999), pp.217–47, at p.222, note 15, notes the irony of Jugurtha's lack of direct speeches. The proportions in Sallust's fragmentary *Histories*, of which we do still have samples from both the speeches and the narrative, cannot, of course, be determined.

50   Cassius Dio 38.18.29. On this episode, see Millar, Fergus, *A Study of Cassius Dio* (Oxford, 1964), pp.49f., and Gowing, Alain M., 'Greek advice for a Roman senator: Cassius Dio and the dialogue between Philiscus and Cicero (38.18–29)', in F. Cairns and Malcolm Heath (eds), *Proceedings of the Leeds Latin Seminar* 10 (Leeds, 1998), pp.373–90.

51   On the incompleteness of Thucydides's history, and analyses of its composition, see p.32 above.

52   So Connor, Walter R., *Thucydides* (Princeton, c.1984), pp.212–18. Contrast Rhodes, Peter J., ' "Epidamnus is a city": On not overinterpreting Thucydides', *Histos* 2 (1998), at http://www.dur.ac.uk/Classics/histos/1998/rhodes.html (accessed on 13 August 2008).

53   On this, see Hidber, Thomas, 'Zeit und Erzählperspektive in Herodians Geschichtswerk', in M. Zimmerman (ed), *Geschichtsschreibung und politischer Wandel im 3. Jh. N. Chr.* (Stuttgart, 1999), pp.145–67.

54   On possible instances of this in Thucydides's portrayal of Pericles and Caesar's depiction of Vercingetorix, see Pitcher, 'Characterisation', p.115.

On Thucydides, see also Pelling, Christopher, *Literary Texts and the Greek Historian* (London, 2000), pp.118, 119.

55 On the mechanics of recording speeches in the ancient and modern worlds, see Greenwood, Emily, *Thucydides and the Shaping of History* (London, 2006), pp.65–6.

56 Seneca the Elder, *Controversiae* 1.19. On considerations of memory, see also Thucydides 1.22 (quoted on p.108 above).

57 For more on this, see Schultze, Clemence E., 'Authority, originalityand competence in the Roman Archaeology of Dionysius of Halicarnassus', *Histos* 4 (2000), at http://www.dur.ac.uk/Classics/histos/2000/schultze1.html (accessed 17 August 2008).

58 Dionysius of Halicarnassus, *On Thucydides* 36 (translated by Stephen Usher).

59 Compare pp.22, 56 and 66–7 above.

60 Polybius 12.25a (translated by W. R. Paton).

61 Polybius 12.25k, omitting some explanation of the circumstances under which Hermocrates made the speech and some of Polybius's opening criticisms of the content of the speech.

62 Hermocrates also delivers a speech on this occasion at the equivalent point in the text of Thucydides (Thucydides 4.59–64). Polybius's failure to mention Thucydides at this point has been taken as evidence that the later historian was not intimately conversant with the text of the earlier (Hornblower, Simon, 'Introduction', in Simon Hornblower (ed), *Greek Historiography* (Oxford, 1994), pp.1–72, at pp.60, 61). But if Polybius regarded Thucydides's speeches as equally fictitious (which was certainly a view held elsewhere in antiquity, as Dionysius demonstrates), there is no particular reason for him to mention one writer of imaginary speeches when he is criticizing another.

63 Walbank, Frank W., *Polybius* (Berkeley, Los Angeles and London, 1972), p.69, note 11, notes Polybius 2.56.10 (criticizing Phylarchus), 3.20.1 (working up to a criticism of the historians Chaereas and Sosylus), 29.12.9–10 and 36.1.2–7 as other examples.

64 Pace Moles, John L., 'Truth and untruth in Herodotus and Thucydides', in C. Gill and T. P. Wiseman (eds), *Lies and Fiction in the Ancient World* (Austin, 1993), pp.88–121, at p.105.

65 Justin 38.3.11 (Justin being the later author who presents a compendium culled from Trogus's works). See also Yarrow, Liv, *Historiography at the*

Notes

End of the Republic: Provincial Perspectives on Roman Rule (Oxford, 2005), p.115.

66 Tacitus's version of the speech is at *Annals* 11.24. The inscription may be found at Dessau, Hermann (ed), *Inscriptiones Latinae Selectae*, five volumes (Berlin, 1892–916), no. 212, and is conveniently available in translation in Levick, B., *The Government of the Roman Empire: A Sourcebook* (London, 1985), no. 159.

67 For interesting comparisons of Tacitus's version with the one on the Lyons tablet, see, for example, Griffin, Miriam, 'The Lyons Tablet and Tacitean hindsight', *Classical Quarterly* 32 (1982), pp.404–18; and von Albrecht, Michael, *Masters of Roman Prose* (Leeds, 1989), pp.136–59.

68 Compare Walbank, *Polybius*, p.45: 'Clearly, as he admits, there has to be some selection; and in the consequent reshaping of material a personal colouring appears ... Sometimes too ... one is forced to choose between the hypothesis that Polybius has in fact had recourse to his imagination or that he has drawn somewhat uncritically on sources that have themselves done just that.' See also Walbank, 'Speeches', p.18, and Marincola, John, *The Greek Historians* (Cambridge, 2001), pp.131–33.

69 A point rightly stressed at Moles, 'Truth and untruth', p.118.

70 See Chapter 2, pp.38–9, on examples of this, especially in the works of Tacitus and Ronald Syme.

71 Thucydides 1.22.1, translated by Richard Crawley.

72 Notable treatments include, but are by no means limited to, Egermann, Franz, 'Thukydides über die Art seiner Reden und über seine Darstellung der Kriegsgeschehnisse', *Historia* 21 (1972), pp.575–602; Wilson, John, 'What does Thucydides claim for his speeches?', *Phoenix* 36 (1982), pp.95–103; Hornblower, Simon, *Thucydides* (London, 1987), p.45f.; and Pelling, *Literary Texts*, pp.114–119. As Pelling remarks (115): 'No sentence in the Greek language can have been taken quite so variously as that on the speeches here. Some scholars think it clear that the guiding principle here is as much historical accuracy as possible, others think it points to a high degree of free composition; the only feature which most interpreters share is their confidence in their own interpretation, and their utter bemusement that others should not see it the same way.'

73 This, for example, seems to be the interpretation of Dewald, Carolyn, 'The construction of meaning in the first three historians', in John Marincola (ed), *A Companion to Greek and Roman Historiography* (Malden, MA, and

Oxford, 2007), pp.89–101, at p.95: 'When he says that he gives us the "necessary parts" (*ta deonta*, 1.22.1) of the speeches he has collected, he is tacitly assuring us that he has selected out the aspects from the hundreds of speeches given that he thought most valuable for understanding the war ... .'

74   For further considerations of this issue, see pp.174–5 below.

75   Hornblower, Simon, *A Commentary on Thucydides Volume I: Books I-III* (Oxford, 1991), p.59, notes an example from Runciman, Steven, *The Crusades*, Vol. 1 (Cambridge, 1951), p.108, note 1: 'in 1095, the speech of Pope Urban II proclaiming the first Crusade was recorded by four chroniclers including one eyewitness, "but it is clear that each author wrote the speech that he thought the Pope ought to have made and added his own favourite rhetorical tricks".'

76   von Ranke, Leopold, *Geschichten der romanischen und germanischen Völker von 1494 bis 1514, Zur Kritik neuerer Geschichtschreiber* (Leipzig and Berlin, 1824), p.27; and Grafton, *The Footnote*, p.43.

77   On Maitland, see the full-length biography: Elton, Geoffrey R., *F. W. Maitland* (New Haven and London, 1985). An approachable introduction may be found in the chapter devoted to him in Annan, Noel, *The Dons: Mentors, Eccentrics and Geniuses* (London, 1999).

78   Pollock, Frederick and Maitland, Frederic W., *The History of English Law Before the Time of Edward I* (Cambridge, 1898), 1.623. For an interesting analysis of this passage in terms of Maitland's own historical context, see Milsom, Stroud F. C., 'Maitland, Frederic William (1850–1906)', *Oxford Dictionary of National Biography* (Oxford, 2004), online edition, May 2007 [http://www. oxforddnb.com/view/article/34837, accessed 19 August 2008].

79   Tacitus, *Annals* 1.9–10, translated by Michael Grant. The extract above is heavily abbreviated. For discussions of this passage, see in particular Syme, Ronald, *Tacitus* (Oxford, 1958), pp.431, 432, and Goodyear, Frank R. D. (ed), *The Annals of Tacitus: Vol 1. (Annals 1. 1–54)* (Cambridge, 1972), pp.154–69.

80   Compare, amongst many other examples, the divided response of the waiting Athenians to Alcibiades' return from exile at Xenophon *Hellenica* 1.4.13f.

81   The examples assembled at Wiseman: 'Late Syme', a study in historiography", p.145, are particularly instructive: ' "the aristocracy seized the

occasion to sharpen and reinforce verdicts normally confined to their clubs and conclaves"; "whatever estimate Caesar Augustus formed (and kept to himself), eager speculation in clubs and salons would fasten on the theme of *capax imperii*"; "men of understanding or hardened intriguers found plenty to talk about in their clubs and circles"; "malice knew no restraint when men congregated at a club, a banquet, or a funeral" ' (Syme, *The Augustan Aristocracy*, pp.38, 408, 341, 441).

82   Tacitus, *Annals* 3.54.1, with Woodman, Anthony J., and Martin, Ronald H. (eds), *The Annals of Tacitus: Book 3* (Cambridge, 1996), p.390. Tacitus himself paints a picture of analyses of the likely succession to the principate at Tacitus, *Annals* 1.13, based on the alleged remarks on the capacities and inclinations of various possible candidates of the elderly Augustus himself.

83   Hopkins, Keith, *A World Full of Gods: Pagans, Jews and Christians in the Roman World* (London, 1999). On this, see, in particular, Simon Swain's review in the *Classical Review* 53 (2003), pp.260, 261.

Chapter 6

1   It was reissued in two volumes in 1965 as *Große Synchronoptische Weltgeschichte*.

2   Anonymous obituary, 'Arno Peters', *The Times* (10 December 2002). Consulted online at http://www.timesonline.co.uk/tol/comment/obituaries/article800223.ece on 20 August 2008.

3   More accurately known, however, as the Gall–Peters Projection, since it was originally developed by the Scottish clergyman James Gall in 1885. Gall, James, 'Use of cylindrical projections for geographical, astronomical, and scientific purposes', *Scottish Geographical Magazine* 1.4 (1885), pp.119–23.

4   For the Mercator projection and its genesis, see Crane, Nicholas, *Mercator: The Man who Mapped the Planet* (London, 2002).

5   Luce, Torrey J., *The Greek Historians* (London and New York, 1997), pp.118–19, characterizes Cyme thus: 'it was not a large or important town, and was saddled with the reputation for stupidity'. This places, perhaps, somewhat too much faith in the casual sarcasms of Strabo (Strabo 13.3.6). As a corrective, see Engelmann, Helmutt, *Die Inschriften von Cyme* (Bonn, 1976).

6   See Chapter 3, pp.66–7.

7   Ephorus *FGrH* 70 F236.

8 Chapter 2, pp.31–2, for the (not insignificant) issue of historians and mortality.

9 Polybius 1.4.6–11 (translated by W. R. Paton).

10 For more on this passage, see Rood, Tim, 'The Development of the War Monograph', in John Marincola (ed), *A Companion to Greek and Roman Historiography* (Malden, MA, and Oxford, 2007), pp.147–58, at pp.149–53.

11 *Oxford English Dictionary*, s. v. 'monograph'. One of the *OED*'s examples of the use of the word 'monography' is its application to the *Bellum Catilinae* and *Bellum Iugurthinum* at Merivale, C. (ed), *Caii Sallustii Crispi Catilina et Jugurtha, an ed. for schools* (Cambridge, 1852), p.xiv. See also Rood, 'Development', p.148.

12 For Diodorus, Chapter 1, pp.21–2.

13 Diodorus 1.3.2 (translated by C. H. Oldfather). He also refers to 'universal' histories as *hai koinai historiai* at Diodorus 1.1.1.

14 He also, at Polybius 12.23.7, calls 'universal history' *hai suntaxeis tōn katholou praxeōn*.

15 Diodorus 1.3.3 (translated by C. H. Oldfather). For the problems with this statement, see Marincola, John, *Authority and Tradition in Ancient Historiography* (Cambridge, 1997), p.242.

16 So Marincola, John, 'Universal history from Ephorus to Diodorus', in John Marincola (ed), *A Companion to Greek and Roman Historiography* (Malden, MA, and Oxford, 2007), pp.171–9, at p.171: 'In antiquity, to write universally comprehended at least two different types of history: first, histories that covered the entire known world ... from earliest recorded times to the author's own day, i.e., universal in time and space; second, histories that treated known events within a restricted time period, i.e., universal only in space.' This contests the more restrictive view of Alonso-Núñez, José M., *The Idea of Universal History in Greece: from Herodotus to the Age of Augustus* (Amsterdam, 2002), p.117, that universal historians might be defined as 'those who study the history of mankind from the earliest times and in all parts of the world known to them'.

17 See Chapter 7, p.150.

18 Polybius 5.33.1–2 (translated by W. R. Paton).

19 Polybius 1.3.3–4. See also Rood, 'Development', p.149. For analysis of Polybius's not altogether self-evident proposition concerning the point at which universal history becomes truly viable, see Walbank, Frank W., *Polybius* (Berkeley, Los Angeles and London, 1972), pp.68–71.

20 Compare Chapter 2, pp.44–5.

21 Cicero, *Letters to his Friends* 5.12.2. Rood, 'Development', p.151, notes the irony here. On Appian, see Chapter 4, pp.81–2.

22 Polybius 7.7.6 (translated by W. R. Paton).

23 For more on Polybius and Timaeus, see pp.22, 56 and 66–7.

24 Polybius 12.23.7.

25 Sallust, *Bellum Catilinae* 8.2–4 (translated by S. A. Handford). On the implications of the passage for Sallust's view of his own achievement, see Kraus, Christina S. and Woodman, Anthony J., *Latin Historians* [New Surveys in the Classics No. 27] (Cambridge, 1997), p.17: 'Here he makes the clear point that the glory of doers depends on writers: it seems to follow that Sallust at 8.2–4 is implicitly arguing for the primacy of writers (and hence of his own, post-conversion self) over doers.'

26 Chapter 2, pp.37–8.

27 Chapter 5, pp.99–100.

28 Chapter 3, pp.52–3.

29 For this, see, in particular, Rich, John W. (ed), *Cassius Dio: The Augustan Settlement (Roman History 53–55.9)* (Warminster, 1990), which provides edition, translation and commentary down to the point where Dio becomes lacunose.

30 For Velleius's account of Augustus, see above all Woodman, Anthony J., *Velleius Paterculus: The Caesarian and Augustan Narrative (2.41–93)* (Cambridge, 1983).

31 For which see the excellent commentary by Carter, John H., *Suetonius: Divus Augustus* (London, 1982), which is useful even to those without Latin. For Nicolaus, see *FGrHist* 90 F125–30.

32 See Brunt, Peter A., and Moore, John M., *Res gestae divi Augusti: the achievements of the divine Augustus* (Oxford, 1967). Apart from bearing out some of the remarks we have already made about the performative element to epigraphy (see above, pp.54–5), the *Res Gestae* neatly trumps its own rhetoric of definitions; at the end of a text which obsessively details the exact numbers involved in Augustus's offices, donations and achievements, the very last word of the document, referring to the scale of his general expenditure on the part of Rome, is 'innumerabilis' ('uncountable').

33 For an example of the difficulties and uncertainties involved in such an enterprise, see Syme, Ronald, *The Augustan Aristocracy* (Oxford, 1986), with

Wiseman, Timothy P., 'Late Syme: a Study in historiography', in T. P. Wiseman, *Roman Drama and Roman History* (Exeter, 1998), pp.135–52, and Chapter 5, pp.99–100.

34 The extant portions of Appian's narrative cover events down to the death of Sextus Pompeius, the son of Pompeius Magnus, in 36 BCE.

35 Diodorus's history for the period from 480 to 302 BCE is fully preserved.

36 In particular, that of the so-called Oxyrhynchus historian, a fragmentary historiographical work discovered on papyri in the course of the twentieth century (*POxy* 842 and PSI 1304) which acts as an interesting alternative to Xenophon for some late fifth- and early fourth-century history. See also Bruce, I. A. F., *A Historical Commentary on the Hellenica Oxyrhynchia* (Cambridge, 1967). For more on such fragmentary texts and the problems involved in handling them, see pp.167–74 below.

37 As a critique of this explanation for the neglect of the Hellenistic age, see, however, Shipley, Graham, *Hellenistic History: A Very Short Introduction* (Oxford, in press), who prefers to see the distaste for the period as arising rather from the perceived 'decline of freedom' amongst the Greek states in this period. He makes some good points, though it is hard to see why interest falls off after the death of Alexander on his reading rather than after the Battle of Chaeronea in 338 BCE.

38 Compare, for example, Syme, Ronald, *The Roman Revolution* (Oxford, 1939), p.4.

39 See below, pp.147–8.

40 Lucian, *How History Ought to be Written* 28. See also Chapter 4, pp.86–7.

41 Lucian, *How History Ought to be Written* 30 (translated by K. Kilburn).

42 For an introduction to de Thou and his work, see Kinser, Samuel, *The Works of Jacques-Auguste de Thou* (The Hague, 1966), Grafton, Anthony, *The Footnote: A Curious History* (London, 1997), pp.135–42.

43 H. G. Wells, *A Short History of the World*, originally published in 1922, and based upon Wells' earlier and much longer (c. 750,000 words) *The Outline of History*. For the reception of this work, see Skelton, Matthew, 'The paratext of everything: Constructing and marketing H. G. Wells's *The Outline of History*', *Book History* 4 (2001), pp.237–75.

44 See Chapter 4, p.76. Gombrich's history was originally written in German in 1935 as *Eine kurze Weltgeschichte für junge Leser*. The most conveniently available edition in English is now Gombrich, E. H., *A Little History of the World* (Yale, 2005).

45   For Nicolaus, otherwise notable for his biography of Augustus (see above, note 31), see *FGrHist* 90, and the extended analysis in Yarrow, Liv, *Historiography at the End of the Republic: Provincial Perspectives on Roman Rule* (Oxford, 2005).

46   Ptolemy Euergetes II *FGrHist* 234; The *History of Philip*, by Theopompus of Chios *FGrHist* 115 F 24–396. For more on Theopompus and this work, see pp.148–9 below. The last 18 books of Ammianus Marcellinus cover a period of only 25 years; see below, pp.122–3.

47   For the debate over the authenticity of the historians satirized in Lucian's *How History Ought to be Written*, see Chapter 4, pp.86–7.

48   For Florus, see Pitcher, L. V., 'The Roman historians after Livy', in Miriam Griffin (ed), *A Companion to Julius Caesar* (Oxford, 2009), pp.268–76, at p.275.

49   For an assessment of the status of Velleius Book One, see Kramer, Emil A., 'Book One of Velleius's *History*: scope, levels of treatment, and non-Roman elements', in *Historia* 54 (2005), pp.144–61.

50   Velleius Paterculus 1.14f, 1.16. For Velleius's handling of material at the end of Book One, see Pitcher, Luke V., 'The stones of blood: Family, monumentality, and memory in Velleius's Second Century', in Eleanor Cowan (ed), *Velleius Paterculus* (Swansea, in press).

51   Velleius Paterculus 2.59f. For this portion of Velleius's narratives, see Woodman, Anthony J., *Velleius Paterculus: The Caesarian and Augustan Narrative (2.41–93)* (Cambridge, 1983), and *Velleius Paterculus: The Tiberian Narrative (2.94–131)* (Cambridge, 1977).

52   Above, p.58.

53   Chapter 4, pp.86–8.

54   Chapter 1, pp.1–2.

55   Compare White, Hayden, *The Content of the Form* (Baltimore, 1987), p.10: 'Every narrative, however seemingly "full", is constructed on the basis of a set of events that might have been included but were left out.'

56   On the foundations of the Confederacy and fourth-century Athenian policies, see Griffith, Guy T., 'Athens in the fourth century', in P. D. A. Garnsey, C. Richard Whittaker (eds), *Imperialism in the Ancient World: The Cambridge University Research Seminar in Ancient History* (Cambridge, 1978), pp.127–44; Cargill, Jack, *The Second Athenian League: Empire or Free Alliance?* (Berkeley, 1981), Hornblower, Simon, *The Greek World: 479–323 BC*, third edition (London, 2002) pp.233f.

57 For discussions of the date of composition of the *Anabasis* and references to earlier bibliography, see Cawkwell, George, 'When, how and why did Xenophon write the *Anabasis?*', in Robin Lane Fox (ed), *The Long March: Xenophon and the Ten Thousand* (New Haven and London, 2004), pp.47–67, at pp.47–50 [supporting the view of a date of composition in the 360s], Rood, Tim, 'Pan-Hellenism and self-presentation: Xenophon's speeches', in the same volume, pp.305–29, at p.307.

58 Chapter 3, p.63.

59 See Lane Fox, Robin, 'Introduction', in Robin Lane Fox (ed), *The Long March: Xenophon and the Ten Thousand* (New Haven and London, 2004), pp.1–46, at pp.43–6, especially 45: 'Some might connect this artful silence with Xenophon's supposed lack of written notes. In my view, it fits neatly with the Xenophon of the essays in this volume: evasive, apologetic, and a master of leaving unwelcome things out.' For other instances of interesting Xenophontic evasions and silences in the *Anabasis*, see pp.23–31 in the same volume.

60 So correctly Pelling, Christopher, *Literary Texts and the Greek Historian* (London, 2000), on the speeches which Thucydides includes in Book Two of his history: 'Had unkind chance robbed us of the first half of Book 2, we should never have expected it to contain a Funeral Speech; that is a staggering departure from his normal practice. When we try to explain it, or any other speech we have, it is only the beginning of an explanation to say that they were really delivered: we also need to ask why Thucydides put them in, given the vast number he must have excluded.'

61 Compare Lewis, David M., 'Sources, Chronology, Method', in D. M. Lewis, John Boardman, J. K. Davies and M. Ostwald (eds), *The Cambridge Ancient History V: The Fifth Century B.C.* second edition (Cambridge, 1992), pp.1–14, at p.5: 'The difficulty here lies in our dependence on what he gives us. This is a great deal, but he has assimilated his source material and concealed his workings.' Thucydides is not quite the only source for this period, however, and Lewis sets out some of the others. On some issues of factual accuracy in Thucydides, see also Marincola, John, *Greek Historians* (Cambridge, 2001), pp.98–9.

62 Hornblower, Simon, 'The religious dimension to the Peloponnesian War, or, What Thucydides does not tell us', *Harvard Studies in Classical Philology* 94 (1992), pp.79–97, is one attempt to explore what Thucydides may not be saying about the conflict that is his main theme.

63 Appian, *Civil Wars* 5.1–2. On this aversion, see Pitcher: 'Caesar', p.273 (where, however, its extent is considerably overstated).

64 Lucian, *How History Ought to be Written*, pp.19, 20.

65 Chapter 1, pp.14–24.

66 Chapter 4, pp.87–8.

67 Compare Lewis: 'Sources, chronology, method', pp.5–6, on Thucydides's selectivity in organizing his narrative of the Peloponnesian War: 'there has inevitably been selectivity, and we should not expect to be told everything that happened ... That Thucydides does not report an event is not a reason for believing that it did not happen, and, if our interests take us that way, we have a duty to try to fill in the gaps.' For two of Thucydides's more interesting possible omissions in the field of political history, the 'Peace of Callias' and the 'First Sacred War', see Hornblower, Simon, *A Commentary on Thucydides Volume I: Books I–III* (Oxford, 1997), pp.179–81 (with the earlier bibliography cited there); and Davies, John, 'The Tradition about the First Sacred War', in Simon Hornblower (ed), *Greek Historiography* (Oxford, 1994), pp.193–212.

68 For a summary of the customary arraignment of Tacitus as a military historian, see Wellesley, Kenneth, 'Tacitus as a military historian', in T. A. Dorey (ed), *Tacitus* (London, 1969), pp.63–98, with the more sympathetic account of Syme, Ronald, *Tacitus,* two volumes (Oxford, 1958), pp.157–75.

69 Contrast the sensible remarks of Whittaker, C. Richard, *Herodian I: Books I–IV* (Cambridge, 1969), p.xliv, who, besides quoting the passage of Lucian used above (p.125), makes a good point from Herodian's own text about the unwillingness of historians to duplicate material readily available at their own time: 'The information was quite often available. For "Many historians, who have made the life of Severus the theme of their entire work, have given detailed treatment to the stages of the march, the speeches that he made at each city ... the topography of each place" ([Herodian] 2.15.6. To do so again was, in Herodian's opinion, superfluous, however regrettable the decision may seem today, when the other sources are lost.'

70 Diodorus 13.84, with Clarke, Katherine, 'Universal Perspectives in historiography', in C. S. Kraus (ed), *The Limits of Historiography: Genre and Narrative in Ancient Historical Texts* (Leiden, 1999), pp.249–79, at p.265.

71 Cassius Dio 43.22.4 (on spectacles); 43.25.1 (on legislation); 42.19.3–4; 43.46.1 (on responses to Caesar's victories). See also Pitcher, 'Caesar', p.270.

72 Herodian 2.15.6 (quoted in note 69 above, in Whittaker's translation).

73 As, for example, when he discusses his arrangement of material at Velleius Paterculus 1.14.1.

74 E.g., Thucydides 2.31.3, on Athenian invasions of the Megarid during the Peloponnesian War. See on this, and similar instances, Lewis, 'Sources, chronology, method', p.5, and Marincola: *Greek Historians*, p.75.

75 On 'author theatre' see Chapter 2, pp.34–9.

76 Chapter 5, p.105.

77 Dionysius of Halicarnassus, *On Thucydides* 9 (translated by Stephen Usher).

78 For a critique of his strictures on Thucydides's handling of the military action at Pylos and Sphacteria, for example, see Rood, Tim, *Thucydides: Narrative and Explanation* (Oxford, 1998), pp.55–7. For an examination of his responses to Thucydides's speeches, see Greenwood, Emily, *Thucydides and the Shaping of History* (London, 2006), pp.71, 72.

79 Marincola, *Authority and Tradition*, p.17, note 81, notes that the 'Oxyrhynchus historian' (p. 103) seems to have emulated Thucydides's structure. A modified form of this system is also adopted after a fashion by Xenophon in his *Hellenica*. See Hornblower, Simon, 'Introduction', in Simon Hornblower (ed), *Greek Historiography* (Oxford, 1994), pp.1–72, at p.30.

80 On the importance of this consideration in Thucydides's narrative, see also Greenwood, *Thucydides and the Shaping of History*, pp.42–3.

81 Appian, *Proem* 45–9 (my translation).

82 Not exactly an unproblematic notion in this context: see below pp.130–1.

83 Hellanicus of Lesbos (*FGrHist* 4), who lived in the fifth-century BCE, is lost apart from approximately 200 fragments, but did write (amongst other things) studies of particular peoples and areas. For more on him, see Hornblower, 'Introduction', pp.23–4, with bibliography.

84 Dionysius of Halicarnassus, *On Thucydides* 9 (translated by Stephen Usher). Again, Dionysius's chosen examples are a little more complicated than he suggests. Herodotus's history could reasonably be described as being organized topographically in the earlier books, but the account of the Persian Expedition of 480–79 BCE, which comprises the last three books, faces narrative issues not so different from those of Thucydides.

85 On such 'rewinds' in historiography, see also Clarke, 'Universal Perspectives', pp.269–70.

86   Appian, *Pun*, p.630. See also Chapter 4, p.82.

87   So, for example, the account of Scipio Aemilianus's conduct of the
      Numantine War opens with the words 'In Rome, the people ... chose
      Cornelius Scipio, *who had captured Carthage*, to be consul again, as the only
      man capable of defeating the Numantians' (Appian, *Iber.* 363; translated by
      J. S. Richardson). Scipio's future conquests of both Carthage and Numantia
      are also given proleptic mention at his first appearance in the book, as a
      subordinate of L. Licinius Lucullus in 151 BCE (Appian, *Iber.* 210). Classical
      historiography was fond of bracketing these two sacks together: compare
      Velleius Paterculus 2.4.3.

88   For one example of how Appian manages to extort a continuous narrative
      of events *across* books and geographical locations, see Luke V. Pitcher,
      review of J. S. Richardson, *Appian: Wars of the Romans in Iberia, with an
      Introduction, Translation and Commentary* (Warminster, 2000), in the *Bryn
      Mawr Classical Review* at http://ccat.sas.upenn.edu/bmcr/2001/2001-08-
      36.html (accessed 24 August 2008).

89   Richardson, *Appian*, p.7, where the reference to the 'sending of regular mag-
      istrates to the area at the end of the *First* Punic War' should actually (as the
      remainder of the discussion makes clear) refer to the Second Punic War.

90   See Drews, Robert, 'Ephorus and history written KATA GENOS', *American
      Journal of Philology*, 84/3 (July 1963), pp.244–55, for a discussion of vari-
      ous theories as to the disposition of Ephorus's history.

91   Weeks, David and James, Jamie, *Eccentrics: A Study of Sanity and Strangeness*
      (London, 1995), pp.38–9.

92   Polybius 15.24a (translated by W. R. Paton). On the positioning of this
      methodological reflection within the text of Polybius, see Walbank,
      Polybius, p.111 with note 75.

93   Diodorus 20.43.7, aptly quoted by Rood, *Thucydides*, p.109.

94   See in particular Scodel, Ruth, 'Zielinski's Law reconsidered', *Transactions of
      the American Philological Association* 138 (2008), pp.107–25, for the oddities
      associated with apparently simultaneous actions in Homer, and Hunter,
      Richard (ed), *Apollonius of Rhodes: Argonautica Book III* (Cambridge, 1989),
      for the way in which simultaneity is managed in a Hellenistic epic.

95   Tacitus, *Annals* 1.31.1.

96   Goodyear, Frank R. D. (ed) *The Annals of Tacitus: Vol. 1 (Annals 1. 1–54)*
      (Cambridge, 1972), p.241. The other considerations he marshals are, as he
      points out, less than compelling, and he concludes by remarking: 'for lack

of precise chronological evidence these matters must remain uncertain. In general, however, we need not doubt the truth of T[acitus]'s presentation of the two mutinies as developing quite independently.'

97 Tacitus, *Annals* 1.16–30.

98 Tacitus, *Annals* 1.31–49. For more on issues relating to the demarcation of these episodes, see O'Gorman, Ellen, *Irony and Misreading in the Annals of Tacitus* (Cambridge, 2000), pp.25–39.

99 For further discussion, see the useful summary at de Jong, Irene, Nünlist, René and Bowie, Angus (eds), *Narrators, Narratees, and Narratives in Ancient Greek Literature* (Leiden, 2004), pp.xv–xvii, from which the quotations above are taken.

100 For examples of its application to the text of Thucydides, see Hornblower, Simon, 'Narratology and narrative techniques in Thucydides', in Simon Hornblower (ed), *Greek Historiography* (Oxford, 1994), pp.131–66, and Rood, *Thucydides*, especially pp.109–30.

101 Tacitus, *Annals* 1.31.1 (my translation).

102 Tacitus, *Annals* 1.31.5 (my translation).

103 See above, pp.130–1, for his presentation of 'rebellions' against Roman rule in Hispania in his book about the Iberian peninsula.

104 Above, pp.127–8.

105 Dionysius of Halicarnassus, *On Thucydides* 9 (translated by Stephen Usher). In the Greek, these phrases are *tou Mutilēnaikou ... polemou, ton pros Aitolous polemon* and *tous epeirōtikous polemous* respectively.

106 Thucydides 3.115.3 (my translation).

107 As, for example, the 'Mantineian and Epidaurian Wars' mentioned at Thucydides 5.26.2.

108 Thucydides 1.1.1 (my translation). For this opening, and its subsequent reception, see Chapter 1, pp.13–14.

109 Thucydides 5.26.1–2. The translation here is based on Richard Crawley's. For further analysis of this passage, see Rood, *Thucydides*, pp.84–8.

110 For the issue of the separateness or otherwise of the first phase of the Peloponnesian War, compare Croix, Geoffrey E. M. de Ste., *The Origins of the Peloponnesian War* (London, 1972), pp.294–5.

111 For the 'long' eighteenth century, see for example, O'Gorman, Frank, *The Long Eighteenth Century: British Political and Social History, 1688–1832* (London and New York, 1997). The 'long' nineteenth century is perhaps best known as the conceptual framework for Eric Hobsbawm's trilogy of

works covering the years 1789–1914: *The Age of Revolution: Europe 1789–1848* (London, *c*.1962); *The Age of Capital: 1848–1875* (London, *c*.1975); and *The Age of Empire: 1875–1914* (New York, *c*.1987).

Chapter 7

1   *Punch*, Vol. 6, p.209, 8 May 1844. See Embree, Ainslie T., 'Napier, Sir Charles James (1782–1853)', *Oxford Dictionary of National Biography* (Oxford, September 2004), online edition, January 2008. http://www.oxforddnb.com/view/article/19748 (accessed 27 August 2008).

2   Most recently in Hurd, Douglas, *Robert Peel: A Biography* (London, 2007), p.294.

3   Kelso, Paul, 'Mayor attacks generals in battle of Trafalgar Square', *The Guardian*, 20 October 2000 (available at http://www.guardian.co.uk/uk/2000/oct/20/london.politicalnews) (accessed on 27 August 2008).

4   Napier, William F. P., *Life and Opinions of Sir Charles Napier* (London, 1857), p.1.

5   For the latest version of Napier's life in this work and links which show the evolution of previous entries, see Embree, 'Napier'.

6   Hurd, *Peel*, pp.293–5.

7   *The Times*, 29 August 1853.

8   Compare Suetonius, *Divus Julius* 51: 'city-folk, lock up your wives; we bring a bald adulterer'. For assessments of these effusions in their cultural context, see Syme, Ronald, *The Roman Revolution* (Oxford, 1939), p.151; Richlin, Amy, *The Garden of Priapus: Sexuality and Aggression in Roman Humor*, revised edition (New Haven and London, 1992), p.95; and Fantham, Elaine, 'Liberty and the people in Republican Rome', *Transactions of the American Philological Association* 135 (2005), pp.209–29, at p.219.

9   Plutarch, *Life of Lysander* 14 (noting that 'this actual story was invented for its neatness' sake').

10 Macaulay, Thomas Babington, *The History of England from the Accession of James the Second*, Everyman Edition (London, 1906), Vol. 1, p.786 and footnote.

11 See Chapter 2, pp.27–8.

12 Chapter 1, pp.11–12.

13 For the student of classics, the most obvious example of historical fiction in the medium of comics is Frank Miller's 1998 work *300*, published by Dark

Horse comics and subsequently converted to the big screen in a 2006 film directed by Zack Snyder. Note also, however, Warren Ellis's *Crécy*, which deals with the eponymous battle of 1346, illustrated by Raulo Cáceres and released by the Avatar Press in 2007.

14 As, for example, Sellar, Walter C. and Yeatman, Robert J., *1066 and all that: A Memorable History of England: Comprising, all the Parts You Can Remember Including One Hundred and Three Good Things, Five Bad Kings, and Two Genuine Dates* (London, 1930); and Pile, Stephen, *The Book of Heroic Failures: Official Handbook of the Not Terribly Good Club of Great Britain* (London, 1979).

15 See above, p.50 and p.208, n7.

16 For Syme, *The Roman Revolution* and its self-conscious relationship with the narrative of Tacitus's *Annals*, see Chapter 3, p.59. For the speculative and reconstructive elements in Syme's *The Augustan Aristocracy* (Oxford, 1986), see Chapter 5, pp.109–10 above.

17 Oxford University Register of Convocation N f. 144. See Stuart Jones, Henry, 'The Foundation and history of the Camden Chair', available at http://www.oahs.org.uk/oxo/vol%208-9/Jones.doc (accessed on 27 August 2008). For this insight into the foundation of the Chair, I am also indebted to the unpublished valedictory lecture given by Fergus Millar on his own retirement from it.

18 See Chapter 6, p.121.

19 *Oxoniana* (edited anonymously by John Walker and published at London without date *c*.1807), iv, 58f.

20 Stuart Jones, 'Foundation', p.6: 'The selection of Florus by Camden was, I expect, suggested by a passage in the writings of Camden's friend Justus Lipsius recommending Florus as an epitome of Roman history for beginners.'

21 MacCaffrey, Wallace T. (ed), *William Camden: The History of the Most Renowned and Victorious Princess Elizabeth Late Queen of England: Selected Chapters* (Chicago and London, 1970), pp.3–8. This is ultimately derived from an analogy of Polybius (Polybius 12.12.3 and possibly 24.4.2 as well). For Camden's erudition as regarded classical historiography, see Collinson, Patrick, 'One of Us? William Camden and the Making of History', *Transactions of the Royal Historical Society*, Sixth Series, 8 (1998), pp.139–63.

22 See Chapter 1, pp.5–14.

23 Plutarch, *Life of Alexander*, p.1 (my translation). For this passage and its relevance to historiography, see the discussion at Pitcher, Luke V.,

'Characterisation in ancient historiography', in John Marincola (ed), *A Companion to Greek and Roman Historiography* (Malden, MA, and Oxford, 2007), pp.102–17, at p.102. As I shall be indicating, however, the lines between biography and history are in fact rather more complicated than that piece suggests.

24 Tacitus, *Annals* 4.32.1–2 (my translation).

25 See Chapter 2, pp.38–9, for further ancient and modern examples of this technique.

26 For a subtle exploration of the ways in which Tacitus fills this alleged void, see Martin, Ronald H. and Woodman, Anthony J. (eds), *Tacitus: Annals Book IV* (Cambridge, 1989), pp.170–1, on this passage.

27 See below, pp.176–8.

28 The story of Pliny the Elder at the eruption of Vesuvius, in which he perished, is told at greatest length by his nephew in one of his letters (Pliny the Younger, *Letters* 6.16). The fact that Pliny the Younger was excerpting Livy (in order to improve his prose style) is revealed in another letter (Pliny the Younger, *Letters* 6.20.5). See also Ash, Rhiannon, '"Aliud Est Enim Epistulam, Aliud Historiam ... Scribere" (Epistles 6.16.22): Pliny the Historian?', *Arethusa* 36.2 (2003), pp.211–25.

29 See below, pp.171–2.

30 See Chapter 6, pp.123–6.

31 Homer, *Iliad* 11.638–41 (for the posset); Homer, *Odyssey* 5.234–61 (for the raft).

32 Thucydides 1.6.3–5. For this perhaps unexpected piece of 'social history' from Thucydides, see Hornblower, Simon, *A Commentary on Thucydides Volume I: Books I–III* (Oxford, 1991), pp.25–7. For an interesting instance of the modern reception of this passage, see also pp.167–71 below.

33 Xenophon, *Anabasis* 4.8.20. On this 'mad honey' and its subsequent history, see Lane Fox, Robin, 'Introduction', in Robin Lane Fox (ed), *The Long March: Xenophon and the Ten Thousand* (New Haven and London, 2004), pp.1–46, at pp.36–9.

34 Polybius 12.3.8–9 (yet another polemic against Timaeus): 'Regarding Corsica, too, he makes the same kind of random statements as in the case of Africa. In the account he gives of it ... he tells us that there are many wild goats, sheep, and cattle in it, as well as deer, hares, wolves, and certain other animals ... The fact is that in this island not only is there not a single

wild goat or wild ox, but there are not even any hares, wolves, deer, or similar animals ... ' (translated by W. R. Paton).

35 Polybius 12.4.5–6 (just after the passage in the previous footnote): 'it is by no means surprising that the animals should obey the call of the trumpet; for in Italy those in care of swine manage matters in the same way as pasturing them' (translated by W. R. Paton).

36 Tacitus, *Annals* 6.28. For discussion, see Keitel, Elizabeth, 'The Nonappearance of the Phoenix at Tacitus *Annals* 6.28', *American Journal of Philology* 120 (1999), pp.429–42.

37 Theopompus of Chios, as reported at Athenaeus 12.517D–18B (*FGrHist* 115 F 204). For analyses of this fragment, see Shrimpton, Gordon S., *Theopompus the Historian* (McGill-Queen's Press, 1991), pp.104f.; and Flower, Michael A., *Theopompus of Chios: History and Rhetoric in the Fourth Century BC* (Oxford, 1997), p.190.

38 See below, pp.170–1.

39 Whittaker, C. Richard (ed), *Herodian I: Books I–IV* (Cambridge, MA and London, 1969), p.xxx. See Chapter 5, pp.103–4, and (on digressions in Herodian) p.150 below.

40 For the focuses of Thucydides's interests, see Chapter 6, pp.125–6.

41 Polybius 38.5.4–9 (see pp.149–50) calls it a *parekbasis*.

42 On Polybian digressions, see Walbank, Frank W., *Polybius* (Berkeley, Los Angeles and London, 1972), pp.46–8.

43 Polybius 38.5.4–9 (translated by W. R. Paton).

44 For the objections of Dionysius of Halicarnassus to this narrative practice in Thucydides and to Appian's resistance to it in plotting the discrete arenas in which the Roman's exercised their virtue, see Chapter 6, pp.127–30. Polybius himself, of course was fully capable of pursuing a line of events to its conclusion when this seemed to assist clarity of exposition (see p.131 above).

45 Polybius 38.5.2 (translated by W. R. Paton).

46 Herodian 6.7.6 (for the freezing of the Danube); Herodian 7.4.4 (for farming conditions in North Africa). On Herodian's digressions and the imprudence of using their subject matter in attempts to determine the composition of his audience, see Whittaker, *Herodian*, pp.xxvii–xxxi.

47 For a discussion of Polybius and the Roman constitution, with further bibliography, see Lintott, Andrew, *The Constitution of the Roman Republic* (Oxford, 1999), pp.16–26.

48 See Chapter 2, pp. 32–3. Polybius states this programme at several points in his history (Polybius 1.1.5–6,1.2.7, 1.4.1, 3.1.4, 3.1.9, 3.2.6, 3.3.9, 3.4.2, 3.118.9, 6.2.3, 8.2.3, 39.8.7).

49 See also Walbank, *Polybius*, p.130.

50 *POxy* 842. For more on the *Hellenica Oxyrhynchia*, its usefulness as a source for early fourth-century BCE Greek history and its fragmentary preservation, see pp.103 and 119.

51 Compare the analysis of Patrick O'Brian's naval fiction at pp.11–13.

52 Canvassed dates range from the first-century BCE to the reign of Hadrian.

53 Morgan, John R., 'Fiction and history: historiography and the novel', in John Marincola (ed), *A Companion to Greek and Roman Historiography* (Malden, MA, and Oxford: Blackwell, 2007), pp.553–64, at p.554: 'The romantic story plays itself out in the interstices of real history.'

54 So for example, Morgan, 'Fiction and history', p.554. This assumption of specifically Thucydidean intertextuality is probably right. Note, though, that Polybius dissects a speech which Timaeus puts into Hermocrates's mouth at Polybius 12.25. Thucydides was not the only historian for whom Hermocrates held an appeal.

55 Chariton 1.10. Compare also 7.2 (Chaereas is speaking to the king of Egypt): ' "You may have heard of Hermocrates, a general who defeated the Athenians at sea?" The Egyptian king nodded to say he had; the whole world had heard of the disaster Athens suffered in the war with Sicily.'

56 Chariton 7.4. The account of the siege of Syene in a later novel, the *Ethiopian Story* of Heliodorus (Heliodorus 9.1f.), illustrates what we have noted as a particular problem of *Quellenforschung* in the absence of reliable chronological data (see Chapter 4, pp.83–4): it remains argued whether Heliodorus's story draws upon narratives of the historical third siege of Nisibis in 350 CE (Julian, *Orations* 1 and 3) or whether the accounts of Nisibis are themselves drawing upon Heliodorus. See Morgan, John R., *A Commentary on the Ninth and Tenth Books of the Aithiopica of Heliodorus* (D. Phil. Thesis, Oxford, 1978), pp.ii–xxxviii (in favour of the first view), Szepessy, T., *Acta Antiquae Academiae Scientiarum Hungaricae* 24 (1976), pp.247–76 (in favour of the second).

57 Gibbon, Edward, *The History of the Decline and Fall of the Roman Empire*, J. B. Bury (ed), Vol. 2 (London, 1896–1900), 523 n.

58 Cicero, *Letters to his Brother* 1.122–4.

59 See Chapter 2, pp.28–30.

60 See Chapter 1, pp.19–24.

61 Lucian, *A True Story* 1.4 (translated by B. P. Reardon).

62 See Chapter 3, pp.63–4 (for autopsy) and pp.57–63 (for oral reports from others).

63 Longus, *Daphnis and Chloe*, Prologue 1–3 (translated by J. R. Morgan).

64 Photius, *Bibliotheca Cod.* 166. The standard edition of what remains of Antonius is Stephens, Susan A. and Winkler, John J., *Ancient Greek Novels: The Fragments* (Princeton, *c*.1995); there is a translation in Reardon, Bryan P. (ed), *Collected Ancient Greek Novels* (Berkeley, 1989).

65 See above, pp.13–14.

66 Lucian, *A True Story* 1.2–3 (translated by B. P. Reardon).

67 On Lucian and Ctesias, see also Wiseman, Timothy P., 'Lying Historians: Seven Types of Mendacity', in C. Gill and T. P. Wiseman (eds), *Lies and Fiction in the Ancient World* (Austin, 1993), pp.122–46, pp.131, 132.

68 On this work, see Lenfant, Dominique, 'L'Inde de Ctésias: Des sources aux représentations', *Topoi* 5 (1995), pp.309–36, with earlier bibliography.

69 Diodorus 2.32.2.

70 Ctesias, *FGrHist* 688 F 45 (15).

71 For contrasting assessments of Ctesias as a historical source, see Braun, Tom, 'Xenophon's dangerous liasons', in Robin Lane Fox (ed), *The Long March: Xenophon and the Ten Thousand* (New Haven and London, 2004), pp.97–130, at pp.12–4, and Lenfant, Dominique, *Ctésias de Cnide: La Perse; L'Inde; Autres fragments* (Paris, 2004), which is perhaps unduly sanguine about his credibility.

72 *FGrHist* 687a T 2. On mendacious historians, see Chapter 2, pp.28–30.

73 'You have been careful not to write in praise of the men of your own time … ' ([Phalaris] *Ep.* 78 = Trapp 60). For further commentary and translation, see Trapp, Michael, *Greek and Latin Letters: An Anthology with Translation* (Cambridge, 2003), p.60.

74 For a good, brief account of the late seventeenth-century controversy over the 'authenticity' of the letters, see Brink, Charles O., *English Classical Scholarship: Historical Reflections on Bentley, Porson and Housman* (Cambridge, 1986), pp.49–60.

75 A possible modern *comparandum* would be the episode of the BBC TV time-travel drama *Doctor Who* called 'The unicorn and the wasp' (written by Gareth Roberts, directed by Graeme Harper, originally broadcast 17 May

2008). In this the (historical) disappearance for several days of the author Agatha Christie is filled in by the sci-fi plot.

76 See Chapter 1, pp.5–14.

77 On the Atthidographers, see Rhodes, Peter J., 'The Atthidographers', in H. Verdin, G. Schepens and E. de Keyer (eds), *Purposes of History: Proceedings of the International Colloquium – Leuven, 24–26 May 1988* (Louvain, 1990), pp.73–81, who rightly stresses the great variety of works which seem to have fallen under this rubric.

78 For more on 'local histories', see Clarke, Katherine, *Making Time for the Past: Local History and the Polis* (Oxford).

79 For these categories and a discussion of the theoretical issues involved in using them, see Marincola, John, *Authority and Tradition in Ancient Historiography* (Cambridge, 1997), pp.1, 2.

80 For a trenchant critique of 'ethnography' as a monolithic concept in antiquity, see Marincola, John, 'Genre, convention, and innovation in Greco-Roman historiography', in Christina S. Kraus (ed), *The Limits of Historiography: Genre and Narrative in Ancient Historical Texts* (Leiden, 1999), pp.281–324, at pp.295–9.

81 Chapter 3, pp.51–2.

82 Chapter 6, pp.127–8.

83 Dionysius of Halicarnassus, *On Thucydides* 5 (translated by Stephen Usher).

84 See below, pp.172–3.

85 Jacoby, Felix, 'Über die Entwicklung der griechischen Historiographie und den Plan einer neuen Sammlung der griechischen Historikerfragmente', *Klio* 9 (1909), pp.80–123 (Jacoby, F., *Abhandlungen zur griechischen Geschichtsschreibung* (ed. H. Bloch) (Leiden, 1956), pp.16–64). For Jacoby's view on how this played out in the career of Herodotus, see Jacoby, Felix, 'Herodotos', in A. F. von Pauly et al. (eds), *Paulys Real-encyclopädie der classischen Altertumswissenschaft*, Suppl. II. (Stuttgart, 1913), pp.205–520, at pp.352–60.

86 For a detailed critique of Jacoby's model, see Fowler, Robert, 'Herodotos and his contemporaries', *Journal of Hellenic Studies* 116 (1996), pp.62–87, at 62, and note in particular p.69: 'Of course Greek historiography developed in some sense, but one must be careful to describe developments in appropriate terms. Rather than thinking of a step-by-step development, we would be wise to think in terms of a long and mutually beneficial exchange of work and ideas between Herodotos and his many contemporaries.'

87 See Chapter 6, pp.114–5.

88 Polybus 12.11.1 (translated by W. R. Paton).

89 Polybius, 8.11.3–4 (translated by W. T. Paton). For more on Polybius and Theopompus's treatment of Philip, see Walbank, F. W., 'The two-way shadow: Polybius among the fragments', in G. Schepens and J. Bollansée (eds), *The Shadow of Polybius: Intertextuality as a Research Tool in Greek Historiography – Proceedings of the International Colloquium Leuven, 21–2 September 2001* (Leiden, 2004), pp.1–18, at p.5. Diodorus, by contrast, adopts the stance that the deeds of a king are ideally contained within discrete units of a multi-volume history for the sake of structural unity: 'In all systematic historical treatises it behoves the historian to include in his books actions of states or of kings which are complete in themselves from beginning to end' (Diodorus 16.1.1, translated by Charles Sherman).

90 See above, pp.144–5.

91 See Chapter 6, pp.116–7.

92 The most notable extant example of this enterprise is the Latin collection assembled in nine books by Valerius Maximus under the reign of Tiberius in the first century CE. For analyses of this, see Bloomer, W. Martin, *Valerius Maximus and the Rhetoric of the New Nobility* (Chapel Hill, 1992), and Gowing, Alain M., *Empire and Memory: the Representation of the Roman Republic in Imperial Culture* (Cambridge, 2005) Chapter Two. For Appian's exemplary mode here, see Henderson, John, 'Three men in a vote: Proscription and the power of the text (Appian, *Bellum Ciuile* 4.1. 1–6. 51)', in *Histos* 1 (1997), available at http://www.dur.ac.uk/Classics/histos/1997/henderson.html (accessed on 31 August 2008).

93 Appian, *Mithridatica* 469, 'to such a pitch of *paradoxology* did Mithridates come' (my translation).

94 The most famous collection of signs and wonders of which we still have substantial remains from antiquity is that by Phlegon of Tralles. See Hansen, William, *Phlegon of Tralles' Book of Marvels* (Exeter, 1996), with the review of John R. Morgan in *Histos* 2 (1998) at http://www.dur.ac.uk/Classics/histos/1998/morgan.html (accessed on 31 August 2008), which adroitly compares instances of 'paradoxography' from the modern world. For an adroit analysis of paradoxography in another historiographer, see Woodman, Anthony J., 'Nero's alien capital: Tacitus as paradoxographer', in A. J. Woodman and Jonathan Powell (eds), *Author and Audience in Latin Literature* (Cambridge, 1992), pp.173–88.

Notes

95 See also Gabba, Emilio, 'True history and false history in classical antiquity', *Journal of Roman Studies* 71 (1981), pp.50–62.

96 See also the remarks at Marincola, 'Genre, convention, and innovation', p.301.

97 The most notable example of an encyclopaedia still substantially extant from antiquity is the *Natural History* of the Elder Pliny, which we have had occasion to quote already in this study (see above, p.204, n64 and 71). For studies in this work, see Bispham, Edward, Roew, Greg and Matthews, Elaine (eds), Vita vigilia est: Essays in honour of Barbara Levick (*Bulletin of the Institute of Classical Studies Supplement* 100: 2007).

98 Consider, for example, the case of Asconius's commentaries on the speeches of Cicero, which have already been discussed above (pp.76–7). See further Lewis, R. Geoffrey (ed), *Asconius: Commentaries on Speeches by Cicero* (Oxford, 2006).

99 *FGrHist* 765 F 18.

Chapter 8

1 Stoppard's later play, *The Invention of Love*, concerned the great textual critic A. E. Housman.

2 Chapter 6, pp.118–20.

3 Gray, Alasdair, *Old Men in Love* (London, 2007), p.167.

4 'Egoom-no-they-san tay protoy kai' and 'exontes, exontes'. The misleading element is that Rees is in fact bemusedly pronouncing the Greek letter 'chi' as the English 'x', whose shape it resembles rather than the 'kh' sound it actually represented. Thus, the last, repeated word would more accurately be rendered as 'ekhontes'.

5 This was taken from Crawley, Richard (trans.), *The History of the Peloponnesian War* (London, 1874).

6 Chapter 7, pp.148–9.

7 On this point, see also Brunt, Peter A., 'On historical fragments and epitomes', *Classical Quarterly* 30/2 (1980), pp.477–94, at p.479.

8 For more on the novel and its preoccupations, see Glass, Rodge, *Alasdair Gray: A Secretary's Biography* (London, 2008), pp.298–303.

9 Yarrow, Liv, *Historiography at the End of the Republic: Provincial Perspectives on Roman Rule* (Oxford, 2005), pp.107–8, notes the consequences of this distribution for our view of the first-century BCE historian Posidonius.

10 For the ways in which Athenaeus can be seen reshaping his 'fragments' of earlier authors, see Pelling, Christopher, 'Fun with Fragments', in David Braund and John Wilkins (eds), *Athenaeus and his World: Reading Greek Culture in the Roman Empire* (Exeter, 2000), pp.171–90.

11 Chapter 6, pp.127–8.

12 Jacoby, Felix et al., *Die Fragmente der griechischen Historiker* (Berlin and Leiden, 1923–58; Leiden, 1958–), usually abbreviated, as elsewhere in this study, to *FGrHist*. Peter, Hermann, *Historicorum Romanorum Reliquiae*, two volumes (Stuttgart, 1906–14), usually abbreviated as *HRR*. Both works are currently in the process of being updated by large teams of scholars: *FGrHist* as *Brill's New Jacoby*, under the editorship of Ian Worthington, and *HRR* as Cornell, Tim J., Rich, John W. and Smith, Christopher J. (eds), *The Fragmentary Roman Historians* (Oxford, in press). For more reflection on the methodological problems involved in Jacoby's enterprise, see Schepens, Guido, 'Jacoby's *FGrHist*: problems, methods, prospects' and Bowersock, Glen W., 'Jacoby's fragments and two Greek historians of pre-Islamic Arabia', in Glenn W. Most (ed), *Collecting Fragments-Fragmente sammeln. (Aporemata: Kritische Studien zur Philologiegeschichte 1.* Göttingen: Vandenhoeck and Ruprecht, 1997), pp.144–72, 173–85.

13 Brunt, 'On Historical Fragments', p.477, therefore prefers the less misleading term 'reliquiae'.

14 Compare Bowersock, 'Jacoby's fragments', p.185: 'The methodological problems of Jacoby's *Fragmente* illustrated here may arguably not warrant a wholesale condemnation of his enterprise. His collection can be viewed as a kind of ladder borrowed from Wittgenstein's philosophy: one uses it to climb up and then throws it away. Or again it may be seen to resemble navigational software for the Internet ... But one point is absolutely secure and that is the necessity to leave Jacoby behind and to examine the original sources for historical fragments (however defined) before bringing any scholarly research on them to a conclusion.'

15 Chapter 6, pp.120–6.

16 Chapter 2, pp.35–6.

17 This is the passage in which Polybius criticizes Callisthenes's account of troop dispositions at the battle of Issus (Polybius 12.17–22).

18 See above, pp.106–7, 116–17.

19 This is an issue which surfaces repeatedly in Schepens, Guido and Bollansée, Jan, (eds), *The Shadow of Polybius: Intertextuality as a Research Tool*

in Greek Historiography – Proceedings of the International Colloquium Leuven, 21–2 September 2001 (Leiden, 2004).

20 Syme, Ronald, *The Roman Revolution* (Oxford, 1939), p.6: 'Pollio, the partisan of Caesar and of Antonius, was a pessimistic Republican and an honest man. Of tough Italic stock, hating pomp and pretence, he wrote of the Revolution as that bitter theme demanded, in a plain, hard style ... ' and so on.

21 Chapter 4, pp.80–1.

22 Polybius 12.25c.1–5 (of, inevitably, Timaeus) translated by W. R. Paton. Polybius himself, of course, would not be entirely immune to a similar observation.

23 For an example of how 'lost' historians can attain an ascendancy over those that have the misfortune to survive more or less intact, compare Sidebottom, Harry, 'Herodian's Historical methods and understanding of history', *Aufstieg und Niedergang der römischen Welt* II.34.4 (Berlin and New York, 1998), pp.2775–836, pp.2827, 2828, on the contrasting receptions of Herodian (mostly intact) and Dexippus (largely gone).

24 One exception would be the endlessly controversial sentence at Thucydides 1.22, discussing the historian's policy with regard to speeches in his history. Chapter 5, pp.107–8.

25 For an interesting case study in how translations can affect historical interpretation, see Woodman, Anthony J., 'Readers and reception: A text case', in John Marincola (ed), *A Companion to Greek and Roman Historiography* (Malden, MA and Oxford, 2007), pp.33–44.

26 Chapter 3, pp.66–7.

27 Chapter 4, pp.87–9.

SUGGESTIONS FOR FURTHER READING

As far as classical historiography is concerned, there is no substitute for assiduous reading and re-reading of the works of the classical historians themselves. Greek or Latin texts of most of the authors handled in this study can be found amongst such series as Oxford Classical Texts, the Bibliotheca Teubneriana, the *Collection Budé* and the Loeb Classical Library. The last-named also carries a facing English translation. Separate English translations of the historians are available in such series as World's Classics and Penguin Classics.

As noted in Chapter 8, individual texts and translations of historians can vary widely in terms of their aims, methodology and reliability. A useful resource in getting a sense for what a particular edition or translation is like is the *Bryn Mawr Classical Review*, at http://ccat.sas.upenn.edu/bmcr/. This reviews classical publications, and has a searchable archive.

In terms of scholarly literature *about* classical historiography, I have tried to suggest in the Notes some useful scholarships relevant to particular authors and topics. The consolidated bibliography at the end of this book also supplies some hints. For general usefulness, the following surveys are a good place to start. Each, in turn, contains further bibliographical suggestions:

Duff, T., *The Greek and Roman Historians* (Bristol, 2003).
Kraus, C. S. and Woodman, A.J., *Latin Historians* (Cambridge, 1997).

Luce, T. J., *The Greek Historians* (London and New York, 1997).

Marincola, John, *Authority and Tradition in Ancient Historiography* (Cambridge, 1997).

——, *Greek Historians* (Cambridge, 2001).

—— (ed), *A Companion to Greek and Roman Historiography* (Malden, MA, and Oxford, 2007).

BIBLIOGRAPHY

Ackroyd, Peter, *The Plato Papers: A Novel* (London, 1999).

Adams, J. N., 'The vocabulary of the later decades of Livy', *Antichthon* 8 (1974), pp.54–62.

Albrecht, M. von, *Masters of Roman Prose* (Leeds, 1989), pp.136–59.

Alonso-Núñez, J. M., *The Idea of Universal History in Greece: from Herodotus to the Age of Augustus* (Amsterdam, 2002).

Annan, Noel, *The Dons: Mentors, Eccentrics and Geniuses* (London, 1999).

Arnott, W. Geoffrey, 'Walter Headlam: Achiever or non-achiever?', in H. D. Jocelyn (ed), *Aspects of Nineteenth-Century British Classical Scholarship*, Liverpool Classical Papers No. 5 (Liverpool, 1996).

Ash, Rhiannon, ' "Aliud est enim epistulam, aliud historiam... scribere" (Epistles 6.16.22): Pliny the historian?', *Arethusa* 36/2 (2003), pp.211–25.

—— (ed), *Tacitus: Histories 2* (Cambridge, 2007).

Asheri, D., Lloyd, A. B. and Corcella, A., *A Commentary on Herodotus I–IV* (Oxford, 2007).

Astin, A. E., *Scipio Aemilianus* (Oxford, 1967).

Baaz, E., *De Herodiani Fontibus et Auctoritate*, Dissertation (Berlin, 1909).

Badian. E., 'The early historians', in T. A. Dorey (ed), *Latin Historians* (London, 1966), pp.1–38.

——, *From Plataea to Potidaea: Studies in the History and Historiography of the Pentecontaetia* (Baltimore and London, 1993).

Bayle, P., *Dictionnaire Historique et Critique* (third edition, Rotterdam, 1697).

Beard, Mary, 'Writing and ritual. A study of diversity and expansion in the Arval Acta', *Proceedings of the British School at Rome* 53 (1985), pp.114–62.

Beck, H., 'The early Roman tradition', in John Marincola (ed), *A Companion to Greek and Roman Historiography* (Malden, MA, and Oxford, 2007), pp.259–65.

Benson, E. F., *As We Were: A Victorian Peep-Show* (London, 1985).

Bispham, Edward, Roew, Greg and Matthews, Elaine (eds), Vita vigilia est: Essays in honour of Barbara Levick (*Bulletin of the Institute of Classical Studies Supplement* 100:2007).

Bloch, M., *The Historian's Craft* (Manchester, 1954).

Bloomer, W. Martin, *Valerius Maximus and the Rhetoric of the New Nobility* (Chapel Hill, 1992).

Bosworth, A. B., *A Historical Commentary on Arrian's History of Alexander*, Vol. 1 (Oxford, 1980), p.43.

Bowen, A. J. (ed), *Plutarch: On the Malice of Herodotus* (Warminster, 1992).

Bowersock, G. W., 'Jacoby's fragments and two Greek historians of pre-Islamic Arabia', in Glenn W. Most (ed), *Collecting Fragments-Fragmente sammeln. (Aporemata: Kritische Studien zur Philologiegeschichte* 1. Göttingen: Vandenhoeck and Ruprecht, 1997), pp.173–85.

Bowie, A. M. (ed), *Herodotus: Histories. Book VIII* (Cambridge, 2007).

Bowie, E. L., 'The Greeks and their past in the Second Sophistic', in *Past and Present* 46 (1970), pp.3–41.

Bowra, C. M., *Memories 1898–1939* (London, 1966).

Braudel, Fernand, *The Mediterranean and the Mediterranean World in the Age of Philip II (La Méditerrannée et le Monde Méditerrannéen à l'époque de Philippe II)*, second edition, two volumes (London and New York, 1966, 1973).

Braun, Tom, 'Xenophon's dangerous liasons', in Robin Lane Fox (ed), *The Long March: Xenophon and the Ten Thousand* (New Haven and London, 2004), pp.97–130.

Brink, C. O., *English Classical Scholarship: Historical Reflections on Bentley, Porson and Housman* (Cambridge, 1986).

Briscoe, John, review of C. P. Jones, *Plutarch and Rome* (Oxford, 1971), *Classical Review* 24 (1974), pp.202–4.

Brosius, M. (ed), *Ancient Archives and Archival Traditions: Concepts of Record-Keeping in the Ancient World* (Oxford, 2003).

Brown, Peter, 'Arnaldo Dante Momigliano 1908–87', *Proceedings of the British Academy* 74 (1988), pp.405–42.

Browning, Andrew, 'Lord Macaulay, 1800–59', *Historical Journal* 2 (1959), pp.149–60.

Bruce, I. A. F., *A Historical Commentary on the Hellenica Oxyrhynchia* (Cambridge, 1967).

Brunt, P. A. (ed), *Arrian: History of Alexander and Indica I* (Cambridge, MA and London, 1976).

—— (ed), *Arrian: History of Alexander and Indica II* (Cambridge, MA and London, 1983).

——, 'On historical fragments and epitomes', *Classical Quarterly* 30/2 (1980), pp.477–94.

——, 'Cicero and historiography', in P. A. Brunt, *Studies in Greek History and Thought* (Oxford, 1993), pp.181–209.

—— and Moore, J. M., *Res gestae divi Augusti: the achievements of the divine Augustus* (Oxford, 1967).

Burke, Peter, *The French Historical Revolution: The 'Annales' School, 1929–89* (Stanford, 1990).

Butterfield, Herbert, *The Whig Interpretation of History* (London, 1931).

Cameron, Averil, *Procopius and the Sixth Century* (Berkeley, 1985).

Capponi, Livia, *Augustan Egypt: The Creation of a Roman Province* (New York, 2005).

Cargill, Jack, *The Second Athenian League: Empire or Free Alliance?* (Berkeley, 1981).

Carr, E. H., *What is History?* (Basingstoke, 1961).

——, *A History of Soviet Russia 12: Foundations of a Planned Economy 1926–1929* (London, 1976), Vol. 3, Part 1.

——, *A History of Soviet Russia 14: Foundations of a Planned Economy 1926–1929* (London, 1978), Vol. 3, Part 3.

—— and Davies, R. W., *A History of Soviet Russia 9: Foundations of a Planned Economy 1926–1929* (London, 1969), Vol. 1, Part 1.

Carter, John H., *Suetonius: Divus Augustus* (London, 1982).

Cawkwell, George, 'When, how and why did Xenophon write the *Anabasis?*', in Robin Lane Fox (ed), *The Long March: Xenophon and the Ten Thousand* (New Haven and London, 2004), pp.47–67.

Chilver, G. E. F., *A Historical Commentary on Tacitus' Histories I and II* (Oxford, 1979).

Clark, J. K., *Goodwin Wharton* (Oxford, 1984).

Clarke, Katherine, 'Universal perspectives in historiography', in C. S. Kraus (ed), *The Limits of Historiography: Genre and Narrative in Ancient Historical Texts* (Leiden, 1999), pp.249–79.

——, *Making Time for the Past: Local History and the Polis* (Oxford, 2008).

Collingwood, R. G., *The Idea of History* (Oxford, 1946).

Collinson, Patrick, 'One of Us? William Camden and the making of history', *Transactions of the Royal Historical Society* Sixth Series, 8 (1998), pp.139–63.

——, 'Elton, Sir Geoffrey Rudolph (1921–94)', *Oxford Dictionary of National Biography* (Oxford, 2004) [http://www.oxforddnb.com/view/article/54946, accessed 30 July 2008].

Connor, W. R., *Thucydides* (Princeton, c.1984), pp.212–18.

Cornell, T. J., 'The formation of the historical tradition of early Rome', in I. S. Moxon, J. D. Smart and A. J. Woodman (eds), *Past Perspectives: Studies in Greek and Roman Historical Writing* (Cambridge, 1986), pp.67–86.

——, Rich, J. W. and Smith, C. J. (eds), *The Fragmentary Roman Historians* (Oxford, in press).

Crane, Nicholas, *Mercator: The Man who Mapped the Planet* (London, 2002).

Crawford, M. H. (ed), *Roman Statutes*, two volumes, (London, 1996).

Crawley, Richard (trans.) *The History of the Peloponnesian War* (London, 1874).

Croix, G. E. M. de Ste., *The Origins of the Peloponnesian War* (London, 1972).

——, 'Aristotle on history and poetry (*Poetics* 9, 1451a36–b11)', in B. Levick (ed), *The Ancient Historian and his Materials: Essays in Honour of C. E. Stevens on his Seventieth Birthday* (London, 1975), pp.45–58.

Culham, Phyllis, 'Archives and Alternatives in Republican Rome', *Classical Philology* 84 (1989), pp.100–15.

Bibliography

Damon, Cynthia, *Tacitus: Histories 1* (Cambridge, 2003).

Davies, John, 'The Tradition about the First Sacred War', in Simon Hornblower (ed), *Greek Historiography* (Oxford, 1994), pp.193–212.

Degrassi, A., *Inscriptiones Latinae liberae rei publicae* (Firenze, 1963).

Dessau, H. (ed) *Inscriptiones Latinae Selectae*, five volumes (Berlin, 1892–1916).

Dewald, Carolyn, 'Pickled heroes, wanton kings, and gnomic founding fathers: Reading the end of Herodotus' histories', in D. H. Roberts, F. M. Dunn and D. Fowler (eds), *Classical Closure: Reading the End in Greek and Latin Literature* (Princeton, 1997), pp.62–82.

——, 'The Construction of meaning in the first three historians', in John Marincola (ed), *A Companion to Greek and Roman Historiography* (Malden, MA, and Oxford, 2007), pp.89–101.

—— and Marincola, John (eds), *The Cambridge Companion to Herodotus* (Cambridge, 2006).

Drews, Robert, 'Ephorus and history written kata genos', *American Journal of Philology*, 84,3 (July, 1963), pp.244–55.

Duff, T., *The Greek and Roman Historians* (Bristol, 2003).

Eck, W., Caballos, A. and Fernández, F., *Das Senatus Consultum de Cn. Pisone Patre* (Munich, 1996).

Egermann, F., 'Thukydides über die Art seiner Reden und über seine Darstellung der Kriegsgeschehnisse', *Historia* 21 (1972), pp.575–602.

Ehrman, J., *The Younger Pitt*, three volumes (London 1969–96).

Ellmann, Richard, *Oscar Wilde* (London, 1987).

Elton, G. R., *The Practice of History* (Sydney, 1967).

——, *F. W. Maitland* (New Haven and London, 1985).

Embree, Ainslie T., 'Napier, Sir Charles James (1782–1853)', *Oxford Dictionary of National Biography* (Oxford, September 2004), online edition, January 2008 [http://www.oxforddnb.com/view/article/19748, accessed 27 August 2008].

Engelmann, H., *Die Inschriften von Cyme* (Bonn, 1976).

Evans, Richard J., *In Defence of History* (London, 1997).

Fantham, Elaine, *The Roman World of Cicero's De Oratore* (Oxford, 2004).

——, 'Liberty and the people in Republican Rome', *Transactions of the American Philological Association* 135 (2005), pp.209–29.

Fehling, Detlev, *Herodotus and his 'sources': citation, invention and narrative art* (Leeds, 1989).

Flory, S., 'The meaning of *to mē muthōdes* (1.22.4) and the usefulness of Thucydides' history', *Classical Journal* 85 (1990), pp.193–208.

Flower, M. A., *Theopompus of Chios: History and Rhetoric in the Fourth Century BC* (Oxford, 1997).

Forsythe, G., *The Historian L. Calpurnius Piso Frugi and the Roman Annalistic Tradition* (Lanham, New York and London, 1994).

Fowler, Don, *Lucretius on Atomic Motion. A Commentary on De Rerum Natura, Book Two, Lines 1–332* (Oxford, 2002).

Fowler, Robert, 'Herodotos and his contemporaries', *Journal of Hellenic Studies* 116 (1996), pp.62–87.

Fox, Matthew, *Cicero's Philosophy of History* (Oxford, 2007).

Gabba, E., 'True history and false history in classical antiquity', *Journal of Roman Studies* 71 (1981), pp.50–62.

Gall, James, 'Use of cylindrical projections for geographical, astronomical, and scientific purposes', *Scottish Geographical Magazine* 1.4 (1885), pp.119–23.

Gelzer, M., 'Über die Arbeitsweise des Polybios', in M. Gelzer, *Kleine Schriften*, Vol. 3 (1964).

Gibbon, Edward, *A Vindication of some Passages in the Fifteenth and Sixteenth Chapters of The History of the Decline and Fall of the Roman Empire* (London, 1779).

———, *The Miscellaneous Works of Edward Gibbon, Esq: With Memoirs of His Life and Writings*, John Holroyd Sheffield (ed) (Dublin, 1796).

———, *The History of the Decline and Fall of the Roman Empire* (J. B. Bury, ed) (London, 1896–1900).

Glass, Rodge, *Alasdair Gray: A Secretary's Biography* (London, 2008).

Gombrich, E. H., *A Little History of the World* (Yale, 2005).

Gomme, A. W., *A Historical Commentary on Thucydides – Volume I: Introduction and Commentary on Book I* (Oxford, 1945).

———, Andrewes, A. and Dover, K. J., *A Historical Commentary on Thucydides – Volume V: Book VIII* (Oxford, 1981).

González, J., 'Tabula siarensis, fortunales siarenses, and the municipia ciuium Romanorum', *Zeitschrift für Papyrologie und Epigraphik* 55 (1984), pp.55–100.

Goodyear, F. R. D., *Tacitus – Greece and Rome New Surveys* (Cambridge, 1970).

——— (ed), *The Annals of Tacitus: Vol. 1 (Annals 1. 1–54)* (Cambridge, 1972).

Bibliography

Gowing, A. M., 'Greek advice for a Roman senator: Cassius Dio and the dialogue between Philiscus and Cicero (38.18–29)', in F. Cairns and Malcolm Heath (eds), *Proceedings of the Leeds Latin Seminar* 10 (Leeds, 1998), pp.373–90.

———, *Empire and Memory: The Representation of the Roman Republic in Imperial Culture* (Cambridge, 2005).

Grafton, Anthony, *The Footnote: A Curious History* (London, 1997).

Grant, Michael, *The Annals of Imperial Rome – Tacitus, Translated with an Introduction by Michael Grant* (London, 1963).

Gray, Alasdair, *Old Men in Love* (London, 2007).

Greenwood, Emily, *Thucydides and the Shaping of History* (London, 2006).

Griffin, M. T., 'The Elder Seneca and Spain', *Journal of Roman Studies* 62 (1972), pp.1–19.

———, 'The Lyons Tablet and Tacitean hindsight', *Classical Quarterly* 32 (1982), pp.404–18.

Griffith, G. T., 'Athens in the fourth century', in P. D. A. Garnsey and C. R. Whittaker (eds), *Imperialism in the Ancient World: The Cambridge University Research Seminar in Ancient History* (Cambridge, 1978), pp.127–44.

Haegemans, Karen and Kosmetatou, Elizabeth, 'Aratus and the Achaean background of Polybius', in G. Schepens and J. Bollansée (eds), *The Shadow of Polybius: Intertextuality as a Research Tool in Greek Historiography* (Leiden, 2004), pp.123–39.

Hahn I., 'Appian und seine Quellen', in G. Wirth (ed), *Romanitas-Christianitas: Untersuchungen zur Geschichte der Römischen Kaiserzeit* (Berlin, 1982), pp.251–76.

Hansen, William, *Phlegon of Tralles' Book of Marvels* (Exeter, 1996).

Hardy, G. H., *A Mathematician's Apology* (Cambridge, 1940).

Harrison, Thomas, 'Herodotus' conception of foreign languages', *Histos* 2 (1998), at http://www.dur.ac.uk/Classics/histos/1998/harrison.html (accessed 4 August 2008).

Haslam, Jonathan, 'Carr, Edward Hallett (1892–1982)', *Oxford Dictionary of National Biography* (Oxford, September 2004), online edition [http://www.oxforddnb.com/view/article/30902, accessed 30 July 2008].

Heath, Thomas, *A History of Greek Mathematics*, two volumes (Oxford, 1921).

Henderson, John, 'Three men in a vote: Proscription and the power of the text (Appian Bellum Ciuile 4.1. 1–6. 51)', in *Histos* 1 (1997), available at http://www.dur.ac.uk/Classics/histos/1997/henderson. html (accessed on 31 August 2008).

——, 'Livy and the invention of history', in John Henderson (ed), *Fighting for Rome: Poets and Caesars, History and Civil War* (Cambridge, 1998), pp.301–19.

Hidber, T., 'Zeit und Erzählperspektive in Herodians Geschichtswerk', in M. Zimmerman (ed), *Geschichtsschreibung und politischer Wandel im 3. Jh. N. Chr.* (Stuttgart, 1999), pp.145–67.

Hobsbawm, E., *The Age of Revolution: Europe 1789–1848* (London, c.1962).

——, *The Age of Capital: 1848–75* (London, c.1975).

——, *The Age of Empire: 1875–1914* (New York, c.1987).

Hollis, A. S. (ed), *Hecale* (Oxford, 1990).

Homeyer, H., *Lukian: Wie man Geschichte schreiben soll* (Munich, 1965).

Hopkins, Keith, 'Taxes and trade in the Roman Empire (200 B.C.–A.D. 400)', *Journal of Roman Studies* 70 (1980), pp.101–25.

——, *A World Full of Gods: Pagans, Jews and Christians in the Roman World* (London, 1999).

Hornblower, J., *Hieronymus of Cardia* (Oxford, 1981).

Hornblower, Simon, *Thucydides* (London,1987).

——, *A Commentary on Thucydides – Volume I: Books I–III* (Oxford, c.1991).

——, 'The religious dimension to the Peloponnesian War, or, what Thucydides does not tell us', *Harvard Studies in Classical Philology* 94 (1992), pp.79–97.

——, 'Introduction', in S. Hornblower (ed), *Greek Historiography* (Oxford, 1994), pp.1–72.

——, 'Narratology and narrative techniques in Thucydides', in Simon Hornblower (ed), *Greek Historiography* (Oxford, 1994), pp.131–66.

——, *A Commentary on Thucydides: Vol. 2: Books IV–V.24* (Oxford, 1996).

——, *The Greek World: 479–323 BC*, third edition (London, 2002).

Housman, A. E., *D. Ivnii Ivvenalis Saturae* (London, 1905).

Howie, G., 'Thukydides' Einstellung zur Vergangenheit: Zuhörerschaft und Wissenschaft in der Archäologie', *Klio* 66 (1984), p.502–32.

Bibliography

Humphreys, S. C., 'Fragments, fetishes, and philosophies: Towards a history of Greek historiography after Thucydides', in G. W. Most (ed), *Collecting Fragments. Fragmente sammeln* (Göttingen 1997), pp.207–24.

Hunter, Richard (ed), *Apollonius of Rhodes: Argonautica Book III* (Cambridge, 1989).

Hurd, Douglas, *Robert Peel: A Biography* (London, 2007).

Hutchinson, G. O., *Cicero's Correspondence: A Literary Study* (Oxford, 1998).

Jackson, H. J., *Marginalia: Readers Writing in Books* (New Haven and London, 2001).

Jacoby, Felix, 'Über die Entwicklung der griechischen Historiographie', *Klio* 9 (1909), pp.80–123.

——, 'Herodotos', in A. F. von Pauly et al. (eds), *Paulys Real-encyclopädie der classischen Altertumswissenschaft*, Suppl. II (Stuttgart, 1913), pp.205–520.

—— et al., *Die Fragmente der griechischen Historiker* (Berlin and Leiden, 1923–58; Leiden, 1958–).

Jaeger, Mary, 'Guiding metaphor and narrative point of view in Livy's *ab vrbe condita*', in C. S. Kraus (ed), *The Limits of Historiography: Genre and Narrative in Ancient Historical Texts* (Leiden, 1999), pp.169–95.

Janko, Richard, *The Iliad: A Commentary*, Vol. 4 (Cambridge, 1990–93).

Jong, Irene de, Nünlist, René and Bowie, Angus (eds), *Narrators, narratees, and narratives in ancient Greek literature* (Leiden, 2004).

Kantorowicz, E. H., *Kaiser Friedrich der Zweite* (Berlin, 1927).

Keitel, Elizabeth, 'The non-appearance of the Phoenix at Tacitus *Annals* 6.28', *American Journal of Philology* 120 (1999), pp.429–42.

Kelly, Christopher, 'A grand tour: reading Gibbon's *Decline and Fall*', *Greece and Rome* 44 (1997), pp.39–58.

Kelso, Paul, 'Mayor attacks generals in battle of Trafalgar Square', *The Guardian*, 20 October 2000 (available at http://www.guardian.co.uk/uk/2000/oct/20/london.politicalnews) [accessed on 27 August 2008].

Kinser, S., *The Works of Jacques-Auguste de Thou* (The Hague, 1966).

Konishi, H., 'Thucydides' *History* as a finished piece', *Liverpool Classical Monthly* 12 (1987), pp.5–7.

Kramer, E. A., 'Book One of Velleius' *History*: Scope, levels of treatment, and non-Roman elements', in *Historia* 54 (2005), pp.144–61.

Kraus, C. S., 'Jugurthine disorder', in C. S. Kraus (ed), *The Limits of Historiography: Genre and Narrative in Ancient Historical Texts* (Leiden, 1999), pp.217–47.

——, 'Caesar's account of the Battle of Massilia (BC 1.34–2.22): Some historiographical and narratological approaches', in John Marincola (ed), *A Companion to Greek and Roman Historiography*, (Malden, MA, and Oxford, 2007), pp.371–8.

—— and Woodman, A. J., *Latin Historians* (Cambridge, 1997).

Krebs, Christopher, *Tacitus' Germania from Humanism to National Socialism* (New York, 2009).

—— and Grethlein, J., 'Introduction', in C. Krebs and J. Grethlein (eds), *The Historian's Plupast* (in press).

Lane Fox, Robin, 'Introduction', in Robin Lane Fox (ed), *The Long March: Xenophon and the Ten Thousand* (New Haven and London, 2004), pp.1–46.

——, 'Sex, gender and the other in Xenophon's *Anabasis*', in Robin Lane Fox (ed), *The Long March: Xenophon and the Ten Thousand* (New Haven and London, 2004), pp.184–214.

Lang, M., 'Participially expressed motivation in Thucydides', *Mnemosyne* 48 (1995), pp.48–65.

Langlois, Charles and Seignobos, Charles, *Introduction to the Study of History (Introduction aux Études Historiques)*, translated by G. G. Berry, (London, 1898).

Lateiner, Donald, review of Bowie (2007) in the *Bryn Mawr Classical Review* (http://ccat.sas.upenn.edu/bmcr/2008/2008-07-34.html#t3, accessed on 9 August 2008).

Lazenby, J., *Hannibal's War: A Military History of the Second Punic War* (Norman, 1998).

Leidl, Christoph, 'Appians "Annibaike": Aufbau-Darstellungstendenzen-Quellen', *Aufstieg und Niedergang der Römischen Welt* 2.34.1 (Berlin, 1972–), pp.428–62.

Lenfant, D., 'L'Inde de Ctésias: Des Sources aux Representations', *Topoi* 5 (1995), pp.309–36.

——, *Ctésias de Cnide: La Perse; L'Inde; Autres fragments* (Paris, 2004).

Levene, D. S., 'Polybius on "seeing" and "hearing": 12.27', *Classical Quarterly* 55.2 (2005), pp.627–9.

Levick, B., *The Government of the Roman Empire: A Sourcebook* (London, 1985).

Lewis, C. S., *The Horse and His Boy* (London, 1954).

Lewis, D. M., 'Sources, chronology, method', in D. M. Lewis, John Boardman, J. K. Davies and M. Ostwald (eds), *The Cambridge Ancient History V: The Fifth Century B.C.* second edition (Cambridge, 1992), pp.1–14.

Lewis, R. G., *Asconius: Commentaries on Speeches by Cicero* (Oxford, 2006).

Lintott, A. W., *Judicial Reform and Land Reform in the Roman Republic: A New Edition, with Translation and Commentary, of the Laws from Urbino* (Cambridge, 1992).

——, *The Constitution of the Roman Republic* (Oxford, 1999), pp.16–26.

Lloyd-Jones, Hugh, 'Wagner' in Hugh Lloyd-Jones, *Blood for the Ghosts: Classical Influences in the Nineteenth and Twentieth Centuries* (London, 1982), pp.126–142.

Lobur, J. A., '*Festinatio* (haste), *brevitas* (concision), and the generation of imperial ideology in Velleius Paterculus', *Transactions of the American Philological Association* 137 (2007), pp.211–30.

Lodge, David, *Author, Author* (London, 2004).

Loomis, Elisha Scott, *The Pythagorean Proposition,* second edition (Washington, DC, 1968).

Lovecraft, H. P., *History of the Necronomicon* (West Warwick, RI, 1980).

Luce, T. J., 'Ancient views on the causes of bias in historical writing', *Classical Philology* 84/1, (1989) pp.16–31.

——, *The Greek Historians* (London and New York, 1997).

—— and Woodman, A. J. (eds), *Tacitus and the Tacitean Tradition* (Princeton, 1993).

Macaulay, Thomas Babington, *The History of England from the Accession of James the Second*, Everyman Edition (London, 1906).

——, *The Letters of Thomas Babington Macaulay,* Thomas Pinney (ed), six volumes (Cambridge, 1974–81).

MacCaffrey, Wallace T. (ed), *William Camden: The History of the Most Renowned and Victorious Princess Elizabeth Late Queen of England: Selected Chapters* (Chicago and London, 1970).

MacLeod, M. D. (ed), *Lucian: A Selection* (Warminster, 1991).

McLoughlin, Kate (ed), *The Cambridge Companion to British and American War Writing* (Cambridge, 2009).

Marincola, John, 'Some suggestions on the Proem and Second Preface of Arrian's *Anabasis*', *Journal of Hellenic Studies* 109 (1989), pp.186–9.

——, *Authority and Tradition in Ancient Historiography* (Cambridge, 1997).

——, 'Genre, convention, and innovation in Greco-Roman historiography', in C. S. Kraus (ed), *The Limits of Historiography:Genre and Narrative in Ancient Historical Texts* (Leiden, 1999), pp.281–324.

——, *Greek Historians* (Cambridge, 2001).

——, 'Speeches in classical historiography', in John Marincola (ed), *A Companion to Greek and Roman Historiography* (Malden, MA, and Oxford, 2007), pp.118–32.

——, 'Universal history from Ephorus to Diodorus', in John Marincola (ed), *A Companion to Greek and Roman Historiography* (Malden, MA and Oxford, 2007), pp.171–9.

Martin, R. H. and Woodman, A. J. (eds), *Tacitus: Annals Book IV* (Cambridge, 1989).

Meritt, B. D., Wade-Gery, H. T. and McGregor, M. F., *The Athenian Tribute Lists*, four volumes (1939–53).

Merivale, C. (ed), *Caii Sallustii Crispi Catilina et Jugurtha, an Ed. for Schools* (Cambridge, 1852).

Millar, Fergus, *A Study of Cassius Dio* (Oxford, 1964).

Miller, N. P. (ed), *Tacitus: Annals Book I* (London, 1992).

Milsom, S. F. C., 'Maitland, Frederic William (1850–1906)', *Oxford Dictionary of National Biography* (Oxford, 2004), online edition, May 2007 [http://www.oxforddnb.com/view/article/34837, accessed 19 August 2008].

Moles, J. L., 'The Interpretation of the Second Preface in Arrian's *Anabasis*', *Journal of Hellenic Studies* 105 (1985), pp.162–8.

——, 'Truth and untruth in Herodotus and Thucydides', in C. Gill and T. P. Wiseman (eds), *Lies and Fiction in the Ancient World* (Austin, 1993), pp.88–121.

Momigliano, A. D., 'The first political commentary on Tacitus', *Journal of Roman Studies* 37 (1947), pp.91–101.

———, 'The rhetoric of history and the history of rhetoric: On Hayden White's tropes', in A. D. Momigliano, *Settimo Contributo alla Storia Degli Studi Classici e del Mondo Antico* (Roma, 1984), pp.49–59.

Mommsen, Theodor, *Römisches Staatsrecht* (Leipzig, 1887–8).

Morgan, J. R., *A Commentary on the Ninth and Tenth Books of the Aithiopica of Heliodorus* (D. Phil. Thesis, Oxford, 1978).

———, review of Hansen (1996), in *Histos* 2 (1998) at http://www.dur.ac.uk/Classics/histos/1998/morgan.html (accessed on 31 August 2008).

———, 'Fiction and history: Historiography and the novel', in John Marincola (ed), *A Companion to Greek and Roman Historiography* (Malden, MA, and Oxford: Blackwell, 2007), pp.553–64.

Morgan, Llewelyn, 'The autopsy of Gaius Asinius Pollio', *Journal of Roman Studies* 90 (2000), pp.51–69.

Motion, Andrew, *Wainewright the Poisoner: The True Confessions of a Charming and Ingenious Criminal* (London, 2000).

Murray, Oswyn, 'Arnaldo Momigliano in England', *History and Theory*, 30/4, Beiheft 30: *The Presence of the Historian: Essays in Memory of Arnaldo Momigliano* (December, 1991), pp.49–64.

Namier, Lewis, *The Structure of Politics at the Accession of George III* (London, 1957).

Napier, W. F. P., *Life and Opinions of Sir Charles Napier* (London, 1857).

Nissen, H., *Kritische Untersuchungen über die Quellen der vierten und fünften Dekade des Livius* (Berlin, 1863).

O'Brian, Patrick, *The Mauritius Command*, paperback edition (London, 2002).

———, *The Ionian Mission*, paperback edition (London, 2003).

O'Gorman, Ellen, 'On Not Writing About Augustus: Tacitus' Annals Book 1', *MD* 35 (1995), pp.91–114.

———, *Irony and Misreading in the Annals of Tacitus* (Cambridge, 2000).

O'Gorman, Frank, *The Long Eighteenth Century: British Political and Social History, 1688–1832* (London and New York, 1997).

Oliver, Revilo P., 'The first Medicean MS of Tacitus and the titulature of ancient books', *Transactions and Proceedings of the American Philological Association* 82 (1951), pp.232–61.

Ondaatje, Michael, *The English Patient* (London, 1992).

Pelling, Christopher, *Plutarch: Life of Antony* (Cambridge, 1988).

———, 'Childhood and personality in Greek biography', in Christopher Pelling (ed), *Characterization and Individuality in Greek Literature* (Oxford, 1990), pp.213–44.

———, 'Epilogue', in C. S. Kraus (ed), *The Limits of Historiography: Genre and Narrative in Ancient Historical Texts* (Leiden, 1999), pp.325–60.

———, *Literary Texts and the Greek Historian* (London, 2000).

———, 'Fun with fragments', in David Braund, John Wilkins (eds), *Athenaeus and his World: Reading Greek Culture in the Roman Empire* (Exeter, 2000), pp.171–90.

———, 'Truth and fiction in Plutarch's lives', in Christopher Pelling (ed), *Plutarch and History: Eighteen Studies* (London, 2002), pp.143–70.

Peter, H., *Historicorum Romanorum Reliquiae* (Stuttgart, 1906–14).

Peters, A., *Synchronoptische Weltgeschichte* (Hamburg, 1965–70).

Petzold, K-E., 'Cicero und Historie', *Chiron* 2 (1972), pp.253–76.

Pile, Stephen, *The Book of Heroic Failures: Official Handbook of the Not Terribly Good Club of Great Britain* (London, 1979).

Pitcher, L. V., 'Narrative technique in the lives of the ten orators', *Classical Quarterly* 55 (2005), pp.217–34.

———, 'Characterisation in ancient historiography', in John Marincola (ed), *A Companion to Greek and Roman Historiography* (Malden, MA, and Oxford, 2007), pp.102–17.

———, review of G. Schepens and J. Bollansée (eds), *The Shadow of Polybius: Intertextuality as a Research Tool in Greek Historiography* (Leiden, 2004), in *Bryn Mawr Classical Review* (http://ccat.sas.upenn.edu/bmcr/2007/2007-08-62.html), accessed on 2 November 2009.

———, 'The Roman historians after Livy', in M. Griffin (ed), *A Companion to Julius Caesar* (Oxford, 2009), pp.268–76.

———, 'Classical war literature', in Kate McLoughlin (ed), *The Cambridge Companion to British and American War Writing* (Cambridge, 2009), 71–80.

———, 'The stones of blood: Family, monumentality, and memory in Velleius's second century', in E. Cowan (ed), *Velleius Paterculus* (Swansea, in press).

———, 'War stories: The uses of the plupast in Appian', in C. Krebs and J. Grethlein (eds), *The Historian's Plupast* (in press).

Bibliography

——, 'Herodian', in I. de Jong (ed), *Space in Ancient Greek Literature* (forthcoming).

Pollock, Frederick and Maitland, F. W., *The History of English Law Before the Time of Edward I* (Cambridge, 1898).

Pullapilly, Cyriac K., *Caesar Baronius: Counter-Reformation Historian* (Notre Dame, 1975).

Purcell, N., 'Atrium Libertatis', in *Proceedings of the British School at Rome* 61 (1993), pp.125–55.

Ranke, L. von, *Geschichten der romanischen und germanischen Völker von 1494 bis 1514, Zur Kritik neuerer Geschichtschreiber* (Leipzig and Berlin, 1824).

——, *Deutsche Geschichte im Zeitalter der Reformation*, P. Joachimsen et al. (eds), Vol. 1 (Munich, 1925–6).

Rawson, Elizabeth, 'Prodigy lists and the use of the *Annales Maximi*', *Classical Quarterly*, New Series, 21/1 (May 1971), pp.158–69.

Reardon, B. P. (ed), *Collected Ancient Greek Novels* (Berkeley, 1989).

Reynolds, L. D. and Wilson, N. G., *Scribes and Scholars: A Guide to the Transmission of Greek and Latin Literature*, third edition (Oxford, 1991).

Rhodes, P. J., 'The Atthidographers', in H. Verdin, G. Schepens and E. de Keyer (eds), *Purposes of History: Proceedings of the International Colloquium – Leuven, 24–26 May 1988* (Louvain, 1990), pp.73–81.

——, 'In defence of the Greek historians', *Greece and Rome* 41 (1994), pp.156–71.

——, ' "Epidamnus is a city": On not overinterpreting Thucydides', *Histos* 2 (1998), at http://www.dur.ac.uk/Classics/histos/1998/rhodes.html (accessed on 13 August 2008).

——, 'Public documents in the Greek states: Archives and inscriptions, Part II', in *Greece and Rome*, Second Series, 48/2 (October, 2001), pp.136–53.

——, 'Documents and the Greek historians', in John Marincola (ed), *A Companion to Greek and Roman Historiography* (Malden, MA, and Oxford, 2007), pp.56–66.

—— and Osborne, Robin (eds), *Greek Historical Inscriptions, 404–323 BC* (Oxford, 2003).

Rich, J. W. (ed), *Cassius Dio: The Augustan Settlement (Roman History 53–55.9)* (Warminster, 1990).

Richardson, J. S., *Appian: Wars of the Romans in Iberia, with an Introduction, Translation and Commentary* (Warminster, 2000).

Richlin, Amy, *The Garden of Priapus: Sexuality and Aggression in Roman Humor*, revised edition (New Haven and London, 1992).

Roger, Nicholas, 'History as fiction in the novels of Patrick O'Brian', in R. S. O. Tomlin (ed), *History and Fiction: Six Essays Celebrating the Centenary of Sir Ronald Syme* (London, 2005), pp.86–99.

Rood, Tim, *Thucydides: Narrative and Explanation* (Oxford, 1998).

——, *The Sea! The Sea! The Shout of the Ten Thousand in the Modern Imagination* (London, 2004).

——, 'Pan-Hellenism and self-presentation: Xenophon's speeches', in Robin Lane Fox (ed), *The Long March: Xenophon and the Ten Thousand* (New Haven and London, 2004), pp.305–29.

——, 'The development of the war monograph', in John Marincola (ed), *A Companion to Greek and Roman Historiography* (Malden, MA, and Oxford, 2007), pp.147–58.

Runciman, S., *The Crusades*, Vol. 1 (Cambridge, 1951).

Russell, D. A., 'Rhetoric and criticism', *Greece and Rome* 14 (1967), pp.130–44.

Sacks, K. S., *Polybius on the Writing of History* (Berkeley, 1981).

——, *Diodorus Siculus and the First Century* (Princeton, NJ, *c.*1990).

Scala, R. von, *Die Studien des Polybios* (Stuttgart, 1890).

Schaeberg, D., 'Social pleasures in early Chinese historiography and philosophy', in C. S. Kraus (ed), *The Limits of Historiography: Genre and Narrative in Ancient Historical Texts* (Leiden, 1999), pp.1–26.

Schepens, G., 'Some aspects of source-theory in Greek historiography', *Ancient Society* 6 (1975), pp.257–74.

——, *L' 'Autopsie' dans la Méthode des historiens grecs du V siècle Avant J.-C.* (Brussels, 1980).

——, 'Jacoby's *FGrHist*: Problems, methods, prospects', in Glenn W. Most (ed), *Collecting Fragments-Fragmente sammeln. (Aporemata: Kritische Studien zur Philologiegeschichte* 1. Göttingen: Vandenhoeck and Ruprecht, 1997), pp.144–72.

——, 'Polybius' criticism of Phylarchus', in G. Schepens and J. Bollansée (eds), *The Shadow of Polybius: Intertextuality as a Research Tool in Greek Historiography* (Leiden, 2004), pp.141–64.

Bibliography

—— and Bollansée, J. (eds), *The Shadow of Polybius: Intertextuality as a Research Tool in Greek Historiography* (Leiden, 2004).

Schmid, Wolfgang, *Historia-Augusta-Colloquium 1964/5* (Bonn, 1966).

Schultze, C. E., 'Authority, originality and competence in the Roman Archaeology of Dionysius of Halicarnassus', *Histos* 4 (2000), at http://www.dur.ac.uk/Classics/histos/2000/schultze1.html (accessed 17 August 2008).

Scodel, Ruth, 'Zielinski's Law reconsidered', *Transactions of the American Philological Association* 138 (2008), pp.107–25.

Scullard, H. H., *Scipio Africanus in the Second Punic War* (Cambridge, 1932).

Sellar, W. C. and Yeatman, R. J., *1066 and all that: A Memorable History of England: Comprising, all the Parts You Can Remember Including One Hundred and Three Good Things, Five Bad Kings, and Two Genuine Dates* (London, 1930).

Shackleton Bailey, D. R. (ed), *Cicero: Epistulae ad Familiares*, Vol. 1 (Cambridge, 1977).

Sherk, R. K., *The Roman Empire: Augustus to Hadrian* (Cambridge, 1988).

Shipley, Graham, *Hellenistic History: A Very Short Introduction* (Oxford, in press).

Shrimpton, G. S., *Theopompus the Historian* (McGill-Queen's Press, 1991).

Sidebottom, H., 'Herodian's historical methods and understanding of history', *Aufstieg und Niedergang der römischen Welt* II.34.4 (Berlin and New York, 1998), pp.2775–836.

Simms, Brendan, 'Butterfield, Sir Herbert (1900–79)', *Oxford Dictionary of National Biography* (Oxford, 2004) [http://www.oxforddnb.com/view/article/30888, accessed 16 July 2008].

Skelton, Matthew, 'The paratext of everything: Constructing and marketing H. G. Wells's *The Outline of History*', *Book History* 4 (2001), pp.237–75.

Smalley, Beryl, *The Study of the Bible in the Middle Ages* (Oxford, 1941).

Stephens, S. A. and Winkler, J. J., *Ancient Greek Novels: The Fragments* (Princeton, c.1995).

Stoppard, Tom, *Arcadia* (London, 1993).

Strachey, Lytton, *Eminent Victorians* (London, 1918).

Stuart Jones, H., 'The foundation and history of the Camden Chair', available at http://www.oahs.org.uk/oxo/vol%208-9/Jones.doc [accessed on 27 August 2008].

Stylianou, P. J., *A Historical Commentary on Diodorus Siculus Book 15* (Oxford, 1998).

Swain, S., review of Hopkins (1999) in *Classical Review* 53 (2003), 260–1.

Syme, Ronald, *The Roman Revolution* (Oxford, 1939).

——, *Tacitus* (Oxford, 1958).

——, *Sallust* (Berkeley, 1964).

——, *Ammianus and the Historia Augusta* (Oxford, 1968).

——, *The Historia Augusta: A Call of Clarity* (Bonn, 1971).

——, 'Tacitus: Some sources of his information', *Journal of Roman Studies* 72 (1982), pp.68–82.

——, *The Augustan Aristocracy* (Oxford, 1986).

Szepessy, T., *Acta Antiquae Academiae Scientiarum Hungaricae* 24 (1976), pp.247–76.

Taplin, Oliver, *Homeric Soundings: The Shaping of the Iliad* (Oxford, 1992).

Tartt, Donna, *The Secret History* (London, 1993).

Taylor, A. J. P., *The Struggle for Mastery in Europe 1848–1918* (Oxford, 1954).

Thomasius, J., *Praeses, Dissertatio Philosophica de Plagio Literario,* resp. Joh. Michael Reinelius (Leipzig, 1692).

Todd, Robert B., review of Arnott (1996) in *Bryn Mawr Classical Review* (http://ccat.sas.upenn.edu/bmcr/1996/96.07.18.html, accessed on 5 August 2008).

Trapp, Michael, *Greek and Latin Letters: An Anthology with Translation* (Cambridge, 2003).

Trevor-Roper, Hugh, *A Hidden Life: The Enigma of Sir Edmund Backhouse* (London, 1976).

——, 'Gibbon's last project' in David Womersley (ed), *Edward Gibbon: Bicentenary Essays, Studies on Voltaire and the Eighteenth Century* 355 (Oxford, 1997), pp.405–19.

Tucci, U., 'Ranke and the Venetian document market', in G. G. Iggers and J. Powell (eds), *Leopold von Ranke and the Shaping of the Historical Discipline* (Syracuse, 1990), pp.99–107.

Bibliography

Usher, Stephen (ed), *Dionysius of Halicarnassus: Critical Essays*, Vol. 1 (London, 1974).

Wagner, Richard, *Die Kunst und die Revolution* (Leipzig, 1849).

Walbank, F. W., 'Polemic in Polybius', *Journal of Roman Studies* 52 (1962), pp.1–12 (Walbank, F. W., *Selected Papers: Studies in Greek and Roman History and Historiography* (Cambridge, 1985), pp.262–79).

——, 'Speeches in Greek historians' (third Myres Memorial Lecture: Oxford, 1965) (Walbank, F. W., *Selected Papers: Studies in Greek and Roman History and Historiography* (Cambridge, 1985), pp.242–61).

——, *Historical Commentary on Polybius – Volume II: Commentary on Books VII–XVIII* (Oxford, 1967).

——, *Polybius* (Berkeley, Los Angeles, and London, 1972).

——, 'Profit or amusement: Some thoughts on the motives of Hellenistic historians', in H. Verdin, G. Schepens and E. deKeyser (eds), *Purposes of History: Studies in Greek Historiography from the 4th to the second Centuries BC* (Leuven, 1990), pp.253–66.

——, 'The two-way shadow: Polybius among the fragments', in G. Schepens and J. Bollansée (eds), *The Shadow of Polybius: Intertextuality as a Research Tool in Greek Historiography – Proceedings of the International Colloquium Leuven, 21–22 September 2001* (Leiden, 2004), pp.1–18.

Walker, A., '*Enargeia* and the spectator in Greek historiography', *Transactions of the American Philological Association* 123 (1993), pp.353–77.

Watson, George, *Lord Acton's History of Liberty: A Study of his Library with an Edited Text of his History of Liberty Notes* (Aldershot, 1994).

Weber, W., *Princeps: Studien zur Geschichte des Augustus* (Stuttgart, 1936).

Weeks, David and James, Jamie, *Eccentrics: A Study of Sanity and Strangeness* (London, 1995).

Weinstein, Lawrence and Adam, John A., *Guesstimation: Solving the World's Problems on the Back of a Cocktail Napkin* (Princeton, 2008).

Wellesley, K., 'Tacitus as a military historian', in T. A. Dorey (ed), *Tacitus* (London, 1969), pp.63–98.

White, Hayden, *Metahistory: The Historical Imagination in Nineteenth-Century Europe* (Baltimore, 1973).

——, *The Content of the Form* (Baltimore, 1987).

Whittaker, C. R. (ed), *Herodian I: Books I–IV* (Cambridge, 1969).

Wilkins, A. S. (ed), *M. Tullii Ciceronis De Oratore Libri Tres – Liber I* (Oxford, 1879).

Willans, Geoffrey, *Down With Skool!* (London, 1953).

Williams, Wynne, 'Reading Greek like a man of the world: Macaulay and the classical languages', *Greece and Rome* 40 (1993), pp.201–16.

Wilson, Edmund, *Patriotic Gore: Studies in the Literature of the American Civil War* (London, 1962).

Wilson, John, 'What does Thucydides claim for his speeches?', *Phoenix* 36 (1982), pp.95–103.

Wilson, Nigel G., 'Thomas William Allen, 1862–1950', *Proceedings of the British Academy* 76 (1990), pp.311–19.

Wilson, Robert A., *Everything is Under Control: Conspiracies, Cults, and Cover-Ups* (London, 1999).

Wiseman, T. P., 'Lying historians: Seven types of mendacity', in C. Gill and T. P. Wiseman (eds), *Lies and Fiction in the Ancient World* (Austin, 1993), pp.122–46.

——, 'Late Syme: A study in historiography', in T. P. Wiseman, *Roman Drama and Roman History* (Exeter, 1998), pp.135–52.

——, 'The prehistory of Roman historiography', in John Marincola (ed), *A Companion to Greek and Roman Historiography* (Malden, MA, and Oxford, 2007), pp.67–75.

Woodman, A. J., *Velleius Paterculus: The Tiberian Narrative (2.94–131)* (Cambridge, 1977).

——, *Velleius Paterculus: The Caesarian and Augustan Narrative (2.41–93)* (Cambridge, 1983).

——, *Rhetoric in Classical Historiography: Four Studies* (London, 1988).

——, 'Nero's alien capital: Tacitus as paradoxographer', in A. J. Woodman and Jonathan Powell (eds), *Author and Audience in Latin Literature* (Cambridge, 1992), pp.173–88.

——, 'Not a Funeral Note: Tacitus, Annals 1.8.5–6', *Classical Quarterly* 52 (2002), pp.629–32.

——, 'Readers and reception: A text case', in John Marincola (ed), *A Companion to Greek and Roman Historiography* (Malden, MA, and Oxford, 2007), pp.33–44.

—— and Martin, R. H. (eds), *The Annals of Tacitus: Book 3* (Cambridge, 1996).

Woodward, B. and Bernstein, C., *Final Days* (New York, 1977).

Worden, Blair, 'Hugh Redwald Trevor-Roper 1914–2003', *Proceedings of the British Academy* 150 (2007), pp.247–84.

Yarrow, L., *Historiography at the End of the Republic: Provincial Perspectives on Roman Rule* (Oxford, 2005).

Yeats, W. B., *Four Years* (Churchtown, Dundrum, 1921).

INDEX

Index

Index